AF539889

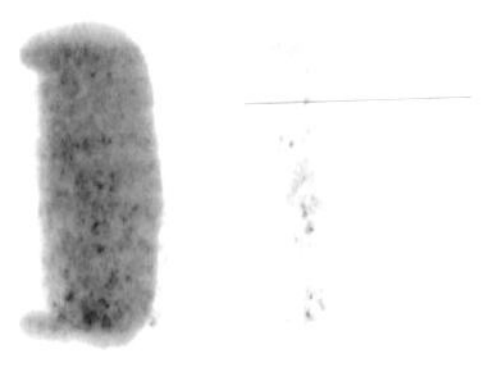

India's Tibet Policy and China

INDIA's TIBET POLICY AND CHINA

Brig. M.N.Sarin

GAURAV BOOK CENTRE PVT LTD
DELHI

Publisher
GAURAV BOOK CENTRE PVT LTD
4832/24, Prahlad Lane, S-207 Ansari
Road, Daryaganj, Delhi-110002
Ph.: 43570976, 23278261
Email: gauravbookcentre@gmail.com

Edition: 2015

ISBN: 978-93-83316-09-0

Laser Typesetting
JEE-VEE Graphics, Delhi

Price: 1195/-

Printed
Vikas Computers, Delhi

Preface

In my years of travelling around the world talking about Tibet; it has been my experience that, more often than not, the audience generally consist of people who are interested in Tibet and already know a great deal about Tibet.

The source of the problem in India-China relations is not Tibet. The problem is rooted essentially in how China perceives Tibet. China's flawed perception on Tibet both colors and distorts its relationship with India. For India, the intractable border dispute is the primary issue inhibiting closer ties. But for China, Tibet is the determining issue, and it perceives India's giving refuge to exiled Tibetans as an anti-China policy.

For India, Tibet has never been a problem. India up until the Chinese invasion in 1950 shared a border with Tibet. Historically, trade, culture and religion linked India to Tibet. More significantly, Tibet got its Buddhist identity from India, and also its written script. In other words, India has been the primary source of Tibetan civilization and identity.

India continues to secretly support separatist activities in the Tibetan Autonomous Region (TAR) through exiled Tibetans while publicly maintaining a 'one China policy', state media said on Monday, adding that this contradiction in New Delhi's policy was harming its relations with Beijing.

As the book addresses this crucial issue quite deftly, it is hoped that it would prove to be a source of great information for the reader.

—*Editor*

Contents

1

India and the Tibetan Tragedy

INTRODUCTION

An apparently insignificant announcement concerning Indo-Tibetan relations was made to the press on September 16, 1952, by the Indian Ministry of External Relations. It stated that the 16-year-old Indian Mission in Lhasa, the capital of Tibet, would be wound up and replaced by a Consulate-General; but that whereas the Mission maintained direct relations between India and Tibet, the new Consulate-General would be accredited to China. In other words, Indian recognition seemed to be entirely withdrawn from Tibet and thus the period of cooperation between the two countries on a basis of equality came to an end. As the initiation of this cooperation was one of the cornerstones of Indian foreign policy under British rule its termination must be the expression of some basic change in policy; and there is no better way of understanding this change than by recalling briefly the history of Indo-Tibetan relations.

Tibet is bordered by Chinese Turkestan and Mongolia in the north; by China in the east; by Burma, India, Bhutan, Sikkim and Nepal in the South; and by India (Punjab and Kashmir) in the west. Bhutan and Sikkim were formerly part of Tibet but are now separate states under Indian suzerainty. Both Tibet and Nepal were under Chinese suzerainty, but whereas the Nepalese threw off Chinese domination, Tibetan efforts to terminate dependence were never completely successful. However, the term Chinese domination calls for explanation. Chinese suzerainty meant at first the overlordship of the Manchu Emperors. With their downfall, Chinese Republican influence in Tibet decreased rapidly and Chinese Communist influence was considered a menace in Lhasa long before the defeat of Chiang Kai-shek.

After the establishment of Buddhism and of the Church of the Lamas, Tibet, once a warring nation, became peace-loving and determined to fend off both Western influence and militarism as a means of avoiding international disputes. There is no other example in history of a nation dominated by a religious creed and priestly organization which was so firm in its policy of avoiding the drawbacks of modern civilization, even if this meant foregoing its benefits. Lacking significant armed forces, Tibet had to safeguard her independence by peaceful means; and this in recent centuries the Lamas succeeded in doing with admirable skill and wisdom. Her neighbors had considerable appetites and tried to find their way to Lhasa. Besides China there was Tsarist Russia, who after having established a hold over Buddhist Mongolia thought of further expanding her influence into Tibet. Russia renounced these intentions in 1907, by a treaty concluded with Great Britain. One of the basic difficulties of all intruders was the complete devotion and allegiance of Tibetans as well as of other Buddhists in that part of the world to the Dalai Lama who combined temporal jurisdiction with spiritual power. None of Tibet's neighbors who had political ambitions was able to overcome the formidable barrier of seclusion, more impenetrable than iron curtains stretched between the pillars of brutal physical force and hostile isolationism.

India's attitude towards Tibet was different from that of any other country. Gotama the Buddha was of Indian origin and the famous Bodhi tree near Gaya in Bihar, beneath which he sat in contemplation, is still today the sacred meeting place of all Buddhists of the world, whether from Tibet, Burma, Ceylon or Japan. All these countries adopted the great faith of the Enlightened, whereas India, his home country, finally rejected him for the Brahmanical religion. India is still to a great extent Brahmanical, and has not much sympathy or understanding for the Buddhist way of life. In shaping their own ideas about Tibet, Indian politicians could not find much enthusiasm in their hearts, political considerations apart, for "heretic" Tibet, for which so many British explorers, traders and travellers developed understanding and even admiration. When British rule established itself in India in the nineteenth century, a number of treaties ensured the settlement of all controversial relations on the northeastern frontier. In a treaty between Great Britain and China, concluded in 1890, the former secured recognition of her protectorate over Sikkim. In 1904, Great Britain concluded a treaty with Tibet securing an open trade route frome Kalimpong in India, to Lhasa. Though direct relations were established between the two countries, Great Britain recognized Chinese suzerainty over Tibet in 1906. In 1910 a British Protectorate over Bhutan was established. Thus India, under British rule, had produced a system of security by which her northeastern frontier could be considered more or less immune against the turmoil of Chinese politics. The main elements of this security system were British India's suzerainty over Bhutan and Sikkim, the free trade route between Kalimpong and Lhasa opened after Colonel Francis Younghusband's expedition to Lhasa in 1904, and friendly relations with Nepal which ceased to be a vassal state in relation to China. Security on her northeastern frontier allowed British India to concentrate on the more difficult problem of her northwestern frontier bordering on Afghanistan.

In view of the constant Chinese infiltration into Tibet, British India had to consider how to maintain a balance of power there. Any sharp increase of Chinese penetration in Tibet was obviously a threat to British India's security; while the elimination of Chinese influence from Tibet would obviously have caused a deterioration of Anglo-Chinese relations, provoked again the danger of Russian infiltration, and increased unnecessarily the responsibility of British India in relation to Tibet. Thus the balance was determined by a policy of keeping Chinese influence in check without eliminating it entirely. It was successful for years in keeping the famous Russian agent, Mr. Dorjeff, at a fair distance from the hearts of the Lamas. The policy was not formally laid down, but it found visible expression in the provisions of the Simla Conference in 1914, where representatives of British India, China and Tibet initialed a Convention of which the chief provisions were the following:

1. Tibet was to be divided into two parts: Outer Tibet, adjoining India and including Lhasa, Shigatse and Chamdo; and Inner Tibet, including the provinces near China and part of Eastern Tibet.
2. The principle of Chinese suzerainty over Tibet was recognized, but China was to observe strictly her limited position as a suzerain. Suzerainty implies that internal sovereignty is vested in the vassal state; in other words China could not, according to the Convention, infringe upon the internal jurisdiction of the Dalai Lama's Government. On the other hand, suzerainty means no external sovereignty in the vassal state. Thus the Convention implied the right of China to conduct Tibet's foreign affairs, with the exception of British India's direct rights in Tibet, essential to the mutual balance in the Indian-Chinese-Tibetan triangle.
3. Great Britain declared that it had no other aspirations in Tibet, and in particular none for territorial expansion or aggrandizement.
4. The division of Tibet into Outer Tibet and Inner Tibet implied the predominant interest of British India in the former and of China in the latter. India always enjoyed the natural security afforded by the Himalayas. The passes leading from the Tibetan plateau into Sikkim and India are important trade routes. Noninterference of China in Outer Tibet best secured freedom of movement on these routes. Thousands of Tibetan traders used to arrive in India yearly over these passes to sell wool, hides and medicinal herbs in exchange for other goods. Thus the firm establishment of the Dalai Lama's jurisdiction in this part of Tibet served the twofold purpose of promoting Indo-Tibetan trade and security of the northeastern frontier of India. British India was allowed to have her trade agents in Outer Tibet and later also established a Mission in Lhasa.
5. In Inner Tibet the Chinese were to keep certain internal rights, including responsibility for the maintenance of order.
6. Finally, the Chinese were to maintain a representative,

called Amban, in Lhasa. The Amban was later matched by the presence of the British Indian Mission to the Dalai Lama.

One of the tasks of the Simla Conference was also to define the northeastern frontier of India, particularly between Tibet and Bhutan, the vassal of British India where Chinese penetration remained a continuous threat.

Two days after the Convention was initialed, the Chinese Government refused to sign it. The British then informed China that they considered the Convention as in force between themselves and Tibet. A few weeks later the First World War broke out and Tibetan affairs were duly shelved. But the principles of the Simla Conference remained a reliable guide to British Indian policy in Tibet, based as it was on genuine friendship and on a mutually respected balance of power by which no more would be given to or withdrawn from either China or Tibet than was inherent in the balance itself.

Tibet was obviously to serve as a buffer state without giving up its autonomy in its own internal affairs. It was also obvious that British India's action was dictated not only by British Commonwealth interests but by the natural requirements of any future Indian policy, whether connected with British rule or not. Problems of security and trade aside, there was also an increased need after the First World War for vigilance against the Bolshevist penetration which Chinese soldiers tended to import into Tibet. Communism was always less popular in Tibet than in India and Nepal, the reason being that the Dalai Lama's Government was, and still is, primarily spiritual, abhorring physical force as a means of leading people to happiness and salvation.

The need for India to play an active part in protecting her security and interests in the northeast is all the greater today because of the strongly imperialist policies adopted by Communist China and the U.S.S.R. The ostensible objective of the Chinese invasion of Tibet is the "liberation" of the Tibetan people. But in fact Mao Tse-tung has assumed the expansionist role formerly played by the Manchu Emperors. In other words, Tibet in Chinese eyes is once again a province of China, composed of the present

Tibetan territory plus all the areas which originally were Tibetan and later were lost to India or Nepal. Years ago, Tibet owned all of Sikkim down to Siliguri in India, including Darjeeling; it also owned Bhutan, now an Indian vassal state, and had Nepal as a protectorate. Nepal discontinued her quinquennial missions to Peking only about 40 years ago, and shook off Chinese suzerainty.

Thirty years ago, Sir Charles Bell, one of the greatest experts on Tibet, made clear in his work, "Tibet, Past and Present," that if the Chinese should disturb the Tibetan balance of power as laid down in the Simla Convention, both Nepal and India would be threatened. He also expressed grave concern about the future of the system of security initiated by the British in the event that India were to become independent. He foresaw that with a transfer of power from the British to an independent India the Simla policy would automatically break down, since, he thought, independent India whether through lack of interest or lack of firmness would not support Tibet against Chinese imperialism (yellow or red). In such circumstances Tibet would have to break away from the Indian environment, and Nepal, Bhutan and Sikkim would find it difficult to continue in friendly partnership with India; for when the inhabitants of these countries saw that India had abandoned the effort to maintain a balance of power in Tibet, and had assumed a passive attitude there, they would be tempted to turn to China of their own accord. One of Sir Charles Bell's practical recommendations for delaying Chinese penetration in Tibet was to prevent Chinese agents from entering that country through India. He also noted that the lines of communication direct from Peking to Lhasa are highly inadequate and emphasized that if ever Chinese troops and officials succeeded in seizing Tibet the export of rice or other food grains and supplies to them through India should be prevented. It is significant that at the present time all Chinese missions enter Tibet via Calcutta and Kalimpong, and that Tibetan missions to China do not travel from Lhasa direct to Peking but take the same roundabout route by way of Kalimpong and Calcutta.

Let us now look at events in the last two years in the light of the above warnings and recommendations. The Chinese invasion of Tibet started at the end of 1950. It embraced at first only part of what the Simla Convention had designated as Inner Tibet. At the end of December in that year the young Dalai Lama left Lhasa and moved to Yatung in the Chumbi valley, only 15 miles from the border of India, thereby making clear that he was ready to become an exile in India, as his predecessor had done 30 years before. As soon as this happened the Chinese invasion stopped and Lhasa remained temporarily free. The next development was that a delegation of the Tibetan Government was invited to Peking. On arriving there they were told that Chinese military headquarters would be set up in Lhasa, and when they protested they were informed that Tibet had become a province of China and that they would do well to recognize the fact. Then a treaty was submitted to them for signature. They first said they would take it to Yatung and ask the Dalai Lama for instructions, but under pressure they were forced to sign immediately. One is reminded of the procedure applied by Hitler in 1938 to the unfortunate President of Czechoslovakia, and later to other victims.

After signing the treaty the Tibetan delegation left Peking and travelled back to Lhasa via Calcutta and Yatung. Meanwhile the Chinese had captured the Dalai Lama, with the help of a few bribed lamas, and brought him to Lhasa. For some time the Chinese generals in Tibet worked under the cloak of the Dalai Lama's authority; but having consolidated their power in the first half of 1952 they forced the Dalai Lama to dismiss all his supporters in the government and remain completely isolated. Furthermore, the Panchen Lama, next in importance to the Dalai Lama, was brought to Lhasa as his rival. When the two became friends they were again separated. Finally the Chinese Government invited India to withdraw her Mission from Lhasa in order to destroy the last trace of Tibetan independence.

The Indian Government has now complied with Chinese wishes and sent a Consul General to Lhasa who is accredited to China and not to Tibet. Thus with a stroke of the pen India relinquished the old policy of security in the northeast, worked out during years of effort and negotiation. Indian public opinion is as yet unaware of the historical consequences of this move. The

Chinese penetration of all the previous dependencies of the Chinese Emperors is likely to increase. The exact sequence of events cannot be foreseen, but it seems that Nepal is already involved in serious internal troubles (not without Communist participation) and that Communist pressure in Sikkim, Bhutan and Darjeeling is increasing.

India, whatever her motives in abandoning a genuine Indian policy as initiated under British rule, has to wake up to the reality on her northeastern frontiers and to events which are likely to follow. Tibet is now definitely behind the Iron Curtain and news as to what is going on beyond the Himalayan passes is scanty. It is, however, certain that the Chinese are building a strategic road from Lhasa to the frontier of India and Sikkim. This is the same track along which Colonel Francis Younghusband's army pushed in more primitive conditions in 1904 from India to Lhasa, and there is no reason why it could not be used for aggressive purposes in the other direction. Accounts of Younghusband's expedition mention the significant fort of Phari on the track below the peak of Chomo Lhari. The Chinese are reported to be building near the old fort a modern fort located in Galingk'a. They are also reported to be building, with the help of Soviet experts, several air bases all over Tibet, one at Lhasa and one on the plain between Lake Manasarowar and Lake Rukas, which is only 300 miles from New Delhi. It has been officially admitted by Indian politicians that there are Chinese military detachments stationed all along the Indian frontier. There are also rumors of atomic experts conducting investigations in uranium deposits in southern Tibet. The Chinese have printed a geographical map of China in which Bhutan and Sikkim are shown as part of China or Tibet. The matter has been recently discussed in the Indian Parliament and is, in spite of Chinese denials, a serious cause for anxiety. It is difficult at the moment to separate reliable evidence from hearsay. However, one thing certain is that the previous intercourse between India and Tibet has come to an end and that India has found herself close up against the Iron Curtain. In case of armed conflict, a southward Communist thrust might take place in the first instance from China and Tibet into Burma. Even so, considerable Indian armed forces would be immobilized on the Himalayan passes and south of them. If these passes and the adjoining strategic areas are not adequately defended, another Communist thrust could, in case of war, follow from the north and east directly into the plains of India.

Whatever the future, the period of balance of power by political manœuvring is over; and if physical force is behind the unbalance it can be opposed only by physical force. A former Congress President emphasized in a speech in the Indian Constituent Assembly that compulsory military service would be one of the best safeguards of independence. Its purpose, in the first instance, would be the creation of a strong and efficient army and, moreover, the strengthening of national discipline essential to face hard facts.

UNDERSTANDING THE TRAGEDY OF TIBET

A nation that has stood tall for more than two thousand years with a thriving civilization and significant cultural and political influence over large parts of Asia has suddenly come under an assault, which from all counts is tragic. When countries around the world, especially in Asia at the end of the Second World War were gaining independence as a result of the process of decolonization, shadows of dark clouds were looming large over the roof of the world – Tibet. No sooner did the Mao's revolutionary forces declared victory and China became a communist nation in 1949, Eastern parts of Tibet started coming under siege. As the world rejoiced freedom of many countries, the country at the roof of the world silently mourned its invasion by foreign forces. Not only is the nature and consequences of this invasion tragic but also how easily Tibet fell prey to the changing geo-political situations of the time.

It was certainly a most deplorable act of humiliation inflicted by a country which claims to have suffered a century of humiliation. But what was more deplorable was the unpreparedness of the Tibetan leadership of the time to face and challenge such situations. His Holiness the 13th Dalai Lama's realization of the importance of modernization saw the establishment of Tibet's first post office, introduction of currency notes and coins and, more importantly dispatching Tibetans to study abroad in England. As the importance of military strength was most dramatically realized, moves were made to strengthen the military as well. Though late, significant progress was nevertheless in the making but soon Tibet was engulfed into the misfortune of His Holiness' demise in 1933. For more than three centuries, the Dalai Lamas have provided both the political and spiritual leadership to the Tibetans. The Dalai Lamas reincarnate and are not elected and hence, there was more or less a political vacuum after the demise of the previous and the full maturity of the next. His Holiness the 14th Dalai Lama was born in the year 1935. It is appalling to think how in those testing times, China took the unpreparedness of the Tibetan leadership to their advantage and rendered Tibetans victims of its expansionist policy. It is also appalling to know that while small neighbouring countries like Nepal were acquiring membership of the newly established the United Nations Organization, Tibetan leadership had failed to do so. Tibetan tragedy is indeed scripted with misfortune of the Tibetans, naivety of their leadership and China's thirst for power.

Due to the impending threat of full-blown military invasion by China from eastern part of Tibet, His Holiness the 14th Dalai Lama and the Tibetan leadership initially tried to seek help from countries like the USA but to no avail. At this critical juncture, negotiation was indeed deemed most necessary in order to avoid People's Liberation Army's (PLA) further intrusion into Tibet. This led to the signing of the so called, "Seventeen Point Agreement" which gave China the legitimacy and powers to formally carry out its own imperialist policies inside Tibet. Out of the 17 points of the Agreement, China exercised immediate implementation of the terms in favour of their imperialistic pursuits and, displayed a complete disregard to the terms such as Article 4, which declared no alteration to "the existing political system in Tibet" and "the established status, functions and powers of the Dalai Lama". Article 11 declared a promise from the China's side that there would be no compulsion to follow the reforms and that any reform "must be settled through consultation with the leading personnel of Tibet". So, what appears to be Article 17, which says, "This agreement shall come into force immediately after signatures and seals are affixed to it" stands as the greatest deceit by the PRC as is seen on a regular basis that none of these terms have been implemented till date let alone "immediately" in 1951. The Agreement was formally and symbolically repudiated by the Tibetan government in March 1959 in Tibet, and later announced to the media on 18 April, 1959 after the Dalai Lama escaped into India. In a hypothetical situation, even if it were recognized, because of China's non compliance with its own dictated terms the Agreement would stand ipso facto invalid.

As a result of the signing of the so called "Seventeen Point Agreement" between Tibet and China, India decided to take a different stand on Tibet's status. Prior to that India acted against the voices raised by the Guomindang and invited the Tibetan delegation as an independent nation to Asian Relations Conference held in March – April, 1947 in New Delhi. India also raised a strong voice against PLA's intrusion into Tibet in 1950. However, due to fear of security threats from the Himalayan borders, India gave in and signed with China what was called the "Panchsheel Agreement" in 1954. This agreement "sacrificed Tibet's historical status at the altar of Sino-Indian friendship (Hindi Chini Bhai Bhai)". According to the colonial British policy, Tibet was treated as an autonomous buffer state between India and China. Thus, if any country mattered in the status disputes of Tibet other than China, it was India and with the "Panchsheel Agreement", India had fundamentally compromised this historical fact. The fact that Nehru looked perplexed (or even remorseful) when he first met the young Dalai Lama in Peking in 1954 a few months after the Agreement was signed tells the underlying story. Late Prof. Dawa Norbu sums up that "the PRC could establish its full legal claims over Tibet only after Nehru recognized Tibet as part of China in 1954" as a part of the Agreement.

A more desperate event followed the one of 1954. Fear of China's conspiracy on the night when the Dalai Lama was invited to a show with conditions that he should be unguarded and unarmed, led many thousands of Tibetans to surround the Dalai Lama's palace and prevent him from attending the show. This later led to one of the biggest national uprisings against China's invasion and, eventually led to a desperate escape of the Dalai Lama into India. The only consolation in those desperate hours was the sympathy and warmth of India in giving the Dalai Lama and his followers the much needed asylum. Two things were settled in that unforgettable year of 1959. Firstly, Tibetans clearly displayed the un-willingness to stay with and under China under the existing circumstances and secondly, Tibetans as a group of population became geographically divided. More importantly, Tibetan leadership became physically separated from the Tibetan masses inside Tibet and this was further exacerbated by the China's iron-fist policy of virtual lock-down and, isolation of the region from the rest of the world.

Since then, Tibet's issue has attracted widespread attention of many countries and many international organizations. For instance, the United Nations has passed three resolutions on Tibet since 1959, one each in years; 1959, 1960 and 1961 regarding concerns over violation of human rights in Tibet by the PRC. European Union, US Congress and many other countries have likewise often raised voices against the violations of human rights in Tibet. Tibetans have made their own efforts too. In March 1979, when Deng Xiaoping stated "apart from independence, all issues can be discussed," the Dalai Lama and the Tibetan leadership in exile responded with the proposal for a negotiated settlement, what is now commonly known as the "Middle Way Approach." In the same year, the Central Tibetan Administration in Dharamashala, India, started dispatching fact finding delegations to Tibet. Even as such, the situation inside Tibet did not improve. In fact, starting in mid-1980's, the PRC imposed further restrictions resulting in Tibetan mass protests and the Chinese government responded with the imposition of martial law inside Tibet. Formal channels of communication between Dharamshala and Beijing were suspended for about a decade. Partly because of the international pressure and partly because of China's own interests in improving its image in the run up to its WTO membership and the Beijing Olympics, formal communications between the Dalai Lama's envoys and the Chinese government represented by the United

Front Work Department began in 2002. This dialogue process culminated in the Tibetan side presenting the Chinese government with the proposal for the genuine autonomy for the Tibetan people in October 2008. All these efforts only resulted in more accusations of the Dalai Lama being a splittist and the condemnation of the Tibetan proposal for their insincerity. Since January 2010, no further direct communications have been held and both sides have since hardened their positions.

There are three ways to look at the failure of Sino- Tibetan dialogues so far. One is of course that China, notwithstanding its own invitation for dialogue, is completely not ready to engage in a serious one. The other two ways are inter-connected. 1963 saw the introduction of modern system of democratic governance in the Tibetan community in exile with elected representatives. Democratization process had steadily grown since then with the historical event of the Dalai Lama completely devolving his political powers to the elected Tibetan leadership in 2011. So, at least the Tibetans in exile enjoy the values of democracy such as freedom of thought and expression. In a democratic set-up however, consensus on any matter could be seldom seen let alone on matters as big as the issue of national status and struggle. Therefore, as expected, some Tibetans chose to keep the struggle for complete independence alive and some conformed to the middle way approach. The largest non-governmental organization and the most vocal advocate of complete independence of Tibet, the Tibetan Youth Congress was founded in 1970 by prominent members of the Tibetan community.

The point of intersection comes here, when Deng Xiaoping assumed the responsibility of China's paramount leadership in 1978, China had merely begun to recover from the miseries of events such as the Cultural Revolution and the Great Leap Forward. China had just opened up its economy and needed to engage itself in nation rebuilding. This gives us a slight hint that may be Deng's invitation for discussions might have been merely a trick to avoid unresolved issue of Tibet disturbing his leadership. With the strategic thinking coming from those of masters like Sun Tzu, China's strategic thinking stands arguably next to no one. This understood, Deng might have taken it for granted that the Tibetans will never reach upon a consensus – independence or autonomy – and that PRC can reject or disregard the dialogues easily on the basis of such grounds. The total rejection of the Memorandum on the genuine autonomy for Tibetans by the Chinese government with no regard whatsoever to the merit of the proposal may not come as a surprise if one can understand the assumptions with which China handles the Tibet issue. For the Chinese government, it is very easy to dismiss the good intentions of the proposal for genuine autonomy as long as the voice for independence is heard on the streets of Dharamshala. The tragedy here is that it is difficult to tell whether the Chinese government is indeed afraid of the independence movement or they are simply framing up this issue to reject any meaningful conversation.

As this impasse continues, Tibetans inside Tibet are deprived of basic human rights every day. To witness one of the most woeful periods in the history of Tibet's political struggle since PLA's intrusion, a spate of self-immolation protests, at an alarming rate, has reached a toll of around 80.

This is a clear reflection of the failed policies of Beijing and the total rejection of the repressive rule of the Chinese government by the Tibetans inside Tibet. However, the tragedy is that the Chinese government has put the blame squarely on the Dalai Lama and the Tibetan set-up in exile of rousing Tibetan separatist sentiments instead of investigating the real causes of these most desperate acts.

This month, the world has seen the formal unveiling of the new Chinese leadership but nothing new or dramatic is expected of them. Besides being risk-averse, old leaders still pull the strings and exert a tremendous amount of control over the new leadership and the policies of the government.

Yet many believe the change is imminent as one-party rule in China cannot withstand the immense pressure of the ground realities. China scholar Minxin Pei believes, "the CCP may have defied the odds so far, but cannot do so indefinitely". Change in the hardline policies with regards to handling the Tibet issue can only come with genuine acknowledgment of mistakes committed by its policies and thereby making necessary course corrections. However, in a political environment where acknowledgment of mistakes tantamounts to failure, will the CCP and the Chinese government take this risk?

Both the Tibetan leadership and the Chinese leadership are under tremendous pressure to resolve the self-immolation crisis as the situation is getting out of control day by day. Both parties need to declare ceasefire (from taking rhetorical stance) and return to the negotiation table to discuss ways and means to resolve this crisis as urgently as possible. Though an assessment of Tibet's tragedy in Sino-Tibetan relations shows that Beijing does not hesitate to be arbitrary at all times, it is hoped that only this time, the Chinese side shows genuine concern and serious intent.

2

The Tragedy of Tibet

INTRODUCTION

Until 1950 Tibet was a sovereign state. The Tibetans knew themselves to be a distinct people with their own language, culture, religion, history and customs. In 1950 Tibet was invaded by the army of The People's Republic of China. It is occupied by the Communist Chinese to the present day.

The Tibetan people were unwilling to accept Chinese occupation. Unrest escalated throughout the decade after 1950, culminated in the Tibetan Uprising of 1959. According to Chinese sources 80,000 Tibetans died in Central Tibet alone during and immediately after the uprising. It is estimated that since 1959, 1.5 million Tibetans have died as a direct result of Chinese incursion into the country.

During 1959 many thousands of Tibetans, including the Dalai Lama, sought asylum in India. The exodus of Tibetans from Tibet continues to this day.

In 1960, after reviewing accounts of Chinese atrocities in Tibet, including the widespread use of summary execution, torture and general abuse that included the forced sterilization of women, the International Commission of Jurists found that the Chinese were committing genocide and the 16 articles of the Universal Declaration of Human Rights were being violated. According to the Commission the Chinese were guilty of "the most pernicious crime that any individual or nation can be accused of, viz. a wilful attempt to annihilate an entire people."

In the decades following 1959, particularly during the Cultural Revolution, there was wholesale destruction of Tibetan buildings and religious artifacts. All but 12 of more than 6,000 monasteries were destroyed. Many of them were used as target practice by Chinese artillery. A thousand years' worth of priceless Buddhist literature, religious paintings and artifacts were either destroyed or have fetched millions of dollars on the international market in an effort by the Chinese to raise foreign currency and to wipe out Tibet's rich heritage.

Today, more than 200,000 Tibetans, including the Dalai Lama, live in exile in India, Nepal, Bhutan, Switzerland, the United States and Canada, Australia, New Zealand and elsewhere.

TIBET TODAY

In the last decade the Chinese have stepped up their efforts to re-populate Tibet. Today, Tibetans are a minority in their own country — there are now about 7.5 million Chinese to about 6.5 million Tibetans, and inducements of higher pay and other privileges continue to bring a stream of Chinese settlers into the country. The aim of this is to forcibly resolve China's territorial claims over Tibet by means of a massive and irreversible population shift. In May 1993, an official Chinese government document, leaked to the Tibetan Government in Exile, indicated that the Chinese authorities proposed another massive population transfer as one element in what they termed "a final solution" to their "Tibetan problem". In April this year (1996), the *South China Morning Post* reported official sources in Beijing as saying that a further 500,000 ethnic Chinese are to be moved into Tibet.

This large-scale population transfer has resulted in a 300 percent inflation rate in Tibet, a two-class society sharply divided along racial lines, and unprecedented unemployment among Tibetans.

Tibet, once a peaceful buffer state between India and China, has been transformed into a militarized zone. There are at least 300,000 Chinese troops stationed there at any time, as are at least one quarter of China's nuclear arsenal of 350 nuclear missiles at 5 different missile bases.

It is believed that approximately 3,000 religious and political prisoners are held in prisons and forced labour camps where torture is common. There are reports that Tibetan women are subject *en masse* to forced abortions and sterilization. Alexander Solzhenitsyn has described China's administration of Tibet as "more brutal and inhumane than any other communist regime in the world."

There are strong concerns, voiced internationally, that China is using Tibet as a dumping ground for nuclear waste. There were reports that China had made an offer to West Germany in 1984 to dispose of nuclear waste. The offer was not accepted. Recently Tibetan farmers have complained that "fertilizer" they have been forced to use on their fields is destroying crops and killing birds and animals.

Tibet's natural resources and ecology are being irreversibly destroyed. Wildlife, including the rare Tibetan snow leopard and the wild blue Tibetan sheep, has been decimated. Forests have been clear-cut and transported to China (since 1950, 68% of Tibet's forests have been felled, causing grave concern in Bangladesh and India, now both frequently devastated by flooding.)

China severely restricts the teaching and study of Buddhism, an essential core of Tibetan culture. The Communist Party regulates the admission of monks and nuns into the monasteries and "political education" is compulsory. Though for a period after the Cultural Revolution there appeared to be a liberalizing of the Chinese attitude to religious life, a new report released by the International Campaign for Tibet indicates that China has shifted its religious policy to actively suppress and restrict further religious growth. This involves measures to halt unauthorized rebuilding of monasteries destroyed during the Cultural Revolution, setting limits on the number of monks and nuns in all monasteries, enforcing restrictions on youths joining monasteries, prohibiting Tibetan Party members from practising religion, and strengthening the control of the government and the Communist Party over each monastery.

Last year the Chinese authorities reintroduced a ban, current during the Cultural Revolution but lifted in 1979, prohibiting pictures of the Dalai Lama from monasteries and temples. Recently this was widened to include schools and private homes and there are reports of house-to-house searches checking for possession of photographs of the Dalai Lama.

In 1995 the Chinese government kidnapped the six-year-old Gendun Chökyi Nyima and his parents, shortly after he had been recognized by the Dalai Lama as the latest reincarnation of Tibet's second most important spiritual leader, the Panchen Lama. In a resolution of July, 1995, the European Parliament called on China to release the family immediately. This family, like many other groups and individuals who have been detained without trial, remains unaccounted for.

The Chinese authorities meanwhile have appointed another child as the "recognized reincarnation" of the Panchen Lama. In January 1996, nine monks in Tibet were arrested for openly protesting against China's choice.

THE DALAI LAMA'S FIVE-POINT PEACE PLAN FOR TIBET

First presented by the Dalai Lama as part of an address to the US Congress's Human Right Caucus in September 1987, the Five-Point Peace Plan proposes that Tibet be given the status of a 'peace zone' and that the Tibetan people be granted self-determination in their own land. The Peace Plan is still current. The Chinese Government continues to ignore it, and to maintain its particularly repressive policy in Tibet, in the face of mounting international condemnation.)

The Five-Point Peace Plan for Tibet proposes:

1. Transformation of the whole of Tibet into a zone of peace;
2. Abandonment of China's population transfer policy which threatens the very existence of the Tibetans as a people;
3. Respect for the Tibetqn people's fundamental human rights and democratic freedoms;
4. Restoration and protection of Tibet's natural environment and the abandonment of China's use of Tibet for the production of nuclear weapons and dumping of nuclear waste;

5. Commencement of earnest negotiations on the future status of Tibet and of relations between the Tibetan and Chinese peoples.

THE IDEA OF TIBET : A HIGHLAND TRAGEDY

We must begin by situating Tibet. Should we not then ask – where is Tibet? There are many connotations to this question. Let us begin with the most obvious.

Tibet, the common sense answer would hold, is located in between the ancient civilisations of China and India in a high mountainous region that separates the two. But in another sense we could say, Tibet, rather than separating the two unites them. It is all a matter of perspective. Is Tibet the high elevated mountainous zone of physical geography and the strategic imaginations of great powers, or is it an amalgamation of the towns and villages that spring from the innumerable routes of trade and livelihood that criss cross the region? The former is a separator, the latter a synthesiser of cultures, experiences and ways of life. The question we have been asking can be rephrased as this : is Tibet the land or the people? This is a complex question.

The answer to this question will, however, lead to the solution of the riddle we began with – where is Tibet? If, like me, the reader identifies Tibet first and foremost with its people the riddle becomes even more perplexing. The only sensible answers that I can think of now is that Tibet, as an idea, is out of place. The Dalai Lama and his Tibetan government is in exile in Dharamshala but there is another government in the Tibetan Autonomous Region in Western China. This conflict of identities is only a more visible manifestation of the million tragedies, of individuals and families separated from each other and their homes, that continue to haunt the idea of Tibet.

What is this idea of Tibet that I keep referring to? In fact, here lies the germ of the tragedy of Tibet – the idea of Tibet has never been of its own making. Tibet has for a long time been represented and constructed as 'a land that lies in between' and hardly ever in its own right and, in deed, almost never by itself. The 'in-betweenness' is in many ways the tragedy of Tibet which continues in our age. In the popular imagination, Tibet – the sound of this name – resonates with alluring romance, the sonorous ringing of the gong and the mystical whiff of incense – but that is the Tibet of the holiday package or the new age spiritualism industry. Or, one could say that these images and sounds the popular imagination associated with Tibet today is a re-packaging of the past to satisfy our voyueristic curiosities of the Orient, to create an illusion which prevents us from seeing that, in our ways large and small, we are all, in Peter Hopkirk's words, 'trespassers on the roof of the world.' The Tibet we are enchanted by is not, in many ways, its own land. Our Tibet is a construction of circumstances and circumstances which most often have been in control of and moulded by 'Great Powers' for whom the 'roof of the world' has been a mere 'table top' – to use a crass analogy – for another round of the 'Great Game.'

TIBET IN CONTEXT

The impression of Tibet as an inaccessible highland notwithstanding the region has been witness to human presence for a very long time. Some of the earliest humans who inhabited the Indian subcontinent had passed through the Tibetan high plateau more than 20,000 years ago. It is quite astonishing to find that megalithic rock burials from upto 3,000 years ago exist in the higher reaches of Tibet which, even in our age, are difficult to excavate because of their locations. It must have been some feat for our ancestors who leave us these remarkable monuments to their rugged adaptability.

Tibet had emerged as a unified kingdom from a multiplicity of disparate tribes by the 7th century. The hardy Tibetans, once organized, turned up in the region as a formidable miltary power, striking out from their highland ramparts and spreading Tibetan influence far and wide. Tibetan influence, at its farthest, was felt as far north as the Ferghana Valley in Central Asia, the far reaches of Kashmir in the north-west, with Ladakh and Gilgit-Baltistan still largely Tibetan in their cultural orientation, skirmishing with the Kingdoms of Nepal in the west, threatening the Pala kingdoms of Bengal in the South, of the Asom in the south-east, the Chinese regions of Sichuan and Yunnan in the east, and across the Silk Road routes and cities of the Takla-Makan desert to the frontiers of the Mongol tribes.

The 7th century also brought Buddhism to Tibet. Buddhism was to slowly replace, and in many aspects syncretically assimilate the existing Bon religions and other animistic traditions of the disparate Tibetans and drastically change the nature of Tibetan society, in one possible interpretation, giving rise to a Tibetan nation. Tibetan society gradually also became more settled and inward looking. The spread of Tibetan culture, however, only accelerated with this change with lamaism, the Buddhism of Tibet, becoming the dominant religio-cultural tradition of the soon to be powerful Mongolia.

The Tibetan proto-empire was to come to a rapid end after its heyday. The newly organised Mongolian tribes burst out of their Heartland and went on to create the world empire of the Mongols. The Mongols also went on to conquer China establishing the Sinicized Yuan dynasty. Tibet, too, was conquered by the beginning of the 13th century by the Mongols of the Yuan. With this Tibet became, for the first time, a part of the Heavenly Empire of China.

Since this is a current issue, and a very contentious one at that, one must offer a few comments on the association of Tibet with China. Most debates about whether Tibet was, or is, a part of China begin with a national-territorial frame of reference. This is an anachronism. The Chinese Imperial system was organized not on a national-territorial but what can be called an associational-tributary basis. We can understand this system as having three sets of concentric circles – with the Emperor and the Imperial seat at the centre drawing its legitimacy and authority from Heaven, the cultural core of the Han Chinese civilization forming the second circle around the Imperial seat, and a series of associated kingdoms and other pre-state polities forming the third circle around the cultural core. These polities were in an associational-tributary relationship with the Emperor of China, recognising his overpower, paying tributes and other forms of respect and, often, accepting in their courts the authority of a Resident Agent of the Emperor.

The Resident Agent, not to be confused with the role played by an ambassador, was very powerful in these courts when backed by the might of the Imperial army which often intervened when the authority, or commands, of the Emperor were contravened. But whenever the Imperial core was weak or unstable, and unable to impose its authority through arms, the Resident Agents were powerless.

Returning to the narrative, Tibet remained under Yuan suzerainty until the end of the 14th century. From then on, with the power of the Imperial centre weakening, the Yuan dynasty being replaced by the new Ming dynasty after a series of wars, Tibet became more or less autonomous and remained that way till the beginning of the 18th century when it was again brought into the system of the Chinese Empire by the later Qing dynasty.

It was during the interceding years that in Tibet developed the politico-religious organization associated with Tibet during the colonial era. Namely, the Dalai Lama as the head of the state, the 'God-King' as he was called in colonial literature, and the religious bureaucracy of the Buddhist priesthood organizing the functions of the state. Now also began the development of the diplomatic system the region which was so 'irrational' and, consequently, threatening to the new national-territorial order of the British Colonial State.

This system was characterized by a series of overlapping, for want of a better word, authorities. While the individual rulers of the various kingdom represented temporal authority, the Dalai Lama represented both temporal and spiritual authority, somewhat akin to the Pope before Westphalia. So, while temporally his authority was limited within the territories of Tibet, what Charles Bell called political Tibet, even subject to, at times, to external powers, spiritually he was often 'paid respects' by various kingdoms, namely, the Mongols in Central Asia and smaller kingdoms like Sikkim and Bhutan to the south. These relationships were further complicated, for the external observer, when the later Qing dynasty re-asserted Chinese Imperial control over Tibet. Now, a Resident Ambassador – the amban – exercised significant control in Tibet's, especially external, afffairs. This limited, to some extent, the Dalai Lama's overall authority – in both realms. The conflicts of authority manifesting from the relations between political Tibet and the wider cultural Tibet would play a key role in its diplomatic trajectory in the coming years.

Towards the turn of the 18th century, the influence of the Ming Emperor on Tibet began to decline and the amban was reduced to a mere spectator at the court of the Dalai Lama in Lhasa. Now, correspondingly, the Dalai Lama began to assert his authority again. This threatened to come into conflict with British interests especially when the assertion sought to transcend the territorially organized frontier system of British India in the east. Specifically, the frontier buffer-protectorate kingdom of Sikkim. It was a purported Tibetan incursion into Sikkim that was stated as the primary reason for a British invasion of Tibet, under the guise of a diplomatic mission. Subsequent diplomacy ensured Tibet should remain entrenched under the suzerainty of the Chinese Empire, thus, limiting its intentions and operations as an independent actor.

Preliminary Assessment

Before we proceed with the discussion on the British association with Tibet a few comments to set up the frame if reference are in order.

Two factors will be prominent in the British reaction to Tibet. First, a 'cartographic anxiety of blank spaces' – with Tibet being one of the last unknown lands on the British Indian frontier. Second, an Orientalist conception of the inherent duplicitousness of the Asiatic. The first fuels the drive for gaining knowledge of the terrain, the land and its routes of access despite resistance from the Tibetans. The second leads to an implicit denial in dealing directly and honestly with the Tibetans, where British overtures for diplomacy are not diplomacy at all, but an all or nothing demand for accepting the terms they dictate. This is tragically displayed in the so called diplomatic mission, led by Francis Younghusband, to Tibet in 1903-4 which rather than being a diplomatic mission was an expeditionary force with the sole purpose of coercing the Tibetans into accepting British terms and to gain access to Lhasa. The harrowing details of the expedition lead one to wonder whether barbarism and duplicitousness more aptly describe British dealings with Tibet than the other way round.

The details of how these representations and constructions of Tibet played out in actual politics are too vast a subject to be addressed here. However, in British dealings with Tibet these ideas always played very importanт roles in moulding attitudes and expectations. I leave aside this discussion for now. But a brief mention of these imaginations and attitudes is necessary and should engage ones thought, especially as one considers the shifting narratives of Tibet.

It was a complete ignorance of local realities in Tibet that led to successive British policies towards the country. To the ignorance of terrain, we can add, more importantly, the ignorance of the local lived geographies of Tibet. For example, Tibet's denial of access to Lhasa to any foreigners was fundamentally on the basis of the religio-cultural importance of Lhasa, the seat of the Dalai Lama. This, however, was perceived as evidence of conspiracy and intrigue. One wonders, really, what was behind the desire to reach Lhasa. Was it really strategic or merely an urge to shatter the obstinacy of an Asiatic ruler who refused to treat the British with a privilege they thought they rightfully deserved? Also, one should recognize how the 'in-betweenness' of Tibet continues to remain the primary frame of reference. Tibet is never engaged in its own right.

And nowhere is this more evident than in Lord Curzon's views on the strategic importance of Tibet.

INTERPRETATIONS OF TIBET I : THE 19TH CENTURY

The British Colonial state's interest in Tibet was primarily motivated by the intention to secure this aspect of the eastern frontier system. A Tibet which acted as an independent state, fuelled by purported Russian arms and aid, would tend to create instability in the region, especially in cases where there existed a case of overlapping suzerainty, as in Sikkim. Tibet was not, in Curzon's view, a buffer state in the traditional sense. For Curzon a buffer state must have contiguous borders with two great powers, thus, acting as an inviolable frontier between them. The British interest in Tibet must be looked at from a different perspective.

Curzon, in the Romanes lecture, in the section on artificial frontiers stressed the importance of protectorate buffer states in the Indian territorial system, especially the Princely states scattered around the country, most of them as enclaves within the larger geobody of British India. It is interesting to read in the text that most of these states, he gives the example of the Rajput States, were once identified as buffers between the advancing British territorial control and a hostile power – the Maratha hordes during the 18th century before they were pacified or conquered. These states, in Curzon's poetic language, 'were engulfed in the advancing tide, remaining embedded like stumps of trees in an avalanche, or left with their heads above water, like Islands in a flood.' On the east, Curzon adds, Nepal, Bhutan and Sikkim played the same role.

In Curzonian thought, we see two crucially inter-related goals for a frontier system. First, the maintenance of order within the territorial system. Second, the elimination of threats possibly originating from the frontier. An uncontrolled frontier region makes both these concerns very real. We can add two more related concerns, one, the cartographic anxiety of blank spaces, and, two, the instability of an undefined geobody. The interactions between all these factors come into play with regard to Tibet.

These are addressed by the following strategies. First, Tibet is diplomatically bound in treaty with Britain granting access to the Kingdom. Second, China's suzerainty over Tibet is stressed. Third, and leading from the previous two, the status of Sikkim is clarified as within the territorial and sovereign domain of British India.

INTERPRETATIONS OF TIBET II : THE 20TH CENTURY

The strategic thinking on Tibet we have spoken of in the above section draws primarily from Curzon's Romanes lecture delivered in 1905. Since Curzon was instrumental in developing and implementing British India's policy towards Tibet, indeed, all of the 'Indian frontier system,' as he calls it in the lecture the lecture reveals not just the theoretical understanding behind the policy but also reveals future trends in policy.

Curzon speaks of the British commitment to treat Tibet as a part of the Chinese territorial order. This was institutionalised in 1906 by an Anglo-Chinese treaty and in 1907 during an Anglo-Russian convention which recognized Chinese suzerainty over Tibet.

Events in the 20th century, however, unfolded rapidly and the world political situation changed drastically enough for British strategic circles to rethink their Tibet strategy. The most important upheaval was, of course, the First World War. But before that, in 1910-11, the Chinese 'invaded' Tibet to enforce their claim over 'their' province, causing inflicting massive bloodshed and sending the Dalai Lama fleeing, for the first time in the 20th century, into India. Tibet continued to burn with the populace taking to guerilla warfare. The tensions in Tibet abated only when the faltering Chinese Empire was replaced by the Republican government which promised to respect Tibet's autonomy.

However, even this 'newer' situation of affairs was all to brief. For the World War had brought in its wake a new 'spectre' that was to haunt the World for well into the last decades of the century – Communism. With the birth of the Soviet Union and the rising tide of the Maoist 'revolution' in China strategic thinking in Britain about the role of Tibet for the security of India, and even Asia at large, began to change. No one represented this more than Olaf Caroe.

The key-phrase in Caroe's strategic thinking is the 'Defense of Asia' which he believed was centred in India which it would be best if it was British India but even if India was to become independent Caroe hoped for a friendly successor state. In Caroe's view, India's security was fundamentally dependant on a system if buffer states which would prevent any great power from approaching 'too close' to India. He classified two types of buffers – an inner ring, comprising of the borderlands with Afghanistan, Nepal and Bhutan, with Burma added to them, and an outer ring, which included Persia and Tibet. The great powers in Caroe's imagination were Russia, of course, but also, very importantly, China. Caroe felt that China's potential as a great power had been, very negligently in his view, ignored. In this Caroe is largely right as even Curzon, the quintessential frontiersman, had initially rebuffed the idea of China as a great power capable of territorially pressing India or Inner Asia. It was only much later, with the rise of Communism, that strategic thinkers, began to take the threat of China seriously.

For Caroe, Tibet played a key role in the frontier defense system of India with regard to China. Tibet added strategic depth to India's defence if the Himalayas. It was important for this reason that India commit to the maintenance of Tibetan autonomy, a position starkly different from Curzon's prewar approach. His position regarding Tibet's relationship with China was somewhat confused. He regarded Tibet to be more or less under Chinese suzerainty but gradually this relationship had evolved into a nominal, mostly ceremonially associated, one.

Caroe's views on the strategic importance if Tibet represent an important dimension with regard to the strategic imagination associated with Tibet. But again it reminds us if the almost perpetually cogent view of the in-betweenness if Tibet, always conceived of as strategic terrain.

CHINA IN TIBET, TIBET IN CHINA

The People's Liberation Army of the Communist Party of China ultimately rolled into Tibet in 1950. The purported reason was the liberation of Tibet, from colonialism and, curiously, from itself. The underlying justification, of course, was that the new republic of China was merely re-claiming a land which had always been part of the old China. We can also consider other reasons.

For this exercise we can apply the reverse of everything we have consider edge regarding the strategic importance if Tibet to India. The 're- integration' of ungovernable peripheries was, essentially, of the same, if not more, importance to the new Chinese regime. There can be another, psycho-historical, understanding of China's motivations. It was widely believed that throughout history, China was strongest when it was united, when all three circles of the Heavenly Empire were in harmony. Otherwise, China had always been vulnerable to outsider powers. Semi-autonomous, peripheral regions would provide easy entry points to hostile powers which a newly consolidated China could never allow.

THE TRAGEDY OF TIBET: A SAGA OF BETRAYAL, COLONIZATION AND EXPLOITATION

Traditionally, the greatest dependence of corporations on the state has been in the area of security, Above all, global corporations need stability – what some corporate planners like to call a "surprise-free world." It is possible to put up with less-than-satisfactory political ground rules if you can count on some continuity, but it is not possible to do the kind of efficient planning that is the raison d'être of the global corporation when the rules are subject to precipitous change. Thus the World Managers are prepared to do business with "revolutionary" governments when they are firmly in the saddle. (Indeed, as one corporate strategist told us, socialism, far from being the "end of the world," is actually a "big help" because it ensures "stability" in large areas of the world..." Richard J Barnet and Ronald Müller.

The above observation by Barnet and Müller, written in 1974 and largely based on interviews with the "World Managers" and their "corporate planners" cogently describes the situation that exists in regard to China and China's control over Tibet; and why in this writer's opinion it is unlikely that their will be a determined effort to free Tibet in the foreseeable future.

Green Party co-leader and Member of Parliament Russell Norman made world headlines on June 18 from backwater New Zealand when he held up the Tibetan flag before China's Vice President Xi Jinping, as t he Vice President approached Parliament House. Although Norman's predecessor the late Rod Donald had made a habit of such protests, what was different about this occasion was that Chinese security scuffled with Norman, snatched the Tibetan flag and trampled upon it causing many New Zealanders to question the position of their country vis-à-vis China, despite the enthusiastic way this relationship has been marketed by political and business interests as a panacea for New Zealand economy.

While this action again drew attention to the plight of Tibet under Chinese domination, despite the enormous goodwill that exists among people the world over for that hapless ancient nation and culture, little action has been taken in practical terms to support the Tibetans and censure China, in sharp contrast to subversive actions if not outright military confrontation, that have been taken both during and after the Cold War to destroy the Soviet bloc, Serbia, Iraq, etc., for the benefit of global capital. This essay suggests that similar actions to rid Tibet of the Chinese are unlikely to take place in any meaningful way, other than as occasional platitudes by some politicians.

CIA Sabotage

While it is being claimed that there has been a long association between the Dalai Lama and his supporters and the CIA, as is generally the case such a relationship has been duplicitous. In a scenario that seems to be analogous to the CIA relationship with anti-Castro Cubans leading up to the "Bay of Pigs" fiasco, and indeed the manner by which the USA betrayed Chiang Kai Shek to the Maoists (ironically, despite Stalin's best efforts to the contrary), the CIA backed the Tibetan resistance in the early years of China's occupation for what seems to have been the purpose of scuttle. From 1958 the CIA began training Tibetans in Virginia and Colorado's Rocky Mountains, where 259 Tibetans were trained in Camp Hale over the next five years. Lhamo Tsering, a senior resistance leader and the CIA's chief coordinator documented this fateful saga with the Tibetans, which was the subject of a BBC documentary produced by his son Tenzing Sonam and the latter's wife Ritu Sarin.

In a review of the BBC documentary *The Shadow Circus: The CIA in Tibet*, R. Sengupta cites some of those involved as stating:

"We had great expectations when we went to America. We thought perhaps they would even give us an atom bomb to take back," says Tenzin Tsultrim. "In the training period, we learned that the objective was to gain our independence," adds another grizzled veteran. But the Americans had other ideas. "The whole idea was to keep the Chinese occupied, keep them annoyed, keep them disturbed. Nobody wanted to go to war over Tibet...It was a nuisance operation. Basically, nothing more," says former CIA agent Sam Halpern.

In 1959, following a revolt, where Tibetans held control over large areas of the south, the USA assisted with the Dalai Lama's entry into India when arrest by the Chinese seemed likely. There followed a mass exodus, leaving few resistance fighters.

Undeterred, the CIA parachuted four groups of Camp Hale trainees inside Tibet between 1959 and 1960 to contact the remaining resistance groups. But the missions resulted in the massacre of all but a few of the team members.

A familiar scenario for anti-communists backed by the USA and/or CIA follows:

The CIA cooked up a fresh operation in Mustang, a remote corner of Nepal that juts into Tibet. Nearly two thousand Tibetans gathered here to continue their fight for freedom. A year later, the CIA made its first arms drop in Mustang. Organised on the lines of a modern army, the guerrillas were led by Bapa Yeshe, a former monk.

"As soon as we received the aid, the Americans started scolding us like children. They said that we had to go into Tibet immediately. Sometimes I wished they hadn't sent us the arms at all," says Yeshe. The Mustang guerrillas conducted cross-border raids into Tibet. The CIA made two more arms drops to the Mustang force, the last in May 1965. Then, in early 1969, the agency abruptly cut off all support. The CIA explained that one of the main conditions the Chinese had set for establishing diplomatic relations with the US was to stop all connections and all assistance to the Tibetans. Says Roger McCarthy, an ex-CIA man, "It still smarts that we pulled out in the manner we did."

Thinley Paljor, a surviving resistance fighter, was among the thousands shattered by this volte-face. "We felt deceived, we felt our usefulness to the CIA is finished. They were only thinking short-term for their own personal gain, not for the long-term interests of the Tibetan people." In 1974, arm twisted by the Chinese, the Nepalese government sent troops to Mustang to demand the surrender of the guerrillas. Fearing a bloody confrontation, the Dalai Lama sent the resistance fighters a taped message, asking them to surrender. They did so, reluctantly. Some committed suicide soon afterwards.

"The film is for the younger Tibetans, who are unaware of the resistance, as well as for Americans, who don't know how their own government used and betrayed the resistance," says Tenzing. "Though it was a story begging to be told, funding it was almost impossible," adds Ritu.

Hence if certain American-based interests can be seen as being involved in certain pro-Tibet lobbies, this does not mean that one can expect there to be a consistent and effective pro-Tibet policy from the USA, nor that global capital is in accord with a position toward China vis-à-vis Tibet. More likely, any such feigned friendship emanating form the USA will be poison, as in the case of CIA "support."

Soros

Soros interests in Tibet are not quite the same as the actions of his network towards a myriad of other states that have suffered his "color revolutions." For example, Soros' daughter Andrea established the Trace Foundation in 1993 to work in the Tibetan plateau, after having taught as an English teacher in the region. The Trace Foundation clearly works with the Chinese authorities, and would not last five minutes if it did not. While there is every reason to believe that this humanitarian effort is designed to encourage economic development in Tibet according to the Soros agenda of the "open society" this does not appear to equate with Soros' agenda in other states where he has been responsible for "regime change," often preceded with violence. The Trace foundation would more likely be a means of partnership rather than that of subversion.

It can of course be argued that a "color revolution" in China or in Tibet is impossible, nonetheless are there tangible reasons as to why global capital would actually desire "regime change" in either place? As is known Rockefeller and Soros, Goldman Sachs, and others, have intimate business connections with China.

Soros and Rockefeller believe that China can be integrated within the world economic system without the need for "regime change." Indeed, such change would undoubtedly cause wholesale disruption from which China, like the fiasco of American intervention in Iraq, might never recover, and in the instance of China particularly, the world economic system being cultivated by such globalist interests would stand in danger of irredeemable collapse. Soros' own attitudes toward China is in accord with that of the Rockefellers. Asked by the *London Financial Times* what Obama should discuss when he visited China in November 2009, Soros made it clear that he sees China not as a rival (neo-con style) but as a world leader that would supplant the USA economically, which from the perspective of a globalist who does not owe loyalty to any particular nation-state, Soros does not see as a worrying prospect. Soros stated:

> This would be the time because I think you really need to bring China into the creation of a new world order, financial world order... I think you need a new world order that China has to be part of the process of creating it and they have to buy in, they have to own it in the same way as the United States owns...the current order.

Clearly, Soros and other globalist interests have no interest in undermining the stability of China, nor in freeing Tibet from Chinese control. Indeed, what other regime would guarantee the stability and order necessary for international capitalism to operate? Certainly from the viewpoint of Soros, Rockefeller, et al, China does indeed need to be more "open", and this is indeed inexorably taking place. While the investment and opportunities of international capital in China are well known enough or easy enough to discover, not so obvious is the position in regard to Tibet, and why the elimination of Chinese authority over Tibet would not serve the interests of global capital.

TIBET UNDER COMMUNO-CAPITALIST EXPLOITATION

Tibet is China's tenth Special Economic Zone. This means that the Tibetan Autonomous Region has been granted "special" status in being opened up to foreign capital for exploitation in partnership with the Chinese administration. China ensures order and stability and Western-style economic development in Tibet. It does not seem plausible that Western-based business interests would want that situation to change in favour of one that returns Tibet to a feudal state. Such regimes are seen as outmoded hindrances to maximum profits by international capital, one example having been the Afrikaner remnant whose traditional system, however flawed, did not slot into a world economic system, the post-Afrikaner regime now pursuing a policy of privatization. A sovereign, traditional Tibet is precisely the type of regime that Soros and the NED have sought to depose in the post-Soviet bloc states, attempting to halt any shift towards tradition.

Tibet is heavily endowed with mineral resources. While the hapless Milosevic was a target of NATO because of the mineral wealth of Kosovo, the present regime in Tibet is ideal for the exploitation of the region by Big Business.

A recent announcement to "leapfrog" Tibet's economic development was announced by the Chinese, veiled as being in the interests of the Tibetan people, of course:

"Rational and orderly exploitation of Tibet's mineral resources will power the region's 'leapfrog development'," said Dorje (many Tibetans go by a single name). The Communist Party of China (CPC) Central Committee announced plans to achieve "leapfrog development" in Tibet at the fifth meeting on the work of Tibet in January, including building the region into a "strategic reserve of natural resources" with an aim to reduce poverty among the Tibetan people.

Over the last eight years, Tibet has witnessed over 12 percent economic growth annually as 180 billion yuan ($26 billion) was poured into infrastructure in the region, mostly by the central government, he said.

The central government would continue to pour investment into Tibet in an effort to develop the economy of the remote, impoverished region and raise the living standards of its people, said Zhang Qingli, the region's Communist Party secretary.

Tibet has more than 3,000 proven mineral reserves containing 102 varieties of resources. It has China's biggest proven chromium and copper reserves, according to figures from the regional land and resources department....

"But Tibet's mineral industry is still fledgling, contributing about 3 percent to the local economy," Dorje told Xinhua.

...Tibet has marked nine special zones for mineral industries, including a special economic zone centred on the Yulong Copper Mine, one of China's biggest copper mines in the eastern Qamdo Prefecture, and a salt lake area in the northwest that is expected to become a major base for saline minerals and lithium....

While the monopoly-capitalism of yesteryear relied on the weapons and administrations of the old European empires under which they exploited the resources of colonies until capital truly globalized and the empires became too restrictive, today international capital has the military and administrative structures of the USA and in this instance of China. It is unlikely to be a situation that international capital wants changing for the sake of Tibetan freedom and civilization, while China is providing the infrastructure, administration and policing.

The following extracts from a submission to the UN by a consultative NGO are instructive in regard to the capitalist-Chinese axis exploiting Tibet:

The People's Republic of China's (PRC) policy and practice of population transfer into Tibet, in aid of its efforts to develop Tibet economically and exploit its resources, has been well-documented. In June 1999, President Jiang Zemin announced the PRC's "Western Development" campaign. In theory, this refers to a policy of developing western China by improving its economic infrastructure and providing more funds for education, the environment and technological development. In practice, it represents a systematic escalation of the long-standing policy of exploiting natural resources in Tibet and Xinjiang for export to China. In aid of its exploitation of Tibet, the PRC has received, and is seeking, the assistance of transnational corporations.

With the support of international corporations, mining operations in Tibet threaten to violate the Tibetans' right to self-determination; that is, their right to freely determine their economic, social and cultural development. For example, Australian-owned Sino Mining International (SMI) and other foreign investors plan to develop the Tanjiashan gold deposit in northern Tibet. Tibetans, however, are not participating in the decisions to exploit their natural resources. They will not enjoy the economic benefits these activities bring, as the resources are mined for export. Moreover, evidence indicates that such projects are pursued in an environmentally destructive manner, polluting Tibet's lands, forests and waters. Tibetan communities will bear the long-term social and environmental costs of destructive mining practices.

Significant reserves of oil, gas and hydropower are also located in Xinjiang and Qinghai (Tibetan: Amdo) Provinces. China's oil and gas reserves already have lured foreign investment. BP Amoco invested $578 million in the Chinese oil company, PetroChina, to help complete the "Sebei-Lanzhou" pipeline, which now runs 2500 km from Tibet's Tsaidam Basin to Lanzhou. Italian ENI/Agip also assisted in the construction of this pipeline across the Tibetan plateau. This internationally-financed energy project was developed without consulting Tibetans, without providing any compensation to the Tibetans for their natural resources, and without assessing its dramatic environmental and social impact.

China's plan to construct a 4000 km oil pipeline from Xinjiang to Shanghai, known as the "West-East Pipeline" project, similarly exploits the people's resources without their participation or benefit. This pipeline will eventually connect with the Sebei-Lanzhou pipeline. To finance this estimated $18 billion project, the PRC is entering into partnerships with Shell, Exxon/Mobil and other transnational corporations. Without their financial backing, the PRC simply could not guarantee the success of this unprecedented project. According to Business Week, because China views this project as the backbone of its national energy plan and a springboard for future foreign investments, China initially has been willing to pay lip service to examining the project's social and environmental impacts. Nevertheless, the construction of this pipeline raises grave concerns about the importation of Chinese laborers to work on the pipeline, long-term environmental degradation, lack of compensation to Tibetans and Uighurs for their land, and long-term economic control over the region.

Virtually all of the natural resources and material wealth extracted from Tibet are channeled back to enrich China's eastern regions. The proposed Qinghai-Tibet railway will also serve to accelerate the extraction of minerals and other natural resources, as well as promote the "assimilation of Tibet into the motherland" by increasing Chinese migration. The purpose of such large-scale infrastructure projects, according to Tibet Information Network, is to facilitate the extraction of raw materials and goods out of Tibet and into the wealthier, more industrialized eastern Chinese regions. The People's Daily acknowledged that this project will bring an "unprecedented mammoth transfer of resources."...

Another example of transnational corporations participating in violations of the Tibetans' rights to self-determination, to religious and cultural freedom, and to a protected environment, is the Yamdrok Tso hydroelectric project. This project was built over the strong objections of many Tibetans (some of whom were jailed for objecting) as it threatens the environment surrounding a lake considered sacred by the Tibetan people. Without substantial participation by transnational corporations, which supplied equipment and expertise, this project could not have been built. Moreover, the primary purpose of the project is to supply additional electric power to the Lhasa area in order to support the transfer of more Chinese settlers into this region.

In 2003 the official Chinese media reported on the growth of foreign investment in Tibet: Improving investment environment has attracted increasing overseas capital to the Tibet Autonomous Region in southwest China, an official said in Lhasa, Tibet on Sep.16. Tibet has approved 14 joint ventures with contractual overseas investment amounting to 4.31 million US dollars since 2001, with 2.16 million US dollars of it already materialized, said Dopuje, deputy head of the investment promotion bureau with the regional development and reform commission.... Dopuje attributed the growing overseas investment to China's campaign to open up the vast western regions and a range of preferential policies Tibet has introduced for investors.

The regional government revoked more than 60 articles of regulations that restricted economic development, and improved the investment environment by simplifying approval procedures in 2001, said the official.

A 2008 report cited the enormous increase in foreign investment into Tibet, particularly in regard to mineral prospecting: LHASA–Lhasa, the capital of west China's Tibet Autonomous Region, received 455.5 million US dollars of overseas investment in the first seven months of 2008, up 33 percent year-on-year.

The majority of the investment, or 95.3 percent of the total, went into the industrial sector, which includes non-ferrous metal smelting, the manufacturing of machinery and chemical products, food processing and geological prospecting, according to figures from the city's statistics bureau on Monday… In 2010 China initiated a further programme to encourage investment, stating that, "It was known that the foreign-invested enterprises approved by governmental sectors shall enjoy related preferential polices of the state and the autonomous region."

The Chinese regime over Tibet represents the ideal capitalist scenario: a police state protecting and encouraging foreign investment. Why would the business coteries that are generally in control of the USA – and no less so under Obama – want this situation to change? Any statement to the contrary is likely to be meaningless rhetoric.

3

Tibet in Exile: Refugees or Citizens?

INTRODUCTION

When the administration of Lobsang Sangay came into office in 2011, the self-immolations exploded, handing the CTA a rare opportunity to articulate the causes of the escalating crisis in Tibet and the plight of the Tibetan refugees in India and Nepal. Images of burning nationalists in Tibet adds to a fearful tremor racing through Asia about China's rise, with PLA battle ships advancing in in South China Sea and the explosion of hydro-dam construction in Tibet, yoking the Mekong, Brahmaputra and Indus rivers.

But the Tibet movement has always had scant resources compared to the mighty People's Republic of China. Since the 1989 Tiananmen Square Massacre, the PRC has paid millions to retain the services of the New York public relations firm Hill & Knowlton, to clean up their image and promote the party line that the CCP's unique mélange of capitalism and communism is both an economic success and a model of governance.

Unfortunately, it works: despite the tarnishing of the "China Brand", by the recent Bo Xilai and Chen Guangcheng affairs, foreign capital still flows into the China. There will be no international sanctions levied upon the PRC for torturing men, women and children in distant Tibet, whereas the CCP withholds trade and cancels high level meetings with any government that receives HH Dalai Lama, and gets away with it.

At a time when people inside Tibet are burning alive, when after 61 years of occupation the PRC has installed a formidable military infrastructure across the Tibetan plateau, when no UN Peacekeeping Forces or NATO troops will rescue the victims of China's police state, it is time be realistic about how to assist the Tibetan people at this perilous hour.

Resolutions condemning Chinese atrocities in Tibet add symbolic value and keep the issue on the radar screen, but the only Tibetan community that the CTA and Mr. Sangay can directly influence is in exile. The Kashag has just released a list of achievements of the past year. The Tibet Core is a welcome new program, as is the reform of the school system. The most significant achievement is that Indian government has "kindly agreed to extend the validity of the Registration Certificate for Tibetans born in India as well as those who have held RC for twenty years or more to five years."

While this is a positive step, the CTA must reassess the hard facts about the fragile state of the Tibetan exiles. Tibetans cannot remain stateless refugees much longer; at 53 years, 2nd to the Palestinians as the world's longest unresolved refugee crisis. In the 21st century there is less room and tolerance for refugees all across South Asia. Any Tibetan with a refugee card risks life and limb if they go back to Tibet — unless they were recruited to spy for the Chinese Communist Party — thus repatriation to the homeland is out of the question.

I urge Mr. Sangay and the CTA to pay greater attention to matters of utmost importance; the legal status of the Tibetans in exile, expanding options for citizenship in India, and initiating re-settlement programs to other nations.

TIBETANS IN INDIA: PERMANENT REFUGEES?

That Tibetans can now renew Indian residency permits every 5 years provides a measure of security, but it still consigns Tibetans to refugee status, which prevents many educated, talented and integrated individuals from fully participating in Indian society. In the 1970's the Indian government offered to make all Tibetan refugees citizens of India, but the CTA declined the offer. Wangyal, a retired CTA official said; "Many of us who were involved in those discussions now think turning down the generous offer from the Indian government was a mistake. But there was still a belief that we would soon go back to Tibet, which, in hindsight, was unrealistic even then. If this third generation of Tibetans in exile had Indian citizenship, the Tibetan community would have far more resources and be much stronger today."

Previous CTA administrations did not pursue Indian citizenship for Tibetan refugees. A number of Tibetans acquired Indian citizenship on their own, but research indicates that only 1-3% of Tibetans who are eligible for Indian citizenship apply. The Immigration and Refugee Board of Canada and the United States Bureau of Citizenship and Immigration Services report that both Tibetans born in Tibet who escaped to India and those born in India to Tibetan refugee parents, face legal obstacles to obtaining Indian citizenship.

Many Tibetans, Indians and international supporters agree; the exile community should commence a new dialogue with the Indian government on securing citizenship for Tibetans, especially those born in India. In a highly publicized 3-year court case, Namgyal Lagyari of Dehradun attained Indian citizenship, which has inspired other Tibetans born in India to do the same.

Tibetans in India need better access to legal resources and education, to fully understand UN and Indian refugee charters and laws, to know the full scope of rights and restrictions that apply to refugees, and to pursue citizenship or immigration through legal processes.

The Quest for the West

Switzerland was the first nation to grant citizenship to a small number of Tibetan refugees in the 1960's. In the 1970's a visionary Canadian Ambassador in New Delhi took an especial interest in the Tibetan refugees and managed a resettlement project, which brought whole families together. The US Immigration Act of 1990 approved 1000 immigrant visas to Tibetans in India and Nepal. But in the American system, a single individual is selected by a lottery. Many relatives spent years waiting for reunification visas, straining ties already injured by separation from kinfolk in Chinese Occupied Tibet.

Today, after 23 years, an estimated 10,000 Tibetans have legally immigrated to the USA to join the relative who went first. But the "quest for the west" as it is often termed in the *chai* stalls of McLeod Ganj and Majnu ka Tila, has caused serious dislocations and fractures. Many in India, constrained by permanent refugee status into a third generation, feel great pressure to try to go west by any means possible.

Most Tibetan refugees are poorly informed about immigration laws and procedures, and are therefore easily misinformed, exploited and harmed by visa brokers.

Visa Brokers, Passport Rings

Refugee groups are especially vulnerable to exploitation, bribery and coercion, and Tibetans are no exception. There are numerous passport and visa brokers operating throughout the Tibetan exile world, from New Delhi to New York. In many cases large sums are paid to visa brokers, who frequently vanish with the cash. Many "clients" of brokers arrive in Manhattan or London, owning a huge debt, which can take several years to pay off. Tibetans who enter Germany as asylum seekers are given a tiny stipend and must live in restricted housing for months or years before they are granted residency, which was not what they expected when cutting the deal with the broker back in Asia.

The US State Dept. has concerns about passport rings operating from Tibet and India, with a well-worn trick, familiar to consular officers; a passport with a US visa is sent back, the photo is changed and a new person enters the USA without having an interview at any consulate.

In recent years, trends have emerged that have caused considerable harm; newly arrived refugees fabricating their date of birth or parentage, to pass as children of Tibetans who entered India before issuance of resident permits for Tibetans was suspended, and Tibetans from India who enter the US and are lured by brokers to claim asylum by fabricating abuse at the hands of Indian officials, or alter documents to pretend they were born in Tibet and thereby qualified for political asylum. Falsifying one's identity invites disastrous consequences, including deportation and arrest; there are documented cases of INS officials discovering fabricated information and deporting Tibetans back to India.

In the late 1990's aggressive brokers began collecting funds from Tibetans in India promising a green card based on bogus asylum claims. I was asked to write supporting letters for persons who had advanced money to brokers, so I had the opportunity to read many of these narratives, which alleged relentlessly cruel treatment at the hands of Indian officials. When I asked if the narratives were true, I was told they were not: they had been written by the broker.

I did not support these claims; I was concerned they would cause problems in the future. If the Indian government learned of the schemes, it would be rightly offended — to this day India is the largest donor to the Tibetan refugees — and it would offend HH Dalai Lama, who has never sought to leave his exile home and proudly states; "I am a son of India."

The Damage Done

In 1998 I received a call from an official at the fraud department of the US Dept. of State in Washington DC, inquiring about a spike in Tibetan refugee asylum claims from India, asking if Tibetans were indeed at risk in India. I forwarded documents from the Indian Home Ministry and the CTA and independent monitoring agencies, with the history of India's generous care for the Tibetan people and their great esteem for HH Dalai Lama. Surely there are individual cases of exploitation and abuse, but the Indian government deserves praise for its humanitarian service to the Tibetan people and its concern for the preservation of Tibetan culture and religion.

Shortly thereafter, I received a letter from a one Mr. Pema Gashon, then a leader of the Tibetan Youth Congress of New York and New Jersey, and a familiar presence at all New York Tibetan gatherings. Mr. Gashon described his plan to get asylum for Tibetans from India, writing; "we know that our case is not strong so we will pay you any fee you wish if you will get members of

Congress and President Clinton to support us." I made several copies of the letter, provided them to CTA officials and urged them to investigate the matter and question Mr. Gashon about offering a bribe to a relative of a US Senator, in exchange for false information about India, a country where my father had served as the US envoy in the 1970's.

I was not privy to any information about what if any action was taken, but I know of several individuals who obtained green cards via Mr. Gashon, and others who paid him large sums of cash but did not obtain papers.

Over the past 15 years, such brokers have multiplied. The Tibet Justice Center and other groups have gathered anecdotal evidence of how the brokers operate; inducing their clients to lie to officials, withholding passports to obtain more funds, threatening to deport clients back to India or Tibet: persuading US law firms to work pro bono while taking large sums of cash from anxious clients; stealing passports from clients for the broker's relatives and friends. There are reports of Tibetan women sold into prostitution rings to pay off the debt. (This is how illegal passport/ visa rings operate around the globe).

And now, sadly, Tibetans in India who have legitimate opportunities to visit the USA, for education, business or family reunification, cannot obtain visas. Most are automatically rejected without having any review of their files. Even Fulbright scholars cannot get a fair hearing. Addressing the Tibetan Community at the Kalachakra in Washington, DC, in 2011, HH Dalai Lama asked that people follow legal procedures and not falsify any information for the purpose of obtaining asylum.

The CTA and other US based Tibet support groups in the USA should work with the US Embassy in New Delhi to grant Tibetan visa applicants fair hearings, and with the US congress to pass a new senate resolution authorizing a second US resettlement project. During the 1990 project the US offered to take more than 1000, but the CTA declined. The US is in the process of resettling 60,000 Bhutanese refugees of Nepali origin who have been in UNHCR camps since the early 1990's. The Tibetan refugees are a small population with longstanding support in the US Congress, thus a strong case can be made for issuing more immigrant visas, which would put a lot of unscrupulous visa brokers out of business.

A great many Tibetan refugees are now stranded in the USA without papers, manipulated by brokers and scammers, living on the fringes of a struggling immigrant network. Most immigrant groups in the US have legal advisory teams and legal defense funds; the CTA could also establish a program that provides counsel to refugees, educating them about their legal status, rights and options. The CTA can also open dialogues with embassies in New Delhi about resettlement, to research procedures whereby Tibetans can legally immigrate.

TIBETANS IN NEPAL: NO PROTECTION, NO EXIT

Tibetans in Nepal are the most vulnerable, neglected, and at risk. In the past decade, following the assassination of King Birendra and the rise of the Maoists, the CTA has lost any means of protecting the large and influential Tibetan network that flourished in the days of the Hindu kingdom, now under assault from Chinese agents and their Maoists puppets.

Said a retired CTA official now living in Kathmandu, who asked not to be named given the sensitivity of the Tibet issue in Nepal, "Dharamshala made decisions that hurt us badly. They sold off so many businesses, leaving families with no income. When UNHCR was told to remove their protection officer at the Tibet border, by Chinese command, there was no effort made to lobby UNHCR headquarters in Geneva to restore it. When the Tibet office was closed down, the CTA did not negotiate with Nepali, Indian and US officials to save it. Samdhong Rinpoche reduced the number of CTA security staff from 12 to 1, overnight. New refugees from Tibet had to be screened by the CTA security department, to protect the exile community and keep strong relations with India and the USA. So many people are abusing the system to qualify for US visas. Without effective screening there is more abuse. That completely broke down. And now CTA officials are afraid to come to Nepal, even if they have US or Canadian passports. The psychological impact of this has created a refugee victim mentality. We have no leadership."

After the murder of King Birendra in 2001, Tibetans in Nepal lost the protection of the palace. The US Embassy in Kathmandu conducted a research survey, and proposed resettling a large number of Tibetan refugees in the US. News of this project in Nepal created a classic "pull factor", whereby Tibetans from India attempted to insert themselves into the process. Said the former CTA official in Nepal; "Dharamshala asked to review all the applicants, and a number of Tibetans from India appeared on the list with no history of being registered in Nepal. The Nepali government got confused, it got bogged down, the Maoists came to power and now they won't issue exit permits, so it did not happen, which is a great shame."

REFUGEES IN INDIA: LEGAL FRAMEWORK, LAW ENFORCEMENT AND SECURITY

There are numerous aspects pertaining to refugees which are of major importance both to India, as a country and to the refugees, particularly in the context of law enforcement. Given the security scenario prevailing in the country, particularly arising out of the role of some of the neighbours in this regard, an utterly humanitarian matter like the 'refugees' has come to be influenced by considerations of national security. It is a reality that we can ill-afford to overlook this aspect of the matter in any dispassionate deliberation of the subject under review in this article. While law and order is a State subject under the Indian Constitution, international relations and international borders are under the exclusive purview of the Union government. This has resulted in a variety of agencies, both of the Central as well as the State governments, having to deal with refugee matters connected with law enforcement. Also, all policies governing refugees are laid down by the Union government though the impact of the refugee problem as such has to be borne by the State administration to a greater degree if not wholly.

Security personnel at the international borders, immigration personnel at the land check posts, international airports and seaports, besides a host of state police personnel, are all intimately connected with law enforcement affecting refugees one way or another. As the very term 'security' denotes, all the above categories of personnel are entrusted with the onerous responsibility of ensuring national as well as internal security of the country as their first and foremost charge. They have to make sure that the laws of the land are enforced in regard to refugees without in any way ignoring or neutralising security considerations. But, at the same time, it is also their responsibility that the humanitarian overtones so characteristically and inseparably associated with refugees in general, are not lost sight of. It is also well known that every single situation pertaining to 'refugees' is replete with human rights aspects as well. It is obvious that these have also necessarily to be taken due care of by law enforcement personnel.

A proper understanding of the circumstances pertaining to specific refugee situations by the concerned law enforcement agency or even by an individual official, would pave the way for taking care of both the security as well as the humane aspects- from both the humanitarian as well as the human rights angle. At the same time, knowledge on the part of all those who handle refugees- whether they are part of the government machinery or outside it (including international agencies, NGOs etc) of the laws of the land and also how the security and enforcement personnel function, would considerably facilitate looking after the refugees.

REFUGEE- A CREATURE OF CIRCUMSTANCES

It should be appreciated that a person becomes a refugee because of circumstances which are beyond that person's control, often poignant. He/She is left with no other option but to flee from human rights violations, socio-economic and political insecurity, generalised violence, civil war or ethnic strife all these leading to fear of persecution. The import of this observation would be evident when one looks at the definition of a 'refugee'. The term 'Refugee' has a particular meaning in international law and its legal definition is laid down in the United Nations 1951 Convention relating to the Status of Refugees (to be referred to as "1951Convention") and its 1967 Protocol. Article 1 para. 2 of the 1951 Convention defines the 'refugee' as "A person who owing to well founded fear of being persecuted for reasons of race, religion, nationality, membership of a particular social group or political opinion, is outside the country of his nationality and is unable or, owing to such fear, unwilling to avail himself of the protection of that country.". Therefore, the need to give due importance to humanitarian and human rights aspects in dealing with refugees cannot be over-stressed.

Thus, it may be noted that there are well-defined and specific grounds, which have to be satisfied before a person can qualify to be a ' refugee'. These grounds are *well-founded on fear of persecution* and considerations of a number of factors which may operate individually or collectively.

DISTINCTION BETWEEN REFUGEES AND OTHER FOREIGNERS

While all persons who are not Indian citizens are 'Foreigners' including refugees, it is necessary to clearly distinguish the latter from other categories of 'foreigners'. There are considerable misgivings in the minds of many in India because of the failure to clearly understand the difference between 'refugees' and various 'other categories of foreigners'. The consequence of this misunderstanding, particularly because of the large number of 'illegal immigrants' from Bangladesh who have spread into different parts of India; has tended to adversely influence the thinking of many in the country about the basic issues involved in the problem of 'refugees'. Unless the distinction between the 'refugees' on the one hand and all other categories of 'foreigners' on the other, is clearly brought home, our attempts to sensitise people in the various strata of our society will remain inadequate.

There are at least three well-defined groups of foreigners who are different from 'refugees'. It is important that the distinction among them is clearly understood and none of them is confused with or mistaken for a 'refugee'. These categories are:

Temporary Residents, Tourists and Travellers

Persons under this category come to India for a specific purpose and duration with the prior permission of the Government of India. However, in certain circumstances any one in this category could become eligible for being a refugee, if, during their sojourn in India, the situation in their country of origin becomes such as to endanger their lives and liberty if they were to return to their country. Many Iranians who had come to India for studies during the regime of the Shah of Iran, have stayed back in India as refugees after the fall of Shah of Iran and a revolutionary government took his place in 1978. It should be mentioned that no one can automatically claim the right for 'refugee status' under this category. It is the prerogative of the Indian government to satisfy themselves and decide each case according to merits and circumstances.

Illegal Economic Migrants

Any foreigner who might have left his or her country of origin without due authorisation from the authorities concerned, both in the country of origin as well as the country of destination, solely to improve his or her economic prospects, is *not a refugee*. After all, there is no element of persecution or coercion compelling the individual to leave the country of origin. Illegal migrants from Bangladesh are examples of this category. Such persons have to be treated as illegal and unauthorised entrants into the country and dealt with under the appropriate laws applicable to foreigners like Foreigners Act, Indian Passport Act etc. besides the IPC, Cr.PC etc.

Criminals, Spies, Infiltrators, Militants etc

None of these can ever become eligible to be refugees. They have to be dealt with under the provisions of the Indian criminal laws as well as any other special laws in force even though some of them may be in possession of valid travel documents.

Internally Displaced Persons (IDP)

Those persons who are fleeing persecution and human rights violations from one region of the country and have sought refuge in another region of the same country, fall under this category. Such persons cannot be categorised as 'refugees' as they have not crossed any international border. Moreover, they have the protection of their national government. These persons are categorised as 'internally displaced persons' (IDP). Kashmiris who have been forced to flee from Jammu and Kashmir and who have settled in other parts of India fall under this category. Incidentally, in many African countries, the IDPs are also treated as 'refugees' within the ambit of the 1951 Convention.

THE REFUGEE SCENE IN INDIA

A brief look at the refugee scenario in India will help appreciate in the proper perspective, the complexities of law enforcement in a variety of situations impinging upon the refugees.

India has been home to refugees for centuries. From the time when almost the entire Zorastrian community took refuge in India fleeing from the persecution they were then subjected to on religious grounds in Iran, India has, from time to time continued to receive a large number of refugees from different countries, not necessarily from the neighbouring countries alone.

The most significant thing which deserves to be taken note of is that, there has not been a single occasion of any refugee originating from the Indian soil except the transboundary movement of the people during the partition of the country in 1947. On the other hand, it has invariably been a receiving country and in the process, enlarging its multi-cultural and multi-ethnic fabric.

In keeping with its secular policies, India has been the home to refugees belonging to all religions and sects. It is relevant to point out that since its independence India has received refugees not only from some of its neighbouring countries but distant countries like Afghanistan, Iran, Iraq, Somalia, Sudan and Uganda.

The South Asian sub-continent has often witnessed situations where refugees from one or the other neighbouring countries have crossed over to India. Considering the sensitivities of national and regional politics in the sub-continent, the problem of refugees crossing over to India cannot be totally disassociated from the overall security issues relevant locally. At the end of 1999, India had well over 2,51,400 refugees, who do not include those from countries like Afghanistan, Iran, Iraq, Somalia, Sudan and Uganda.

ACCORDING 'REFUGEE STATUS'

Even though India has been the home for a large number and variety of refugees throughout the past, India has dealt with the issues of 'refugees' on a bilateral basis. India, as explained in the earlier pages, has been observing a 'refugee regime' which generally conforms to the international instruments on the subject without, however, giving a formal shape to the practices adopted by it in the form of a separate statute. Refugees are no doubt 'foreigners'. Even though there may be a case to distinguish them from the rest of the 'foreigners', the current position in India is that they are dealt with under the existing Indian laws, both general and special, which are otherwise applicable to all foreigners. This is because there is no separate law to deal with 'refugees'. For the same reason, cases for refugee 'status' are considered on a case-by-case basis. UNHCR often plays a complementary role to the efforts of the Government, particularly in regard to verification about the individual's background and the general circumstances prevailing in the country of origin. That agency also plays an important role in the resettlement of refugees etc.

It may be restated for purposes of clarity and understanding that a refugee is defined as one who is outside the country of nationality (or even country of habitual residence) due to one of the five grounds, namely, a well-founded fear of persecution on the basis of religion, race, nationality or membership of a political or social group. In some countries, a person who flees his home country because of armed conflicts or wars or other generalised violation of human rights and who may not be targeted on account of any of the five grounds specified above, is excluded from the purview of the above definition of 'refugee'. In many countries a difference is sought to be made between persecution effected by State agents and the one effected by non-state agents as may be the case in places where 'rebel' 'terrorist' and such other groups are active. Under such circumstances it is only those who are affected by the action of the State agents who are held to fulfill the definition of 'refugee' and not the latter.

One of the principal elements to satisfy a claim to refugee status is that the claimant must be 'genuinely at risk'. Various legal "tests" have developed which concern the standard of proof that is required to satisfy what constitutes being genuinely at risk or having a genuine well founded fear of persecution. Some of these tests have been articulated by courts in a number of countries. In the case of *INS vs Cardoza Fouseca* interpretation of the "well founded fear" standard would indicate that "so long as an objective situation is established by the evidence, it need not be shown that the situation will probably result in persecution, but it is not enough that persecution is a reasonable possibility..." The above standard was considered in *R vs Secretary for the Home Department*, the case of *ex parte Sivakumaran*. The judgement suggested that the 'test' should consider whether there is an evidence of a "real & substantial danger of persecution". The Canadian Federal Court of Appeal considered the above and disapproved the House of Lords formulation in *Joseph Ayei vs Ministry of Employment & Immigration*. They considered the "reasonable chance" standard. Therefore, in sum, in considering the above 'tests' what can be gleened is a rather liberal standard which requires that if, "....there is an objective evidence to show that there is a reasonable possibility or chance of relevant prosecution in the claimant's state of origin", the claim should be adjudged well founded.

In the case of India, the decision as whether to treat a person or a group of persons as refugees or not is taken on the merits and circumstances of the cases coming before it. The Government of India (GOI) may be often seen as following a policy of bilateralism in dealing with persons seeking to be refugees. For example, Afghan refugees of Indian origin and others, who entered India through Pakistan without any travel documents, were allowed entry through the Indo-Pakistan border till 1993. Most of the refugees had entered India through the Attari border near Amritsar in Punjab. Subsequent to 1993, the Government altered its policy of permitting Afghan refugees freely into India.

In the case of a large number of them (many of them were Afghan Sikhs and Afghan Hindus) who had to flee from Afghanistan under circumstances which fulfilled one or more of the grounds specified earlier for being treated as a 'refugee', the GOI did not officially treat them as refugees. However, the UNHCR with the consent of the GOI, recognised them as refugees under its mandate and is rendering assistance to them. In such cases, even though the local Government is kept in the picture, the UNHCR becomes responsible to look after them as well as 'administer' them and also to ensure that such refugees do not in any way violate the code of conduct governing them.

In contrast, in 1989, when the Myanmar authorities started suppressing the pro-democracy movement in that country and about 3,000 nationals of that country sought refuge in India, the GOI declared that in accordance with well accepted international norms defining refugee status, no genuine refugee from Myanmar would be turned back and in fact, they were accepted as refugees by the GOI. Similar is the case of Sri Lankan Tamil refugees crossing the sea to enter the southern Indian State of Tamil Nadu. The Government of India followed a specific refugee policy regarding Sri Lankan refugees and permitted them entry despite the fact that the refugees did not have travel documents.

In cases where the Government of India recognises the claim of refugee status of a particular group of refugees, there is minimal interference if any, caused to the refugees. This is the case even though there may be no official declaration of any policy of grant of refugee status to that group. However, there are instances where refugees recognised by the Government of India and issued with valid refugee identity documents by the government, are later prosecuted for illegal entry/over stay. The National Human Rights Commission had taken up successfully the cause of a number of Sri Lankan Tamil refugees who had been likewise prosecuted.

EVIDENCE REQUIRED TO ESTABLISH A REFUGEE CLAIM

In order for a claimant refugee to put forward a genuine claim for determination of refugee status, it is crucial to accumulate all the documents that the claimant can muster in support of the grounds of persecution or fear thereof resulting in flight from country of origin. The documentation may be in the form of an identity card of employment with some governmental agency in the country of origin, or an identity card indicating membership of a particular group. Production of the same would be evidence of a claim of involvement with particular groups and would also serve to prove the claimant's identity. Any other information that the claimant may be able to gather to prove specific persecution or fear thereof, such as names of persecutors, leaders of groups involved in committing persecution, details of areas where persecution is committed will help strengthen the case of the claimant. Similarly, the claimant must be able to establish all his statements to interviewing authorities in a consistent manner, without discrepancies. If there are obvious contradictions between the statements made by the claimant himself at different times to different persons, his claim to refugee status may be rejected. The statements made by the claimant must also not be contradictory to the general information available on the country of origin. Corroboration and confirmation of facts pertaining to persecution is an essential factor in determining refugee status. Efforts are made by authorities to gather background human rights data from a broad cross section of official and non-governmental sources in order to supplement whatever evidence may be adduced by the claimant himself. Thus, circumstantial evidence that persons similarly situated to the claimant are at risk in the country of origin, is essential.

To establish a fear of persecution, the term "fear" is not to be judged on the basis of the emotional reaction of the claimant. Instead, "fear" must be employed to mandate a forward looking assessment of risk. Therefore, persons who had already suffered persecution in their country of origin, as well as those who may be judged to face prospective risk of persecution in event of return to their country of origin, would be able to claim refugee status.

The heart of the refugee determination process is the careful consideration of the claimant's own evidence, whether provided orally or in documentary form. It is ideally required that all claimants for refugee status receive an opportunity to be heard by the authority responsible for the adjudication of their case. All the materials thus collected and collated are then tallied with independent, internationally acknowledged information available on the region from which the claimant has arrived. In possible circumstances and cases, the information thus obtained is also reconfirmed from the UNHCR office in the country of origin.

Along with making claims for refugee status, refugees may also seek redressal of immediate basic problems facing them, such as food, shelter, legal aid etc. In regard to such matters the UNHCR plays a major role by providing in suitable and deserving cases, a "Subsistence Allowance" to destitute refugees and their dependents. The UNHCR also helps in enabling the refugee to find his own accommodation or to share a tenanted accommodation with another similarly placed refugee. When a refugee seeks legal aid for himself or for his dependent, the UNHCR may provide the assistance or recommend an Advocate who is familiar with handling refugee matters, to help sort out the problem faced by the refugee. In cases where the refugee is to be deported back to his country of origin, the UNHCR officials may request the Central Government to stall deportation proceedings, pending UNHCR attempts at resettlement of the refugee in a safe country. In order to make such resettlement possible, the UNHCR takes up such cases with the Embassies of other countries for grant of travel to and stay facilities in their countries.

INDIA'S INTERNATIONAL COMMITTMENTS

India does not have on its statute book a specific and separate law to govern refugees. In the absence of such a specific law, all existing Indian laws like The Criminal Procedure Code, The Indian Penal Code, The Evidence Act etc. apply to the refugees as well. Even though India is not a signatory to the 1951 Convention on refugees and also the 1967 Protocol, India is a signatory to a number of United Nations and World Conventions on Human Rights, refugee issues and related matters. India's obligations in regard to refugees arise out of the latter. India became a member of the Executive Committee of the High Commissioner's Programme (EXCOM) in 1995. The EXCOM is the organisation of the UN, which approves and supervises the material assistance programme of UNHCR. Membership of the EXCOM indicates particular interest and greater commitment to refugee matters. India voted affirmatively to adopt the Universal Declaration of Human Rights which affirms rights for all persons, citizens and non- citizens alike. India voted affirmatively to adopt the UN Declaration of Territorial Asylum in 1967. India ratified the

International Covenant on Civil and Political Rights (ICCPR) as well as the International Convention on Economic, Social and Cultural Rights (ICESCR) in 1976. India ratified the UN Convention on the Rights of the Child in 1989. India ratified the Convention on the Elimination of All Forms of Discrimination Against Women (CEDAW) in 1974 under which Article 1 imposes legally binding obligation. India accepted the principle of *non-refoulement* as envisaged in the Bangkok Principles, 1966, which were formulated for the guidance of member states in respect of matters concerning the status and treatment of refugees. These Principles also contain provisions relating to repatriation, right to compensation, granting asylum and the minimum standard of treatment in the state of asylum.

In order to get a clear understanding of the rights which devolve on the refugees on account of India's international commitments mentioned above and their relevance to law enforcement, it is pertinent to enumerate some of the more important rights accruing to refugees under the above mentioned Conventions. Article 13 of the Universal Declaration of Human Rights guarantees 'Right to Freedom of Movement', Article 14 'Right to Seek and Enjoy Asylum' and Article 15 the 'Right to Nationality.' Article 12 of the ICCPR deals with 'Freedom to leave any country including the person's own' and Article 13 'Prohibition of expulsion of aliens except by due process of law'. Under Article 2 A of the UN Convention on the Rights of the Child, the State must ensure the rights of "each child within its jurisdiction without discrimination of any kind"; Article 3 lays down that "In all actions concerning children the best interest of the child shall be a primary consideration"; Article 24 relates to 'Right to Health'; Article 28 to 'Right to Education' and Article 37 to 'Juvenile Justice'.

REFUGEES AND THE INDIAN LEGAL FRAMEWORK

Refugees encounter the Indian legal system on two counts. There are laws which regulate their entry into and stay in India along with a host of related issues. Once they are within the Indian territory, they are then liable to be subjected to the provisions of the Indian penal laws for various commissions and omissions under a variety of circumstances, whether it be as a complainant or as an accused. These are various constitutional and legal provisions with which refugees may be concerned under varying circumstances.

Constitutional Provisions

There are a few Articles of the Indian Constitution which are equally applicable to refugees on the Indian soil in the same way as they are applicable to the Indian Citizens.

The Supreme Court of India has consistently held that the Fundamental Right enshrined under Article 21 of the Indian Constitution regarding the Right to life and personal liberty, applies to all irrespective of the fact whether they are citizens of India or aliens. The various High Courts in India have liberally adopted the rules of natural justice to refugee issues, along with recognition of the United Nations High Commissioner for Refugees (UNHCR) as playing an important role in the protection of refugees. The Hon'ble High Court of Guwahati has in various judgements, recognised the refugee issue and permitted refugees to approach the UNHCR for determination of their refugee status, while staying the deportation orders issued by the district court or the administration.

In the matter of *Gurunathan and others vs. Government of India* and others and in the matter of *A.C.Mohd.Siddique vs. Government of India and others,* the High Court of Madras expressed its unwillingness to let any Sri Lankan refugees to be forced to return to Sri Lanka against their will. In the case of *P.Nedumaran vs. Union Of India* before the Madras High Court, Sri Lankan refugees had prayed for a*writ* of mandamus directing the Union of India and the State of Tamil Nadu to permit UNHCR officials to check the voluntariness of the refugees in going back to Sri Lanka, and to permit those refugees who did not want to return to continue to stay in the camps in India. The Hon'ble Court was pleased to hold that "since the UNHCR was involved in ascertaining the voluntariness of the refugees' return to Sri Lanka, hence being a World Agency, it is not for the Court to consider whether the consent is voluntary or not." Further, the Court acknowledged the competence and impartiality of the representatives of UNHCR.

The Bombay High Court in the matter of *Syed Ata Mohammadi vs. Union of India,* was pleased to direct that "there is no question of deporting the Iranian refugee to Iran, since he has been recognised as a refugee by the UNHCR." The Hon'ble Court further permitted the refugee to travel to whichever country he desired. Such an order is in line with the internationally accepted principles of '*non-refoulement*' of refugees to their country of origin.

The Supreme Court of India has in a number of cases stayed deportation of refugees such as *Maiwand's Trust of Afghan Human Freedom vs. State of Punjab* ; and, *N.D.Pancholi vs. State of Punjab & Others*. In the matter of *Malavika Karlekar vs. Union of India,* the Supreme Court directed stay of deportation of the Andaman Island Burmese refugees, since "their claim for refugee status was pending determination and a *prima facie* case is made out for grant of refugee status." The Supreme Court judgement in the Chakma refugee case clearly declared that no one shall be deprived of his or her life or liberty without the due process of law. Earlier judgements of the Supreme Court in *Luis De Raedt vs. Union of India* and also *State of Arunachal Pradesh vs. Khudiram Chakma,* had also stressed the same point.

Arrest, Detention and Release

There is yet another aspect of *non-refoulment* which merits mention here. The concept of 'International Zones' which are transit areas at airports and other points of entry into Indian territory, which are marked as being outside Indian territory and the normal jurisdiction of Indian Courts, is a major 'risk factor' for refugees since it reduces access of refugees to legal remedies. This legal fiction is violative of the internationally acknowledged principle of *non-refoulement*. In the matter of a Palestinian refugee who was deported to New Delhi International Airport from Kathmandu was sent back to Kathmandu from the transit lounge of the Airport. He was once more returned to New Delhi International Airport on the ground of being kept in an 'International Zone'. Such detention is a classic case on the above point barring legal remedies to the detained refugee. The only relief in such a case is through the administrative authorities.

Articles 22(1),22(2) and 25(1) of the Indian Constitution reflect that the rules of natural justice in common law systems are equally applicable in India, even to refugees. The established principle of rule of law in India is that no person, whether a citizen or an alien shall be deprived of his life, liberty or property without the authority of law. The Constitution of India expressly incorporates the common law precept and the Courts have gone further to raise it to the status of one of the basic features of the Constitution which cannot be amended.

The Indian Constitution does not contain any specific provision which obliges the state to enforce or implement treaties and conventions. A joint reading of all the provisions as well as an analysis of the case law on the subject shows international treaties, covenants, conventions and agreements can become part of the domestic law in India only if they are specifically incorporated in the law of the land. The Supreme Court has held, through a number of decisions on the subject that international conventional law must go through the process of transformation into municipal law before the international treaty becomes internal law. Courts may apply international law only when there is no conflict between international law and domestic law, and also if the provisions of international law sought to be applied are not in contravention of the spirit of the Constitution and national legislation, thereby enabling a harmonious construction of laws. It has also been firmly laid that if there is any such conflict, then domestic law shall prevail.

GROUND REALITIES - SOME ASPECTS

Role of Border Guarding Forces and Law Enforcement Officials

It will be useful to acquaint oneself with the realities on ground when a refugee attempts to cross or actually crosses over to India. The Border Security Force (BSF) which guards the India-Pakistan and the India-Bangladesh borders, the Indo-Tibetan Border Police Force (ITBPF) which is deployed along the India-Tibet (China) border and the Assam Rifles (AR) which is deployed along the India-Myanmar border, are usually the first representatives of the

Indian system which refugees may encounter when they enter or exit India by land routes.

Vastness and, sometimes even the treacherous nature of the border terrain make it difficult to physically man the entire international borders of India. The gaps in the border left unguarded, are often used by refugees to illegally enter/exit the Indian territory. If caught while entering illegally, the authorities may return the refugee across the border, sometimes even without ascertaining relevant refugee claims of persecution in the country of origin, though this is not in strict conformity with the internationally acknowledged principle of *non-refoulement*. When this happens, the refugee may face 'forced return' to the country where he/she came from. In the alternative, the border guarding force may interrogate and detain the person as permissible under the law of the land, at the border itself, pending decision by the administrative authorities regarding his plea for refuge/ asylum. In all such cases, the person will have to be ultimately handed over to the local police who will exercise their powers under relevant provisions of the Criminal Procedure Code (Cr.PC).

It goes without saying that there will be circumstances and occasions when the authorities may have to be satisfied about the *bona fides* of the person concerned. It is part of the duty and responsibility of the authorities to rule out any criminal or anti-national taking the plea of a 'refugee' and entering the country for *mala fide* purposes. If caught while illegally exiting India, the person (refugee) may be handed over to the local police for investigation and for further action according to law. In cases where the refugee is found in possession of invalid travel documents or in cases of violation of any other Indian law, the refugee may be detained by the border authorities at the border post itself and handed over to the local police for investigation. In all such instances, after the registration of a case on the basis of a First Information Report, the police would lodge the accused refugee in the area prison and produce him/her in the local court for trial in conformity with the provisions of CrPC..

The position of law as well as the procedure that is followed in two specific circumstances. *Mehmud Ghazaleh*, an Iranian refugee registered with UNHCR, was detained while illegally exiting India for Nepal via the Sonauli border in District Maharajgunj, U.P. The refugee was travelling on forged & fabricated travel documents. He was detained by the border authorities who *prima facie*discovered that his travel documents were forged. They handed the refugee over to the local police station at Sonauli for investigation and registration of FIR u/s 419/420/468/471 IPC read with Sec 3/6 of the Passport Act and Sec.14 Foreigners Act. He was subsequently interned at the Gorakhpur district jail. In another case two Afghan refugees, Shah Ghazai and his minor son Assadullah, were apprehended by the authorities at the Attari border at Amritsar, Punjab while attempting to illegally exit India for Afghanistan via Pakistan. They were handed over to the local police in Gharinda, district Amritsar for investigation and registration of FIR and were subsequently interned at the Amritsar Central Jail.

NGOs and Human Rights activists look for instances and often intervene through legal action in courts, in cases of suspected illegal detention of refugees, particularly in cases where it is alleged that formal FIR is not recorded by the concerned law enforcement authorities even after such a detention.

It is sometimes alleged that such a situation obtains in cases where the refugee is suspected to be a spy or a terrorist entering the Indian borders with the deliberate and *mala-fide* intent to cause harm to the stability and integrity of the country or a person suspected to be engaged in trans-border crime like smuggling etc. In such cases allegations are made that the refugee's detention would not be recorded until the authorities are in a position to know the credentials of the individual(s) concerned. The following case is illustrative of the above, even though the circumstances pertaining to it may be somewhat different. An Iranian refugee, Syed Ata Mohamadi, recognised by UNHCR, was apprehended at the Bombay International airport en route to Canada. He was detained at the immigration lounge of the airport for travelling on an assumed name, on a false passport. His detention lasted over a month, he was released only on the intervention of the Bombay High Court.

Immigration and Custom officials come into the scene at the point of entry into India through seaports and airports. In cases where a refugee is detected while entering/ exiting established seaports and airports on Indian territory, without valid travel documents, he/she is immediately detained by the Immigration/ authorised Custom officers and *prima facie* investigated. In cases of illegal entry, the immigration authorities usually take steps to deport the refugee immediately to the country where he or she last came from. This, it may be mentioned, is not in conformity with the principle of *non-refoulement*. Pending deportation, the refugee is detained at a detention cell in the immigration section of the airport, seaport etc. In such an eventuality, the refugee has to arrange to buy his/her own meals and other requirements from resources at his/her disposal. In addition, when deported, the cost of the ticket is also required to be paid by the refugee, which often renders him/her a destitute. The following is a case of this kind. A Palestinian refugee *Majid Ahmad,* was deported from Kathmandu to New Delhi. He was again sent back to Nepal and was once again deported back, thus amounting to four trips in two days. He was subsequently detained at the Immigration lounge of the International Airport at New Delhi for over 25 days. All the expenses for his food as well as his forced travels including his final deportation to Bangladesh were met from his personal resources, which no doubt was almost fully depleted.

Forged/Fabricated Travel Documents, Invalid and Expired Documents etc.

In the event of violation of any other law, such as forgery/ fabrication of travel documents by a refugee, the immigration/ custom officials hand over the accused refugee to the local police where a First Information Report is registered against the accused refugee and taken into police custody. He/she would be produced in the local sessions court and may be ordered to be lodged in the local prison awaiting trial. A case of this kind is cited here. A 17 year old Sri Lankan Tamil refugee, Winston Venojan registered with UNHCR, was separated from his family in Madras and came to Delhi, where he received information that his father was in London. In an attempt to reach London, he was duped by a travel agent who fabricated a passport for him. The forgery was detected at the New Delhi International Airport, and the refugee was handed over by the custom authorities to the area police for investigation and registration of FIR. The refugee was produced before the concerned Metropolitan Magistrate who remanded him to judicial custody in Tihar jail.

In instances where the immigration/ custom authorities suspect discrepancies in the travel documents of a refugee when he or she enters the country, they may send the purported documents for further investigation to the local Foreigners Regional Registration Office (FRRO) and direct the refugee to tender appearance at the FRRO the next day. An Iraqi refugee, was detained at the New Delhi International Airport for holding alleged false travel documents. He was released from detention, but his travel documents were seized and he was asked to approach the local FRRO for reclaiming them the next day. However, he was later arrested and a FIR was lodged against him u/secs.419/ 420/ 468/ 471 of the Indian Penal Code.

In cases where refugees initially enter India with valid travel documents which in the ensuing period expire, or in cases where discrepancies in the travel documents are detected subsequent to his/her entry into India, the refugee may be arrested on expiry of the said documents, or when the said discrepancy is detected. Often, refugees fail to obtain renewal of their visas/ residential permit from the local Foreigners Regional Registration Office and random checks are routinely conducted by the local police, amongst foreigners, including refugees, at places commonly frequented by them such as hotels, restaurants, religious places, markets etc. Those refugees who do not comply with the mandatory requirement of renewal/obtaining residence permits, are arrested and produced before the local sessions court which may direct that they may be lodged in the local prison pending trial.

'Leave India' Notices

The police usually do not consider any pleas of claim of refugee status, persecution in country of origin etc. Further, the administrative authorities vide sec. of the Foreigners Act, 1946 may issue *Leave India Notice* to refugees who have failed to obtain extension of their travel permits, or who are ordered to be deported by the court. In such cases the refugee may be arrested if apprehended, and may be forcibly deported. *Gurinder Singh and Karamjit Singh*, two Afghan Sikhs of Indian origin, who had fled persecution from Afghanistan were registered as refugees with UNHCR in New Delhi. They were issued Leave India Notices by the FRRO to leave India within 7 days of receipt of the notice. The only remedy under such circumstances is through legal action in the appropriate court. In this instance, a criminal writ petition was filed in the Punjab & Haryana High Court at Chandigarh and interim stay of the Leave India Notice was obtained.

INDIA'S MEASURES FOR FULFILLING INTERNATIONAL OBLIGATIONS

India has taken numerous steps and measures to fulfill its international obligations in respect of refugees.

Entry into India

The Government of India have followed a fairly liberal policy of granting refuge to various groups of refugees though some groups have been recognised and some other groups have not been, often keeping in view the security concerns of the nation. However, the emerging trend of past refugee experiences bear testimony to the fact that entry into India for most refugee groups is in keeping with international principles of protection and*non-refoulement*. Further, such entry is not determined by reasons of religion or any other form of discrimination. It may be pointed out that India has granted refuge to Buddhist Tibetans, Hindus and Christians of Sri Lanka, Hindus and Muslims from the then East Pakistan, Hindus, Muslims, Christians and Buddhists from Bangladesh and Sikhs and Muslims from Afghanistan etc.

Work Permits

There is no concept of work permits in India, although refugees who are granted residence permits do find employment in the informal sector, without facing any objection from the administration. In fact, Tibetan refugees have been granted loans and other facilities for self- employment. Similarly, most Sri Lankan Tamils have been granted freedom of movement within the camp areas, enabling work facilities for them as casual labour. Similarly, Chakma and Afghan refugees have also been engaging in gainful, even if it is in minor forms of employment.

Freedoms

Generally, refugees are allowed freedom concerning their movement, practice of religion and residence. In case of refugees whose entry into India is either legal or is subsequently legalised, there is limited interference by the administration regarding these basic freedoms. However, those refugees who enter India illegally or overstay beyond permissible limits, have strict restrictions imposed upon them in accordance with the statutes governing refugees in India i.e., The Foreigners Act, 1946, Foreigners Order, Passport Act etc.

Handling Refugees Legally

From the moment of entry of a refugee into the Indian territory, the laws of India would apply to him/her. Therefore, enforcement and security personnel who have to deal with refugees, cannot overlook the legal requirements which have to be adhered to by them. In the following paragraphs an attempt has been made to identify some common situations which may be faced by enforcement and security personnel in dealing with refugees. An attempt has also been made to suggest possible courses of action within the legal framework.

The main purpose of this attempt is twofold. Firstly, it will help to focus on the need for showing due concern for human rights. Secondly, it is also important to create awareness about the unavoidable compulsions, which forced the person concerned to take refuge in the country and the inherent and unmistakable poignant human situation in the entire episode. It is pertinent to remember that the circumstances and facts pertaining to each refugee may be peculiar and different from the rest. In such cases, therefore, it is extremely important to ascertain, understand and appreciate the background of the compelling circumstances of each of the cases so that the law of the land may be applied in the most appropriate manner. It is in this context that the legal provisions, directions and guidelines, if any, issued by competent courts as also the practical experience gained in dealing with such cases, would come in handy.

Keeping the above aspects in view, some of the more important situations relevant to security personnel are enumerated below. An attempt has been made to highlight the more feasible options which could be considered in dealing with refugees. It goes without saying that these options have to be exercised within the legal frame-work of the country.

At the Point of Entry

Refugees may enter India by land, air and/or sea. Depending upon the point of entry, they will come into initial contact with immigration authorities at airports or sea-ports or with the border guarding authorities at the border check-posts. It is relevant to point out that more often than not, a refugee would be without valid travel documents or valid identity documents making his/her entry into the country 'illegal'. Since India has not yet incorporated the principle of *non-refoulement* in its legal statutes, the person concerned would have to face the prospect of being arrested and prosecuted as per the laws of the land. However, this should not be held against the intending refugee to debar entry as a matter of course. Therefore, the agency which comes into contact with the refugee initially, will have to satisfy itself about the bonafides of the intending refugee instead of pre-emptorily refusing entry. Under the circumstances, the ends of justice would be met if the person seeking refuge does not have valid travel documents, is arrested and produced in a court of law for appropriate judicial action. In the meanwhile, even as that person is under judicial detention, the security agency will have opportunity to verify his claims and also to notify the concerned competent authority in government to take decision in the matter. In such cases the help of the UNHCR could also be sought so that that agency would be in a position to help speed up the process of verification and also to render suitable help in finalising the legal process.

Detention

A refugee may face detention as soon as he/she illegally crosses the international border into India. It is pertinent to appreciate that the refugee has at that moment just entered an unknown country, after fleeing to save his/her life from his/her own country of origin. He/she may have undergone severe trauma of loss of family and friends in his/her homeland or en route India. The refugee in such situations may be unable to explain his/her background during initial interrogation, giving rise to apprehension on the part of local authorities regarding the genuineness of his/her subsequent refugee claim.

He/she may be suspected to be a spy or infiltrator in the light of inconsistent statements that may have been made by him/her to the authorities. This is bound to be further compounded if the refugee is not in possession of the usual 'travel documents'. In fact, it would be very unreasonable to expect him/her to possess valid travel documents, considering the background of his/her having to escape from his/her own country.

The same may result in further interrogation and continued detention pending registration of FIR (First Information Report, which is usually the basis of the start of 'investigation'). In such a situation there may be no course of action open to the refugee to follow, since he/she has no family to lean on locally and who may be aware of his/her plight. Further, the refugee would not be in a position to get a message across to any person outside regarding his/her predicament. What is more, because of the peculiarities of the circumstances, the refugee may be detained in a remote place further compounding an already difficult and unnerving situation.

In such circumstances it would be quite justified for the security agency to register a case under the provisions of IPC/Foreigners' Act etc. and even arrest the refugee and forward him/her to the court having local jurisdiction. In case the refugee desires legal help it is desirable that the local 'legal-aid cell' may be allowed to be contacted by the refugee. Where such facilities are not available and the refugee is not in a position to hire legal services on his/her own, the court may be requested to notify the UNHCR to render help to the refugee to seek legal assistance. If any local NGO is available and willing, their services may also be sought to help out the refugee.

Lack of Medical Aid in Detention

While in detention the refugee may be suffering from some physical ailment requiring immediate medical attention. In the event that the detaining authority does not provide the requisite medical aid, the same may result in devastating consequences. In some cases court's directions can be obtained and appropriate medical attention and treatment given to the refugee. Here again, NGOs can play a very useful role. In the case of a Palestinian refugee who was detained at the international airport in New Delhi consequent to a deportation order pending against him, a writ petition was filed to obtain the Delhi High Court's order that the refugee be provided at least the basic necessities like food and medical care. Knowledge of such cases would help security personnel to foresee and where necessary, seek the help of an agency like the UNHCR or a local NGO to render necessary help to the refugee.

Detention of Women Refugees

Most courts are of the opinion that in cases where there has been no grave breach of law by the accused woman (refugee), she may be released on bail pending trial. In the specific case of Marui, an Iraqi refugee who fled persecution from Iraq with her husband and children, the family was arrested in New Delhi. However,.Marui being a woman, was released on bail soon thereafter though her husband continued to be in detention till much later. Even after such a release, it is quite possible that the woman may find herself in some predicament having been suddenly isolated in a foreign country. In such specific cases, it would make the task of the security officials easier if they liaised with the UNHCR or any local NGO to provide the much needed psychological support to the refugee woman. Also, in such cases where deportation orders are passed by the courts, the UNHCR can help to rehabilitate the concerned refugee in another sympathetic country. Knowledge on the part of security and enforcement officials of such available options would help in perpetuating humanitarian attitude on the part of security officials.

Detention of Refugee Children

Refugee children face many problems which deserve to be treated with due sensitivity, care and caution by the authorities concerned. Usually, access is provided to detained mothers to meet their children and tend to their needs. There are, however, cases of sufficiently grown up refugee children who may be between the ages of 15 and 18 years of age and who may be detained for non possession of valid travel documents. Such a problem mostly arises due to the fact that children are not granted separate residential permits but are included in their parent's permits. In cases involving children who do not possess separate residential permits, the UNHCR may be in a position to help sort out the problem, particularly because in cases where refugee children are separated from their families, UNHCR makes all possible attempts to reunite them. Therefore, it will be advantageous if the security agency concerned seeks the help and assistance of the UNHCR in such matters.

In the specific case of Winston Venojan, a Sri Lankan Tamil refugee, thanks to the UNHCR, the 17 year old boy, who had got separated from his parents, was reunited with them. In this case the boy was arrested on landing at New Delhi. Bail was, however, granted to him within a short time. In genuine cases of this kind, the security agency should always consider not to oppose bail. In the meanwhile, the UNHCR got clearance from the British Immigration and Nationality Department for the boy to travel to the UK.

However, the refugee could not be permitted to leave the country till the disposal of the case for the violation of some of the legal provisions under the Indian laws. Luckily this matter was speedily disposed off on the intervention of the Delhi High court. Once the court's orders were obtained, the refugee was provided with Red Cross travel documents to travel to London. The security agency can further help in such genuine case by speedy investigation and filing of charge sheet in time.

Securing that the Refugee is not Untraceable on Release from Detention

Release of a refugee from detention is often fraught with legalities. Courts are sometimes reluctant to direct release of the refugee without ensuring about securing his/her presence in a specific place. The primary concern of courts while barring the deportation of refugees is that the refugee should not become "untraceable". In some cases of this kind, courts have agreed that the refugee may be handed over into the "care of UNHCR". This would ensure that the refugee will be available whenever wanted. In addition, the UNHCR would take care of the refugee till the legal issue is disposed of. In cases where the UNHCR refuses to take custody of the said refugees, there will be no alternative but to send the refugees back to Jail.

Securing against Re-arrest on Release from Detention

The refugee on release from prison after serving his/her sentence may still not be having valid travel documents. In such circumstances, the refugee may face the risk of re-arrest while commuting from the prison to secure residential permit/refugee certificate etc., Hence the authorities are often requested to provide police escort to the refugee to enable him to reach the authorised place safely and to secure documents for valid stay in India. This measure would help speed up to regularise the stay in India, which is desirable from both the point of view of security as well as humanitarian considerations.

Timely filing of Charge Sheet by the Prosecution to Enable Pleading Guilty

The need for timely filing of charge-sheet in courts of law cannot be over emphasised, particularly in the cases of refugees. Only when the charge sheet is filed it is possible for the refugee to be aware of the charges against him and to plead guilty to the same. In some cases the refugee may require early disposal of his/her case, hence filing of charges at an early stage is crucial.

4

Events Leading to the Sino-Indian War

INTRODUCTION

A long series of events triggered the Sino-Indian War in 1962. According to John W. Garver, Chinese perceptions about the Indian designs for Tibet, and the failure to demarcate a common border between China and India (including the Indian Forward Policy) were important in China's decision to fight a war with India.

Friendly Relations

Numerous changes occurred in the late 1940s. With the independence of the Republic of India and the separate Islamic Republic of Pakistan's creation in 1947, and the establishment of the People's Republic of China (PRC) in 1949. One of the most basic policies for the Indian government was that of maintaining cordial relations with China. The Indian government wished to revive its ancient friendly ties with China. When the PRC was declared, India was among the first countries to give it diplomatic recognition.

After coming to power, the PRC announced that its army would be occupying Tibet. India sent a letter of protest to China proposing negotiations on the Tibet issue. The newly formed PRC was more active in posting troops to the Aksai Chin border than the newly formed Indian republic was. India decided to take moves to ensure a stable Indo-Chinese border. In August 1950,

China expressed its gratitude to Indian attempts to "stabilize the Indo-Chinese border". To clear any doubts or ambiguities, Prime Minister Nehrustated in Parliament in 1950 that "Our maps show that the McMahon Line is our boundary and that is our boundary...we stand by that boundary and we will not let anyone else come across that boundary". China expressed no concerns at these statements.

By 1951, China had extended numerous posts in Aksai Chin. The Indian government, on the other hand, concentrated its military efforts on stopping Ladakh from being taken by Pakistani troops and did not establish itself in Aksai Chin. On various occasions in 1951 and 1952, however, the government of China expressed the idea that there were no frontier issues between India and Chinese Tibet to be worried about.

Later, in September 1951, India declined to attend a conference in San Francisco for the conclusion of a peace treaty with Japan because China, which India viewed as an important factor in this treaty, was not invited because of its status as an international pariah. In the coming years India strove to become China's representative in world matters, as China had been isolated from many issues. India vigorously pressed, since the start of the 1950s, for the PRC to be included within the UN.

The People's Liberation Army defeated the Tibetan army in a battle at Chamdo in 1950 and Lhasa recognized Chinese sovereignty over Tibet in 1951. The Indian army asserted control of Tawang at this time, overcoming some armed resistance and expelling its Tibetan administrators. In 1954, the China and India concluded the Five Principles of Peaceful Coexistence under which India acknowledged Chinese sovereignty in Tibet. Indian negotiators presented a frontier map to the Chinese that included the McMahon Line and the Chinese side did not object. At this time, the Indian government under Prime Minister Nehru promoted the slogan *Hindi-Chini bhai-bhai* (India and China are brothers).

"By allowing the Chinese to take possession of Lhasa, the Prime Minister has practically helped them bring their border down to the Indian border... Aggression might well be committed by people who are

always in the habit of committing aggression." — B. R. Ambedkar in the Indian Upper House, 1954

On July 1, 1954 Nehru wrote a memo directing that the maps of India be revised to show definite boundaries on all frontiers, where they were previously indicated as undemarcated. The new maps also revised the boundary in the east to show the Himalayan hill crest as the boundary. In some places, this line is a few kilometres north of the McMahon Line. These new maps also revised the maps to show the countries of Bhutan and Sikkim as part of India.

Beginning in 1956, the CIA used Indian territory to recruit Tibetan guerrillas to fight Chinese troops, with a base in Kalimpong, India. The Indian public was outraged when it learned in 1958 that China had built a road between Xinjiang and Tibet through Indian territory in Aksai Chin (historically a part of Indian state of Ladakh).

In 1956, Nehru expressed concern to Zhou Enlai that Chinese maps showed some 120,000 square kilometres of Indian territory as Chinese. Zhou responded that there were errors in the maps and that they were of little meaning. He stated that the maps needed revising from previous years where such ideas were considered to be true. In November 1956, Zhou again repeated his assurances that he had no claims based on the maps.

TIBET DISAGREEMENTS

According to John W. Garver, Nehru's policy on Tibet was to create a strong Sino-Indian partnership which would be catalyzed through agreement and compromise on Tibet. Garver believes that Nehru's previous actions (befriending China on such issues as war in Korea, the PRC's U.N. admission, the peace treaty with Japan and transfer of Taiwan to the PRC, Indochina, and decolonization and the Afro-Asian movement) had given Nehru a confidence that China would be ready to form an "Asian Axis" with India. Much misunderstanding between the two nations led to diplomatic spats over Tibet, with Nehru's move to accommodate the Dalai Lama overshadowing his other actions and opinions on Tibet, including the opinion that an armed resistance movement in Tibet would be suicidal and counterproductive. While China treated India's concerns with Tibet as expansionist, Some in India claim that its concerns were in fact sentimental and culturally-linked, as Buddhist Tibet had been under influence of Indian culture for many years.

Top PRC leader Mao Zedong was humiliated by the reception the Dalai Lama obtained in India when he fled there in March 1959. The Tibet disagreements heightened in the Chinese media, with Mao himself asking Xinhua News Agency on 19 April to produce commentary on unknown Indian expansionists operating in Tibet. Mao decided on April 25 to openly criticize Nehru for his Tibet policy:

"Be sharp, don't fear to irritate him [Nehru], don't fear to cause him trouble. Nehru miscalculated the situation believing that China could not suppress the rebellion in Tibet and would have to beg India's help. – Mao Zedong addressing a Politburo Standing Committee

Tensions steadily increased between the two nations when Mao implied that the Lhasa rebellion in Tibet was caused by Indians. On 6 May 1959, Mao published "The Revolution in Tibet and Nehru's Philosophy" where he accused Nehru of openly encouraging Tibetan rebels. This publication was evident of China's perception of India as a threat to its rule of Tibet, which became an underlying reason for triggering the Sino-Indian War. India had become the imperialist enemy, with Nehru and his "big bourgeoisie" striving to "prevent China from exercising full sovereignty over its territory of Tibet" to form of a buffer zone. On the same day, Zhou Enlai lashed out at Nehru's "class nature".

"Nehru and people from the Indian upper class oppose reform in Tibet, even to the extent of saying that reform is impossible...[They want] Tibet to remain for a long time in a backward state, becoming a 'buffer state' between China and India. This is their guiding mentality, and also the center of the Sino-Indian conflict. – Zhou Enlai

India continued negotiations about Tibet. According to the Indian official history, India wished to express goodwill to China and stop the claims of it having a hostile design in Tibet.

In August 1959, the Chinese army took an Indian patrol prisoner at Longju, which falls north of the McMahon Line coordinates drawn on the Simla Treaty, signed in 1914, map (27°44'30"N), but claimed by India to lie directly on the McMahon Line. There was another bloody clash in October at Kongka Pass in Aksai Chin in which 9 Indian frontier policemen were killed. Recognizing that it was not ready for war, the Indian Army assumed responsibility for the border and pulled back patrols from disputed areas.

On October 2, Nikita Khrushchev defended Nehru in a meeting with Mao. The Soviet Union's siding with Nehru, as well as the United States' influence in the region, gave China the belief that it was surrounded by enemy forces. On 16 October, General Lei Yingfu reported on Indian expansionism on the Thag La Ridge. On 18 October, the Chinese government approved the PLA's plan of a "self-defensive counterattack" against India because of its actions in Tibet.

However, Mao decided against further escalation because he feared that India would retaliate by permitting the U.S. to station U-2 surveillance aircraft on its territory. This would allow the CIA to photograph China's nuclear test site at Lop Nor in Xinjiang. A few days after Kongka Pass, Chinese Prime Minister Zhou Enlai proposed that each side withdraw 20 kilometres from a "Line of Actual Control". He defined this line as "the so-called McMahon Line in the east and the line up to which each side exercises actual control in the west". Nehru responded with a proposal to turn the disputed area into a no man's land.

Chinese studies of the 1990s still maintain that India was planning aggression in Tibet. Most Chinese scholars believe that the root cause of the war was India's plan to seize Tibet and turn it into a protectorate or colony of India. The official Chinese history of the war states that Nehru was planning to create a "great Indian empire". It was also insisted that there were right wing nationalist forces that influenced Nehru to pursue the goal of controlling Tibet. Zhao Weiwen, of the Chinese Ministry of State and Security, places emphasis on Nehru's "dark mentality".

China's policy on Tibet did much to heighten the conflict and tensions between the two nations. The perceptions of India as a capitalist expansionist body intent on the independence of Tibet to create a buffer zone between India proper and China was fundamentally erroneous. The negative rhetoric led to what Zhou himself called the Sino-Indian conflict. Because of these false fears, China treated the Indian Forward Policy of the 1960s, which India admits as a fundamental mistake, as the beginning of Indian expansionism into Tibet.

BORDER NEGOTIATIONS

China's 1958 maps showed the large strip of land between Ladakh and Bhutan (the Aksai Chin) as Chinese. In 1960, Zhou Enlai proposed that India drop its claim to Aksai Chin and China would withdraw its claims from NEFA. According to John W. Garver, Zhou's propositions were unofficial and subtle. Zhou consistently refused to accept the legitimacy of India's territorial claims; he proposed that the any negotiations had to take into account the facts on the ground. Zhou tried many times to get Nehru to accept conceding Aksai Chin, he visited India four times in 1960. However, Nehru believed that China did not have a legitimate claim over both of those territories and was not ready to give away any one of them. However, they had different opinions as to the legality of the Simla agreement which eventually led to the inability to reach a decision. Nehru's adamance was seen within China as Indian opposition to Chinese rule in Tibet, as China needed the highway through Aksai Chin to maintain an effective control over the Tibetan plateau.

According to Neville Maxwell, Nehru wasn't ready to simply concede the territory and leave negotiations at that. He was open to continued negotiations, but did not accept the idea of Indian troops withdrawing from their claimed regions. Nehru stated "*We will negotiate and negotiate and negotiate to the bitter end. I absolutely reject the approach of stopping negotiations at any state.*" He remained firm that there would be no boundary negotiations until Chinese troops withdrew from Aksai Chin and areas south of the British McMahon Line. This was unacceptable to the Chinese, which never recognized the legal validity of the McMahon Line. Nehru stated "*We will never compromise on our boundaries, but we are prepared to consider minor adjustments to them and to talk to the other side about them.*" In light of these comments, the international community rallied behind Nehru in claiming that China was at fault in failing to conduct proper negotiations. Maxwell argues that Nehru's words were ambiguous.

According to the official Indian history: "Nehru did not agree to barter away the Aksai Chin area, under illegal occupation of China, in return for China giving up its unreasonable claim to Indian territory south of the McMahon Line."

After the talks, India produced its official reports on the talks and translated the Chinese report into English. India believed it would improve a feeling of understanding between the nations. China saw it as an unreasonable attempt by India to secure its claim lines. Nehru's adamance that China withdraw from Aksai Chin and thus abandon the highway was seen as further Indian attempts to undermine China's presence in Tibet. According to John W. Garver, China reached the incorrect conclusion that Nehru was continuing his "grand plans in Tibet".

Forward Policy

At the beginning of 1961, Nehru appointed General B.M. Kaul QMG but he was influential in all army decisions. Kaul reorganized the general staff and removed the officers who had resisted the idea of patrolling in disputed areas, although Nehru still refused to increase military spending or otherwise prepare for war. In the summer of 1961, China began patrolling along the McMahon Line. They entered parts of Indian administered regions and much angered the Indians in doing so. After May 1961 Chinese troops occupiedDehra Compass and established a post on the Chip Chap River. The Chinese, however, did not believe they were intruding upon Indian territory. In response the Indians launched a policy of creating outposts behind the Chinese troops so as to cut off their supplies and force their return to China. According to the Home Minister in Delhi on February 4, 1962:

"If the Chinese will not vacate the areas occupied by her, India will have to repeat what she did in Goa. She will certainly drive out the Chinese forces."

This has been referred to as the "Forward Policy". There were eventually 60 such outposts, including 43 north of the McMahon

Line. Kaul was confident through previous diplomacy that the Chinese would not react with force. According to the Indian Official History, Indian posts and Chinese posts were separated by a narrow stretch of land. China had been steadily spreading into those lands and India reacted with the Forward Policy to demonstrate that those lands were not unoccupied. India, of course, did not believe she was intruding on Chinese territory. British author Neville Maxwell traces this confidence to Mullik, who was in regular contact with the CIA station chief in New Delhi. Mullik may therefore have been aware of Mao's sensitivity concerning U-2 flights.

The initial reaction of the Chinese forces was to withdraw when Indian outposts advanced towards them. However, this appeared to encourage the Indian forces to accelerate their Forward Policy even further. In response, the Central Military Commission adopted a policy of "armed coexistence". In response to Indian outposts encircling Chinese positions, Chinese forces would build more outposts to counter-encircle these Indian positions. This pattern of encirclement and counter-encirclement resulted in an interlocking, chessboard-like deployment of Chinese and Indian forces. Despite the leapfrogging encirclements by both sides, no hostile fire occurred from either side as troops from both sides were under orders to fire only in defense. On the situation, Mao Zedong commented,

Nehru wants to move forward and we won't let him. Originally, we tried to guard against this, but now it seems we cannot prevent it. If he wants to advance, we might as well adopt armed coexistence. You wave a gun, and I'll wave a gun. We'll stand face to face and can each practice our courage.

OTHER DEVELOPMENTS

At a Communist Party conference in Beijing in January 1962, Chinese President Liu Shaoqi denounced the Great Leap Forward as responsible for widespread famine. The overwhelming majority of delegates expressed agreement, but Defense Minister Lin Biao staunchly defended Mao. A brief period of liberalization followed while Mao and Lin plotted a comeback. Jung Chang writes that

China was prepared for war with India after the border clashes in May and June, but were concerned about the Nationalists, which had been making active preparations for invasion from Taiwan, and had moved large forces to the south-east coast.

Transcripts from the decision for war was not made by China's leaders until early October 6, 1962, and only then were war plans drawn by China's Central Military Commission. Roderik McFarquhar states, "In May–June 1962, the main concern in Beijing was over the threat of an invasion from Taiwan... Chinese leaders would have been reluctant to provoke hostilities in the Himalayas, which might have meant diverting military resources from the main danger point along the Fujian coast."

The Indian military was not ready for full-scale combat. India had just annexed the Portuguese State of India or, Goa and was facing border disputes with Pakistan in Kashmir. TheIndian National Congress proposed non-violent means to solving India's problems, and Indian military leaders, who proposed that India should prepare for a full scale attack, were ignored or dismissed.

Early Incidents

Various border conflicts and "military incidents" between India and China flared up throughout the summer and fall of 1962. According to Chinese sources, in June 1962, a minorskirmish broke out between the two sides, and dozens of members of the People's Liberation Army killed and wounded. Units of the Indian and Chinese militaries maintained close contact throughout September 1962; however, hostile fire occurred only infrequently.

On May 2, 1962 the Directorate of Military Operations in India had suggested that the air force should be readied for use in NEFA and Ladakh. The Air Force was considered a feasible way to repel the unbalanced ratio of Chinese troops to Indian troops and the Chinese air force was assessed as only capable of limited strategic raids which could be countered by the Indian air force. Indian Air Force soon started reconnaissance flights over the NEFA border. On May 7, 1962 Chinese troops shot down an Indian Dakota plane in which young officer B. P. Tiwari was lost. Following this incident, the Indian Air Force was told not to plan for close air support.

In June, 1962, the Indian Intelligence Bureau said it received information about a Chinese military buildup along the border which could result in a war. Information was also received that Pakistan was considering to attack simultaneously in the west. Chinese airfields in Tibet and Yunnan were addressed as a threat to Indian cities, as the PLAAF could conduct heavy bombings through their use of Soviet aeroplanes.

On July 8, the Chinese initiated another diplomatic communication, to protest against an alleged Indian incursion into the Galwan Valley. According to China Quarterly, the Government of India released press reports to the public indicating that Indian had gained 2,000 mi^2 of territory from the Chinese. However, in their diplomatic reply to the Chinese, India denied that any incident had taken place.

On July 10, 1962, 350 Chinese troops surrounded an Indian post at Chushul, in the Galwan Valley, north of the MacMahon Line. They used loudspeakers to obtain contact with the Gurkha forces stationed there. The Chinese troops attempted to convince the Gurkhas that they should not be fighting for India, to cause an abandonment of the post. After a fiery argument the 350 Chinese withdrew from the area.

July 22, 1962 saw a change in the Forward Policy, according to the official Indian history of the war. While the Forward Policy was initially intended to prevent the Chinese from advancing into empty areas (by occupying them first), "it was now decided to push back the Chinese from posts they already occupied." Whereas Indian troops were previously ordered to fire only in self-defense, all post commanders were now given discretion to open fire upon Chinese forces if threatened.

In August, 1962, the Chinese military improved its combat readiness along the McMahon Line, particularly in the North East Frontier Agency, Tibet and Xinjiang. In Tibet, there were constructions of ammunition dumps and stockpiling of ammunition, weapons and gasoline, though there were no indications of a manpower buildup. China's preparedness for war strongly contrasted with India's, which had largely neglected its military throughout the 1950s. Nehru believed that the Himalayas were a large enough defense against China, however, the Korean war had provided China with practice in mountain combat. This neglect on behalf of India would decide numerous pivotal battles where logistical inadequacy and lack of leadership led to defeat after strong starts.

Confrontation at Thag La

In June 1962, Indian forces had established an outpost at Dhola, on the southern slopes of Thag La Ridge, overlooking the village of Le in Tibet. Based on the treaty map of the 1914 Simla Convention, the McMahon Line lay at 27°44'30''N. However, Dhola post lay about one mile (1.6 km) north of the McMahon Line The Indian government maintained that the *intention* of the McMahon Line was to set the border along the highest ridges, and that the international border fell on the highest ridges of Thag La, about 3 to 4 miles (4.8 to 6.4 km) north of the line drawn by Henry McMahon on the treaty map. Brigadier John Dalvi would later write of this claim: "The Chinese had raised a dispute about the exact alignment of the McMahon Line in the Thag La Ridge area. Therefore the Thag La-Dhola area was not strictly territory that 'we should have been convinced was ours' as directed by the Prime Minister, Mr. Nehru, and someone is guilty of exceeding the limits prescribed by him."

In August, China issued diplomatic protests which accused India of violating even the McMahon Line, and Chinese soldiers began occupying positions at the top of Thag La, north of Indian positions.

On September 8, 1962, a 60-strong PLA unit descended from the heights and occupied positions which dominated one of the Indian posts at Dhola. Neither side opened fire for 12 days. Nehru had gone to London to attend a Commonwealth Prime Ministers' Conference and, when told of the act, said to the media that the Indian Army had instructions to "free our territory".

According to the official Indian history, a decision was made on September 9 to evict the Chinese from the southern part of the Thag La Ridge, by force, if necessary. Two days later, it was decided that "all forward posts and patrols were given permission to fire on any armed Chinese who entered Indian territory". According to author Neville Maxwell, officers at the Indian Defense Ministry had expressed the concern that Indian maps showed Thag La as Chinese territory; they were told to ignore the maps. However, Nehru's directives to Defense Minister V.K. Krishna Menon were unclear, and the response, code named Operation LEGHORN, got underway only slowly. As the Chinese numbers were exaggerated to 600 instead of about 50 or 60, the 9 Punjab battalion, numbering 400 riflemen, was sent to Dhola.

By the time the Indian battalion reached the Thag La Ridge in the Chedong region on September 16, north of the McMahon Line, Chinese units controlled both banks of the Namka Chu River. The day after, India's Chief of the Army Staff Gen P N Thapar ordered his men to re-take the Thag La Ridge. According to the official Indian history, on September 20, Indian eastern command ordered all Indian posts and patrols to engage any Chinese patrols within range of their weapons. On September 20, at one of the bridges on the river a firefight developed, killing nine Chinese and Indian soldiers. Skirmishes continued throughout September.

On 3 October, Zhou Enlai visited Nehru in New Delhi, promising there would be no war between the nations and reiterating his wishes to solve the dispute diplomatically.

On October 4, a new corp was created 4 corp, under Lt. Gen. B.M. Kaul, tasked with evicting the Chinese from Dhola-Thag La October 10 was the planned date for Operation Leghorn. Because of the difficulties involved in directly assaulting and taking Thag La, Kaul made the decision instead to occupy nearby Yumtso La to the west, to position his troops behind and dominate the Chinese positions.

Brigadier John Dalvi, tasked with taking Yumtso La, argued that he lacked necessary supplies and resources to take the pass. On October 9, Kaul and Brigadier Dalvi agreed to send a patrol of 50 soldiers to Tseng Jong, the approach to Yumtso La, to occupy the position and provide cover before the rest of the battalion would move forward for the occupation of Yumtso La. On October 10, these 50 Indian troops were met by an emplaced Chinese position of some 1,000 soldiers. The Chinese troops opened fire on the Indians believing that the Indians had intruded upon Chinese land. The Indians were surrounded by a Chinese positions which used mortar fire. However, they managed to hold off the first Chinese assault, inflicting heavy casualties. In the second assault, the Indians began their retreat, realising the situation was hopeless. The Indian patrol suffered 25 casualties, with the Chinese suffering 33. The Chinese troops held their fire as the Indians retreated, and then buried the Indian dead with military honors, as witnessed by the retreating soldiers. This was the first occurrence of heavy fighting in the war.

This attack had grave implications for India and Nehru tried to solve the issue, but by 18 October it was clear that the Chinese were preparing for an attack on India, with massive troop buildups on the border.

EVENTS LEADING UP TO WAR

Tibet and the Border Dispute

The 1940s saw huge change in South Asia with the Partition of India in 1947 (resulting in the establishment of the two new states of India and Pakistan), and the establishment of the People's Republic of China (PRC) in 1949. One of the most basic policies for the new Indian government was that of maintaining cordial relations with China, reviving its ancient friendly ties. India was among the first nations to grant diplomatic recognition to the newly created PRC.

At the time, Chinese officials issued no condemnation of Nehru's claims or made any opposition to Nehru's open declarations of control over Aksai Chin. In 1956, Chinese Premier Zhou Enlai stated that he had no claims over Indian controlled territory. He later argued that Aksai Chin was already under Chinese jurisdiction, implying that there was therefore no contradiction with his earlier statement, since China did not regard the region as "Indian controlled", and that since the British hand-over, China had regarded the McCartney MacDonald Line as the relevant border. Zhou later argued that as the boundary was undemarcated and had never been defined by treaty between any

Chinese or Indian government, the Indian government could not unilaterally define Aksai Chin's borders.

In 1950, the Chinese People's Liberation Army annexed Tibet and later the Chinese extended their influence by building a road in 1956–67 and placing border posts in Aksai Chin. India found out after the road was completed, protested against these moves and decided to look for a diplomatic solution to ensure a stable Sino-Indian border. To resolve any doubts about the Indian position, Prime Minister Jawaharlal Nehru declared in parliament that India regarded the McMahon Line as its official border. The Chinese expressed no concern at this statement, and in 1951 and 1952, the government of China asserted that there were no frontier issues to be taken up with India.

In 1954, Prime Minister Nehru wrote a memo calling for India's borders to be clearly defined and demarcated; in line with previous Indian philosophy, Indian maps showed a border that, in some places, lay north of the McMahon Line. Chinese Premier Zhou Enlai, in November 1956, again repeated Chinese assurances that the People's Republic had no claims on Indian territory, although official Chinese maps showed 120,000 square kilometres (46,000 sq mi) of territory claimed by India as Chinese. CIA documents created at the time revealed that Nehru had ignored Burmese premier Ba Swe when he warned Nehru to be cautious when dealing with Zhou. They also allege that Zhou purposefully told Nehru that there were no border issues with India.

In 1954, China and India negotiated the Five Principles of Peaceful Coexistence, by which the two nations agreed to abide in settling their disputes. India presented a frontier map which was accepted by China, and the Indian government under Prime Minister Nehru promoted the slogan *Hindi-Chini bhai-bhai* (Indians and Chinese are brothers). According to Georgia Tech political analystJohn W Garver, Nehru's policy on Tibet was to create a strong Sino-Indian partnership which would be catalysed through agreement and compromise on Tibet. Garver believes that Nehru's previous actions had given him confidence that China would be ready to form an "Asian Axis" with India. This apparent progress in relations suffered a major setback when, in 1959, Nehru accommodated the Tibetan religious leader at the time, the 14th Dalai Lama, who fled Lhasa after a failed Tibetan uprising against Chinese rule. The Chairman of the Chinese Communist Party, Mao Zedong, was enraged and asked the Xinhua News Agency to produce reports on Indian expansionists operating in Tibet.

Border incidents continued through this period. In August 1959, the People's Liberation Army took an Indian prisoner at Longju, which had an ambiguous position in the McMahon Line, and two months later in Aksai Chin, a clash led to the death of nine Indian frontier policemen.

On 2 October, Soviet Premier Nikita Khrushchev defended Nehru in a meeting with Mao. This action reinforced China's impression that the Soviet Union, the United States and India all had expansionist designs on China. The People's Liberation Army went so far as to prepare a self-defence counterattack plan. Negotiations were restarted between the nations, but no progress was made.

As a consequence of their non-recognition of the McMahon Line, China's maps showed both the North East Frontier Area (NEFA) and Aksai Chin to be Chinese territory. In 1960, Zhou Enlai unofficially suggested that India drop its claims to Aksai Chin in return for a Chinese withdrawal of claims over NEFA. Adhering to his stated position, Nehru believed that China did not have a legitimate claim over either of these territories, and thus was not ready to concede them. This adamant stance was perceived in China as Indian opposition to Chinese rule in Tibet. Nehru declined to conduct any negotiations on the boundary until Chinese troops withdrew from Aksai Chin, a position supported by the international community.

India produced numerous reports on the negotiations, and translated Chinese reports into English to help inform the international debate. China believed that India was simply securing its claim lines in order to continue its "grand plans in Tibet". India's stance that China withdraw from Aksai Chin caused continual deterioration of the diplomatic situation to the point that internal forces were pressuring Nehru to take a military stance against China.

The Forward Policy

At the beginning of 1961, Nehru appointed General B. M. Kaul as army Chief of General Staff, but he refused to increase military spending and prepare for a possible war. According to James Barnard Calvin of the U.S. Navy, in 1959, India started sending Indian troops and border patrols into disputed areas. This program created both skirmishes and deteriorating relations between India and China. The aim of this policy was to create outposts behind advancing Chinese troops to interdict their supplies, forcing them north of the disputed line. There were eventually 60 such outposts, including 43 north of the McMahon Line, to which India claimed sovereignty. China viewed this as further confirmation of Indian expansionist plans directed towards Tibet. According to the Indian official history, implementation of the Forward Policy was intended to provide evidence of Indian occupation in the previously unoccupied region through which Chinese troops had been patrolling. Kaul was confident, through contact with Indian Intelligence and CIA information, that China would not react with force. Indeed, at first the PLA simply withdrew, but eventually Chinese forces began to counter-encircle the Indian positions which clearly encroached into the north of McMahon Line. This led to a tit-for-tat Indian reaction, with each force attempting to outmanoeuver the other. However, despite the escalating nature of the dispute, the two forces withheld from engaging each other directly.

Chinese attention was diverted for a time by the military activity of the Nationalists on Taiwan, but on 23 June the U.S. assured China that a Nationalist invasion would not be permitted. China's heavy artillery facing Taiwan could then be moved to Tibet. It took China six to eight months to gather the resources needed for the war, according to Anil Athale, author of the official Indian history. The Chinese sent a large quantity of non-military supplies to Tibet through the Indian port of Calcutta.

Early Incidents

Various border conflicts and "military incidents" between India and China flared up throughout the summer and autumn of 1962. In May, the Indian Air Force was told not to plan for close air support, although it was assessed as being a feasible way to counter the unfavourable ratio of Chinese to Indian troops. In June, a skirmish caused the deaths of dozens of Chinese troops. The Indian Intelligence Bureau received information about a Chinese buildup along the border which could be a precursor to war.

During June–July 1962, Indian military planners began advocating "probing actions" against the Chinese, and accordingly, moved mountain troops forward to cut off Chinese supply lines. According to Patterson, the Indian motives were threefold:

1. Test Chinese resolve and intentions regarding India.
2. Test whether India would enjoy Soviet backing in the event of a Sino-Indian war.
3. Create sympathy for India within the U.S., with whom relations had deteriorated after the Indian annexation of Goa.

On 10 July 1962, 350 Chinese troops surrounded an Indian occupied post in Chushul (north of the McMahon Line) but withdrew after a heated argument via loudspeaker. On 22 July, the Forward Policy was extended to allow Indian troops to push back Chinese troops already established in disputed territory. Whereas Indian troops were previously ordered to fire only in self-defence, all post commanders were now given discretion to open fire upon Chinese forces if threatened. In August, the Chinese military improved its combat readiness along the McMahon Line and began stockpiling ammunition, weapons and gasoline.

Given his foreknowledge of the coming Cuban Missile Crisis, Mao Zedong was able to persuade Nikita Khrushchev to reverse the Russian policy of backing India, at least temporarily. In mid-October, the Communist organ *Pravda* encouraged peace between India and China. When the Cuban Missile Crisis ended and Mao's rhetoric changed, however, Russia reversed course.

Confrontation at Thag La

In June 1962, Indian forces established an outpost at Dhola, on the southern slopes of the Thag La Ridge. Dhola lay north of the McMahon Line but south of the ridges along which India interpreted the McMahon Line to run. In August, China issued diplomatic protests and began occupying positions at the top of Thag La. On 8 September, a 60-strong PLA unit descended to the south side of the ridge and occupied positions that dominated one of the Indian posts at Dhola. Fire was not exchanged, but Nehru said to the media that the Indian Army had instructions to "free our territory" and the troops had been given discretion to use force. On 11 September, it was decided that "all forward posts and patrols were given permission to fire on any armed Chinese who entered Indian territory".

However, the operation to occupy Thag La was flawed in that Nehru's directives were unclear and it got underway very slowly because of this. In addition to this, each man had to carry 35 kilograms (77 lb) over the long trek and this severely slowed down the reaction. By the time the Indian battalion reached the point of conflict, Chinese units controlled both banks of the Namka Chu River. On 20 September, Chinese troops threw grenades at Indian troops and a firefight developed, triggering a long series of skirmishes for the rest of September. Some Indian troops, including Brigadier Dalvi who commanded the forces at Thag La, were also concerned that the territory they were fighting for was not strictly territory that "we should have been convinced was ours". According to Neville Maxwell, even members of the Indian defence ministry were categorically concerned with the validity of the fighting in Thag La.

On 3 October, a week before the start of the war, Zhou Enlai visited Nehru in New Delhi promising there would be no war. On 4 October, Kaul assigned some troops to secure regions south of the Thag La Ridge. Kaul decided to first secure Yumtso La, a strategically important position, before re-entering the lost Dhola post. Kaul had then realised that the attack would be desperate and the Indian government tried to stop an escalation into all-out war. Indian troops marching to Thag La had suffered in the previously unexperienced conditions; two Gurkha soldiers died of pulmonary edema. On 10 October, an Indian Punjabi patrol of 50 troops to Yumtso La were met by an emplaced Chinese position of some 1,000 soldiers. Indian troops were in no position for battle, as Yumtso La was 16,000 feet (4,900 m) above sea level and Kaul did not plan on having artillery support for the troops. The Chinese troops opened fire on the Indians under their belief that they were north of the McMahon Line. The Indians were surrounded by Chinese positions which used mortar fire. However, they managed to hold off the first Chinese assault, inflicting heavy casualties.

At this point, the Indian troops were in a position to push the Chinese back with mortar and machine gun fire. However, Brigadier Dalvi opted not to fire, as it would mean decimating the Rajput who were still in the area of the Chinese regrouping. They helplessly watched the Chinese ready themselves for a second assault. In the second Chinese assault, the Indians began their retreat, realising the situation was hopeless. The Indian patrol suffered 25 casualties, and the Chinese 33. The Chinese troops held their fire as the Indians retreated, and then buried the Indian dead with military honours, as witnessed by the retreating soldiers. This was the first occurrence of heavy fighting in the war.

This attack had grave implications for India and Nehru tried to solve the issue, but by 18 October, it was clear that the Chinese were preparing for an attack on India, with massive troop buildups on the border. A long line of mules and porters had also been observed supporting the buildup and reinforcement of positions south of the Thag La Ridge.

SINO-INDIAN TERRITORIAL PROBLOEMS

In terms of "the rise of China" and its "implications for India", the title of this book, the Sino-Indian territorial dispute represents an immediate arena in which India is having to face the uncomfortable implications from having an increasingly stronger neighbour. For India, the ability of China to deny India's hopes of territorial settlement on India's terms has become ever clearer in the wake of China's rise in military power in and around their disputed territory, which remains the biggest amount of land still in dispute in Asia. As such, "the 4,056—kilometre (2,520 miles) frontier between India and China, one of the longest inter-state borders in the world, remains ... not defined, let alone demarcated, on maps or delineated on the ground". Here, the judgement over a century ago of Lord Curzon, British Viceroy of India 1898-1905 still seems relevant; the most urgent work of Foreign Ministers and Ambassadors ... is now the conclusion of Frontier Conventions in which sources of discord are removed by the adjustment of rival interests or ambitions at points where the territorial borders adjoin", for "frontiers are indeed the razor's edge on which hang suspended the modern issues of war or peace, of life or death to nations". Admittedly, the territorial issue has been officially decoupled from the wider Sino-Indian relationship; as with the PRC rhetoric that "China and India have already reached consensus on the border issue. Before it is completely resolved, both countries will endeavour to maintain peace and stability in the border areas and will not let the border issue affect the general picture of China and India's cooperation". However, in reality their territorial issues do affect their wider relationship, in PRC terms "the existence of immense territorial disputes between China and India".

In dispute terms, this chapter argues that, in International Relations (IR) theory terms, the territorial disputes between India and China involve *classical geopolitics* entwined with *critical geopolitics*. Each strand of geopolitics, in their different ways, both involve the respective "position" that India and China hold for themselves and for each other in their immediate and extended neighbourhood. Whilst each side argues from history, the chapter argues that in reality the evidence from history is rather ambiguous and inconclusive for both sides' territorial claims. Indeed, history is a sterile area to argue from, as one Indian commentator put it, "can we go beyond history to look at solutions which do not hark back to the past?" The chapter argues that, from the outside, resolution of the issue seems feasible enough in terms of simple seeming territorial trade offs involving Arunachal Pradesh and Aksai Chin; but is complicated by smaller geographic issues surrounding Tawang, and wider geopolitical issues surrounding Tibet and indeed the balance of power in Asia between India and China.

The two main areas of dispute along this Himalayan frontier are the *Western Sector* (Aksai Chin, around 37,250 square kilometres/

14,380 square miles); and the *Eastern Sector* (Arunachal Pradesh, around 83,740 square kilometres/ 32,330 square miles). On the one hand, Arunachal Pradesh is inhabited by over a million people, Indian citizens, and includes important Buddhist centres like Tawang. On the other hand, Aksai Chin is a virtually uninhabited bleak barren plateau with no permanent settlements. It is the place "where not a blade of grass grows" as Jawaharlal Nehru once dismissively said; but where China's National Highway 219 runs through Aksai Chin as a key geopolitical infrastructure link for the PRC between its provinces of Tibet and Xinjiang. One further complication is China's occupation of the Shaksgam valley; around 5,180 sq kilometres/1,930 square miles, to which Pakistan relinquished its Baltistan-related claims in 1963, but over which India maintains its own Kashmir-derived claims. Smaller pockets of disputed territory are found, the *Middle Sector* fringes of Himachal Pradesh and Uttar Pradesh. Elsewhere along the Himalayas, lingering uncertainty over China's recognition of Sikkim's incorporation into India in 1975 is entwined with continuing PRC claims to the "Finger Area" in the north of Sikkim, with 71 supposed incidents reported of Chinese troop "incursions" in 2008. Nearby territorial disputes between China and Bhutan around the Chumbi Valley triangulation point with India are of further concern to New Delhi, given the Chumbi Valley's location looking down onto the India's sensitive Siliguri corridor which links India's northeastern states with the rest of India.

Wider nuances arise with India's Foreign Secretary (2004—2006) Shyam Saran, and his comments about *the logic of geography*. In front of one audience, it was a question for Saran of "geopolitical reality" in which "I would like to focus particularly on Asia, where the interests of both India and China intersect. It is said that the logic of geography is unrelenting. Proximity is the most difficult and testing among diplomatic challenges a country faces", where "to those who harbour any skepticism about this fact, it would suffice to remind that we share one of the longest [and disputed] land borders in the world with China. In front of another audience, it was again a question that "it is said that the logic of geography is unrelenting and proximity is the most difficult and testing among diplomatic challenges a country faces"; with the following gloss that "frontiers with neighbours are where domestic concerns intersect with external relationships. This is where domestic and foreign policies become inextricable and demand sensitive handling", and in which "it is important for us to look at the [disputed] boundary question from the long-term and strategic perspective of India-China relations, rather than as a mere territorial issue.

The territorial issues between India and China form one of the biggest land disputes in Asia, and are of significance not only for the size of area under dispute, but also because the two disputants are the big countries most evidently on the rise in Asia. Alongside this *logic of geography*, there is then what Neville Maxwell called "the logic of power"; a *logic of power* whereby powerful states "in their expansive phases push out their frontiers until they meet the resistance of a strong neighbour or reach a physical barrier which makes a natural point of rest". In geopolitical terms, the current point of rest is along the Himalayas/Karakoram range, but in the long term where exactly is the "natural" point of rest between them? Amidst talk of mutual IR *security dilemma* dynamics, China's strengthening of military forces and related infrastructure in Aksai Chin and Arunachal Pradesh zones is now a spur to India's own more halting augmentation of military forces and related infrastructure. Meanwhile, both countries are seeking to expand their wider strategic space at a time when their immediate mountain borders remain unresolved.

NEGOTIATING STRATEGIES

One repeated emerging criticisms of India's negotiating strategy is that "unilateral concessions" have been made too often by India, without similar concessions being made by China. When PRC military forces started moving into Tibet in 1950, the Republic of India quickly moved to (a) give up the Forward Rights inherited from the days of British India, which stemmed from the Simla Convention and Anglo-Tibetan Agreement of 1904; and (b) instead recognise Chinese control over Tibet in stronger terms than the hitherto used term "suzerainty". In effect, a "Tibet Card" was there to be played at a time of PRC uncertainties. A robust Indian intervention might have maintained Tibet as an effective buffer between India and China, or at least enabled concessions to be won by India on the Himalayan—Karakoram borders. This is the reverse logic behind recent Indian comments that "China has failed to appreciate that if Arunachal is claimed to be the southern part of Tibet Autonomous Region (TAR), India cannot accept Tibet to be within China. India's formal position on Tibet articulated in 1954 and 2003 is therefore a tentative and unilateral diplomatic offer that can only be sustained and the circle completed once China recognizes Arunachal as part of India". Reinvoking such a "Tibet Card" has been floated in some Indian circles in the past few years.

Having lost that opportunity, the next criticism of Indian negotiating strategy is that, faced with an immediate PRC military presence in Tibet and renewed Chinese claims over Aksai China and Arunachal Pradesh, Nehru ignored the chance of a trade-off seemingly offered by China in 1960; whereby Aksai China would have gone to China and Arunachal Pradesh would have gone to India. Instead, India refused to engage in sovereignty negotiations in the 1950s, maintained its claims to the fullest, neglected to build up its own military forces, yet still engaged in adventurist forward probing movements in the late 1950s. At the time, Nehru rejected the idea of territorial trade-off; India "will not concede one piece of territory in return for another in the same manner as a similar dispute between China and Burma was settled this year"; for "there is no question of barter in these matters ... facts are facts". His formal position was, in the formal *Indian Note* of June 16 1962; quite simply that "this boundary is well known and well recognized and has been so for centuries and cannot be the subject of any negotiations". The trouble was the precise boundaries were not well known, were not well recognized, and had not been in shape for centuries. The irony is that the territorial agreement reached between Burma and China in 1960 involved China following the MacMahon Line alongside other mutual concessions and swapping of territory; as did the 1963 Agreement between China and Pakistan with regard to mutual concessions over claims and territory in the Karakoram reaches.

Nehru might have said "facts are facts" but the fact of the matter is that China's military superiority and continuing occupation of Aksai Chin created a very different subsequent set of facts in the wake of India's military defeat at the hands of China in 1962. The problem for consideration of negotiated resolution of the territorial dispute is that demands and offers have shifted. From the outside, an obvious trade off would be between the *Western* Sector and the *Eastern Sector*; which is where Noorani argued that "there is no territorial dispute which has been, and still is, more susceptible to a solution than India's boundary dispute with China. Each side has its non-negotiable vital interest securely under its control. India has the McMahon Line; China has Aksai Chin" In other words, China's *de facto* control of Aksai Chin could be reflected in agreed *de jure* sovereignty for China, and India's *de facto* control of Arunachal Pradesh could in turn be reflected in agreed *de jure* sovereignty for India. This had been Zhou Enlai's seeming suggestion in 1960, and was the "Package Plan" floated by Deng Xiaoping during 1980. The problem is that the Indian government has never taken up such trade-off offers, with Chinese comments made about the weakness of the Indian governments in taking any compromise deal to the Indian public. The separate *sector-by-sector* approach advocated by India when discussions resumed in the 1980s, rather than *overall package* trade-off deals suggested by China, has not worked, it has merely led the PRC to maintain its particular claims in all Sectors.

Another possible example of unilateral concessions was Rajiv Gandhi's visit to Beijing in 1988. Various concessions were made by him. He agreed that the settlement of the border dispute no longer was necessary as a precondition for improvement of bilateral relations, secondly he agreed that some members of the Tibetan community in India were engaged in anti-China activities, and thirdly he agreed that Tibet was an internal affair for China. Ganguly considered the results were "clearly asymmetric" as no support on the Kashmir issue was received from China, which "underscored the stark debility of India's negotiating capabilities vis-à-vis China". On the other hand, the earlier unequivocal support for Pakistan's case in Kashmir was moderated by a more neutral position by the 1990s, the PRC eventually announcing it was "not taking sides on Kashmir".

A final example of "unilateral concessions" came in the 2003 *Declaration on Principles for Relations and Comprehensive Cooperation between India and China,* in which India explicitly recognised the sovereignty of China over Tibet. A careful look at the text shows one-way agreement, one-way obligations, one-way concessions. On the one hand, it stated that "The Indian side recognizes that the Tibet Autonomous Region is part of the territory of the People's Republic of China and reiterates that it does not allow Tibetans to engage in anti-China political activities in India"; before going on to immediately say, on the other hand, "The Chinese side expresses its appreciation for the Indian position and reiterates that it is firmly opposed to any attempt and action aimed at splitting China and bringing about "independence of Tibet". As can be seen, there was no recognition of Indian territory (Arunachal Pradesh?) by China; not even return recognition by China of India's sovereignty claims over Sikkim, the Princely State reincorporated into the Republic of India in 1975, an incorporation which China had refused to recognise. Indian commentators may have read the accompanying *Trade Memorandum* designating Natu La as a border trade post as recognition by China of India's sovereignty over Sikkim, but that was implied rather than explicit, *de facto* rather than *de jure*.

Meanwhile, New Delhi has refused to lay out its formal position, other than the reiteration of its full claims of the Indian Parliament in November 1962, a unanimous vote to get China to vacate all Indian-claimed territories that China occupied. Specific territorial negotiations involving sensitive political climb downs or concessions might well be conducted in private out of the public gaze, yet there seems no indications of this either. India could then indicate some sort of territorial trade-off, short of this maximalist reiteration of its full claims which China is unlikely to accept. Of course, India indicating a territorial trade-off would not necessarily meet with Chinese acceptance, given Indian suspicions that China is happy enough to avoid definitive frontier settlement; but at least it would clarify the issue, and in such an eventuality enable India to more straightforwardly strengthen her own presence and power towards China along the border. In IR terms, if *engagement* proved unsuccessful in leading to territorial settlement, then India could go for a degree of *internal balancing* through building up its military presence and power in Arunachal Pradesh and Ladakh. Some Indian commentators have suggested that "when the Agni-III is finally ready for deployment, it is likely that the Chinese will come down to the table for negotiations and there is likely to be further progress on the border dispute". It could also go for a degree of *external balancing* with others vis-à-vis China but that is a much wider issue. It could try adjusting its bigger policy on Tibet, in effect playing a "Tibet Card" to engineer geopolitical shifts in the future; though would be a much more high risk strategy immediately bringing it up against China's perceived "core interest" of averting internal fragmentation.

If India's strategy over the disputed territories has been hesitant, this has been exacerbated by the very opaqueness, the "Chinese whispers" coming from Beijing. What exactly does China really want, what is its bottom line? For example, are PRC reiterations of claims over the whole of Arunachal Pradesh, re-invoked with greater vigour since the 1990s, just a maximalist initial tactic to end up with the Tawang pocket, thereby strengthening its control over Tibet, a line of argument by Chinese commentators like Ma Jiali and others. Are some suggestions in PRC circles of a different trade-off, Aksai Chin to India and Arunachal Pradesh to China, serious? Did China's acceptance in 2003 of Nathu La as an official border trade post between India and China represent full and definitive acceptance by China of Sikkim's incorporation into India; and what is the significance of rising "incursion" incidents into Sikkim during 2008 by Chinese troops; uncertainties that undermine Wen Jiabao's assertions in 2005 that "Sikkim is no longer the problem between China and India?" Is talk in the PRC that "China won't make any compromises in its border disputes with India" a tactical ploy by China to get India to make compromises? If it is, then a trade-off deal is likely at some point. If it is not, then indefinite deadline/stand off is likely, unless one or the other disputant state attempts to decide it on the military battlefield.

One emerging line from the PRC, with implications for India, is PRC emphasis and definition of a "core interests" diplomacy, reflecting the rise of China; "as the country becomes stronger, China is now on the trajectory to develop its own doctrine of diplomacy". This has been a development in the last couple of years, overlapping with rising friction along the disputed Himalayan reaches; generally what the PRC calls "the recalibration of its strategic focus in diplomacy to 'core interests'", over which it is taking a more obstructive/assertive line. This sense of "core interest" can be primarily seen at stake for the PRC in Taiwan and also Xinjiang. It can also be seen with PRC statements with regard to Tibet, whereby "Tibet related issues remain a core interest of China that refers to state sovereignty and territorial integrity. This is neither a religious issue nor a human right issue". The question is how far China's "core interest" framework may be "expanding". If such a "core interest" linkage is also invoked for Arunachal Pradesh (or in PRC eyes *Zang Nan* "Southern Tibet") as "Tibet-related issues", then one would have less expectations of territorial agreements being reached between India and China, and more likelihood of armed resolution in the future. Such trends were the spur for Barat Verma at the *India Defence Review* to warn that for the PRC "the most attractive option is to attack a soft target like India and forcibly occupy its territory in the Northeast...Beijing's cleverly raising the hackles on its fabricated dispute in Arunachal Pradesh to an alarming level, is the preparatory groundwork for imposing such a conflict on India"; a scenario dismissed in China as a "provocative and inflammatory illusion". Nevertheless, IR security dilemma dynamics may indeed lead to increasing military tension as both sides reinforce their military positions, and "war talk" about the disputed territories increases.

Concerned voices are easy to find as "tensions over a boundary dispute between the two sides are escalating". One reason for Indian concerns is the increasing number of "incursion" incidents along the border, though denied by China. The official India leadership downplays such trends, India's Foreign Secretary Niripuma Rao thus asserting in September 2009 that "there has been no significant increase in intrusions across all Sectors of the Line of Actual Control (LAC)", but that such India-perceived incursions were "because there is no mutually agreed or delineated border". This ignores the earlier increase the previous year, whereby the number of India-perceived "incursions" by the PRC has increased from 140 in 2007 to 280 in 2008, with a similar number in 2009. Such incursion incidents involved not just the *Eastern Sector* around Arunachal Pradesh but now also the *Western Sector* around Aksai Chin/Ladakh; a particular widening development that Indian commentators like Bhaskar Roy have found "sinister" and which Kanwal sees as "aggressive tactical posturing" on the part of China. Admittedly, such border incursions, reflecting different perceptions of where the LAC actually is, have often been trivial in themselves; for example Chinese troops painting rocks in red paint or cross-LAC sheep grazing. Chinese troop movements near and around the narrow Siliguri corridor "chicken's neck" linking north-east India to the rest of India do though cause immediate geopolitical concerns to India.

Certainly, a substantive military build up along the Aksai Chin and Arunachal Pradesh borderlines has also been evident. Partly this has been an infrastructure race, in which India has been belatedly trying to catch up and match China's better established road, and now railway, infrastructure in these disputed borderlands. It has also involved increasing military deployment, again by India to match China's already established forces in places like Linzi airbase. This is reflected in India increasing its ground forces in the border regions facing China. In the *Eastern Sector,* this has also involved the Indian Air Force (IAF) deploying advanced long range Sukhoi Su-30 warplanes to Tezpur for potential cross-LAC operation; complemented by six surface-to-air Akash missile squadrons. In the *Western Sector,* this has also involved the Indian Air Force reactivating disused high altitude airstrips like Daulat Beg Oldi and Fukche. Such reinforcements have been picked up in the PRC, and denounced as "unwise military moves".

Meanwhile, Brahma Chellaney asked the question in 2006 "will India—China border talks ever end"? He argued that "after a quarter century of unrewarding negotiations with Beijing, India ought to face up to the reality that it is being taken round and round the mulberry bush by an adversarial state that has little stake in an early border resolution"; in which "the more the talks have dragged on, the less Beijing has appeared interested in resolving the border disputes other than on its terms". His prognosis was simple, "it is time for it to draw the line, at least in the negotiations" and "to re-evaluate the very utility of staying absorbed in a never-ending process". Three years later, in the wake of the 2009 talks, his sense was the same, "the latest round of the unending and fruitless India—China talks on territorial disputes was a fresh reminder of the eroding utility of this process". The PRC may indeed wish to keep the issue open as a way of distracting and threatening India; but other dynamics may be leading the PRC to postpone decisive border negotiations. The PRC may well consider tightening its hold on Tibet itself as a greater priority, shaken during the disturbances that swept across Tibet and Tibetan areas in the spring of 2008? The PRC may also want to delay decisive border territorial resolution with India until it has resolved the Taiwan issue first? Garver also has wondered how far Beijing's apparent slowdown and readiness to avoid territorial resolution with India, is because of "understanding between Pakistan and China that neither will settle their territorial disputes with India independently of the other". Such a consideration point to the wider Pakistan—China—India triangle interplay around the disputed territories that stretch along the Himalayas from Arunachal Pradesh in the east to Aksai Chin and Kashmir in the west, which overlap with basic power balancing by the China—Pakistan "nexus" against India. The overlaps between the varied territorial disputes was shown in 2009 when China gave visas for the entry of Kashmiri separatists to visit China, in the wake of India giving permission to the Dalai Lama to visit Arunachal Pradesh.

What is certain is that any quick decisive territorial resolution between India and China is unlikely. Following rising border frictions, the PRC media reported "China—India border dispute turns sour", with hard hitting nationalist blogs being noticeable in the Chinese official and state controlled media in the autumn of 2009. Admittedly, the Indian and Chinese leadership did again reaffirm dialogue in autumn 2009. However, this reaffirmation was in cautious terms "to gradually narrow differences on border issues between the two countries ... to continue talks, with the aim of incrementally removing the barriers to a solution that was fair and acceptable to both sides". Despite the euphemistic headline from the official Chinese media that the two countries had reached "concensus on narrowing border differences"; in reality this merely indicated the existence of a gap without showing how and when it would be resolved. Talk of "gradually" and "incrementally removing" barriers to a solution flags up the slowness of any likely process, whilst offering nothing on what solutions could then emerge once such barriers have been, incrementally, removed.

What of solutions? Could outside arbitration be one way forward? Nehru himself had offered such a route in the immediate aftermath of war in the shape of the International Court of Justice (ICJ) at The Hague. However this was badly received in Parliament and Nehru then backed away immediately from this. In reality the ICJ seems ill equipped to deal with direct large scale territorial disputes between major powers, whilst China's reluctance to have outside bodies disposing of sovereignty issues is higher even than India's.

One bilateral solution which we can return to, involves a *logic of geography,* the "watershed/crestline" line along the Himalayas/ Karakoram. It has a degree of clearness, "the advantage of having a border on such a prominent line as the high watershed of the Himalaya is that it is easily identifiable, historically traditional and politically neutral". It may also be sellable to both parties. Thus, "as far as the Indian public is concerned, they have been brought up to believe that the Himalaya is the traditional boundary and they will be willing to concede any territory that lies beyond it without demur"; whilst "such a boundary should also be acceptable to China as it is based on the same watershed principle which they have accepted in defining their boundaries with Myanmar, Sikkim and Nepal. This watershed principle was an angle suggested by Zhou Enlai in the abortive 1960 discussions. In effect, applying the watershed principle would leave Aksai Chin to China and almost all Arunachal Pradesh with India.

Admittedly, Tawang remains problematic. The Tawang District's 2,085 square kilometres is around 2.5% of Arunachal

Pradesh's entire 82,743 area, and its population of 38,924 is around 3.6% of Arunachal Pradesh's 1,091,120 inhabitants (2001 figures), relatively small shares on paper. Neutralization of the entire Tawang subdivision pocket might be an option. Within the Tawang District, given that the Tawang Subdistrict and the District capital Tawang (27°34'47"N) itself lies north of the Se la Pass and the Ka crest line (27°32'26"N), whereas the Lumla and Jang Subdistricts lie on the southerly India-facing slopes of that crest line; could a division of Tawang District be carried out, with the Tawang Subdistrict allocated to China and the Lumla and Jang Subdistricts allocated to India? However, local opinion at the District capital Tawang, population c. 20,000, would probably vote in favour of staying in 'India' rather than going into the 'PRC', though an independent 'Tibet' option would provide an interesting third option. Having Tawang subdivision inhabitants relocate further south if they wished might be another solution, though ugly in political and human terms. Meanwhile, if the Dalai Lama's death was followed by any proclaimed rebirth at Tawang, a not impossible scenario, the situation would be still more complicated with the PRC.

Failing dramatic regime change scenarios of regime collapse/ democratization in the PRC, and re-establishment of a genuinely autonomous or independent Tibet, and Tawang notwithstanding; some sort of trade off involving Aksai Chin and Arunachal Pradesh seems the most likely way forward. In using relatively clear cut neutral geographic principles, the deadlocked politics and unclear history could perhaps be sidelined? Such a trade off would give neither side too much geopolitical advantage, but also ensure a degree of security for each? A *logic of geography* for the future for the national leaderships that would enable these two neighbours to get past the inconclusive divisive *logic of history* between them, and would provide a mutually satisfactory *logic of power* in terms of geopolitical equilibrium outcomes. Failing resolution of their territorial issues, the grinding tectonic plates along the Himalayas will continue to have their geopolitical counterpart as the two Asian giants look at each other across these disputed areas.

5

A New India's Tibet Policy

THE BRITISH POLICY ON TIBET

The British were good strategists, nobody can deny this. It has not always been the case of the Indians, especially with issues related to Tibet as we shall see in this chapter. On November 5, 1945, as World War II ended, the British Cabinet issued a little-known Statement on Tibet. It reiterated: "The attitude of His Majesty's Government towards the Tibetan question is defined in a memorandum by the Secretaries of State for Foreign Affairs and for India dated 23rd June, 1943."

What was this memorandum of 1943? It was a policy statement about Tibet sent by Antony Eden, the then British Prime Minister to Dr. T. V. Soong, China's Foreign Minister: "When you visited me on 26th July, you spoke of Tibet and enquired as to our attitude. I have pleasure in sending you the accompanying informal memorandum which I trust will serve to clear this matter up".

The well-known Memorandum represented the British policy towards Tibet for several decades. It starts thus: "Since the Chinese Revolution of 1911, when Chinese forces were withdrawn from Tibet, Tibet has enjoyed *de facto*independence. She has ever since regarded herself as in practice completely autonomous and has opposed Chinese attempts to reassert control. "

It is necessary to mention some of the points highlighted in the 1945 British Cabinet's Statement:

- Until the Chinese Revolution of 1911, Tibet acknowledged the suzerainty of the Manchu Emperors and a measure of control from Peking which fluctuated from military occupation to a more nominal link.

- His Majesty's Government made repeated attempts after 1911 to bring the Chinese Republic and the Tibetan Government together on the basis that Tibet should be autonomous under the nominal suzerainty of China, but these attempts always broke down on the question of the boundary between China and Tibet, and eventually in 1921, His Majesty's Government presented the Chinese Government with a declaration to the effect that they did not feel justified in withholding any longer their recognition of the status of Tibet as an autonomous State under the suzerainty of China, and that they intended dealing on that basis with Tibet in the future.
- ...we have promised the Tibetan Government to support them in maintaining their practical autonomy which is important to the security of India and to the tranquility of India's north-eastern frontier.

The Statement admits that the alliance with China during World War II made it difficult to give 'effective material support' to Tibet. Lhasa was however informed that London "would be prepared to give them only diplomatic support against China."

The Statement points to an interesting development; in August 1945, Chiang Kai-Shek made a declaration in the Chinese Assembly: "I solemnly declare that if the Tibetans should at this time express a wish for self-government our Government would, in conformity with our sincere traditions, accord it a very high degree of autonomy. If in the future, they fulfill economic requirement of independence, the nation's Government will, as in the case of Outer Mongolia, help them to attain this status".

The British commented: "There would seem to be nothing irreconcilable between this offer of 'a very high degree of autonomy' and the attitude of His Majesty's Government. It is clear however, from conversations which took place between British and Chinese representatives in Lhasa in 1944 that with regard to Tibet, there is a considerable difference between the British and the Chinese conceptions of the word 'autonomy'."

The conclusion of the British Cabinet was that two factors would govern the Tibetan question for London:

- Tibet has in practice regarded herself as autonomous and has maintained her autonomy for over 30 years;
- Our attitude has always been to recognize China's suzerainty, but on the understanding that Tibet is regarded as autonomous by China.

This was the Government of India's position when the country became independent in August 1945.

INDEPENDENT INDIA HAVE TIBET POLICY

This brings another question: had India a Tibet Policy at the beginning of 1950, when Communist China was preparing the 'liberation' (invasion in fact) of Tibet? The answer is a clear 'no'. The 1950 events in Tibet should have triggered a chain of reactions which could have resulted in a well-defined policy. It was not to be the case.

In India, the demise of Sardar Patel, the Deputy Prime Minister who had a pragmatic view on the security issues for the Indian borders, stopped the search for a Tibet Policy. The disastrous consequences are still visible more than 60 years later. During October and November 1950, India had the choice between two directions: either to bend with the 'east wind' and ally with China or stand and defend her own interests. The letter from Patel to Nehru, which could be considered his political testament, was resolutely in favour of the second path.

What probably started the exploration for a Tibet Policy was a report of Sir Girja Shankar Bajpai, the General Secretary of the Ministry of External Affairs and Commonwealth. We know of the report's existence only through a letter that Patel wrote to Bajpai on November 4, 1950. The Deputy Prime Minister tells Bajpai: The Chinese advance into Tibet upsets all our security calculations. Hitherto, the danger to India on its land frontiers has always come from the North-West. Throughout history we have concentrated our armed might in that region. For the first time, a serious danger is now developing on the North and North-East side; at the same time, our danger from the West or North-West is in no way lessened.

This creates most embarrassing defense problems and I entirely agree with you that a reconsideration of our military position and a redisposition of our forces are inescapable.

A few days later, Patel send his above-mentioned letter to Jawaharlal Nehru. The clarity of Patel's perception and the strategic implications of Tibet's invasion for India have been masterfully outlined in the following lines:

We have also to take note of a thoroughly unscrupulous, unreliable and determined power practically at our doors.....[the invasion of Tibet] in my judgment, entitles us to treat them with a certain amount of hostility, let alone a great deal of circumspection. In these circumstances, one thing, to my mind, is quite clear; and, that is, that we cannot be friendly with China and must think in terms of defense against a determined, calculating, unscrupulous, ruthless, unprincipled and prejudiced combination of powers, of which the Chinese will be the spearhead. Twelve years later, this last sentence would resound in the Indian mind. Was the China of 1950 very different from 1962's China? Or was it the same China who had already decided in 1949 who would be the new leader of Asia and was ready to use all available means to achieve its plans.

In a way, Patel's letter was the first (and only) draft Tibet Policy for India. The letter goes on to analyse, with great lucidity, the defence and other strategic and political issues facing India. For example, Patel lists the problems which need immediate action:

- a military and intelligence appreciation of the Chinese threat to India both on the frontier and the internal security.
- An examination of our military position and such redisposition of our forces as might be necessary, particularly with the idea of guarding important routes or area which are likely to be subject to dispute
- An appraisal of the strength of our forces
- A long-term consideration of our defence needs
- The question of Chinese entry into the UNO
- The future of our mission in Lhasa and trade posts at Gyantse and Yatung

- The policy in regard to the McMahon Line.

Six months later, as a first consequence of the new policy of non-interference of the Government of India, a 17 Point Agreement would be forced 'under duress' on the Tibetans. The first consequence was that the Indo-Tibetan border in the western and eastern sector became the Indo-Chinese border. It is what the British had tried to avoid at any cost.

NEHRU'S NOTE ON TIBET POLICY

Nehru did not respond directly to Sardar Patel's letter, but a few days later, he dictated a Note that would become the corner stone of India's Tibet Policy until the Prime Minister's death, and in a way, till today. We shall look at this Note to try to understand Nehru's fears and motivations.

In November 1950, Nehru had already accepted that the frontier between India and Tibet had de facto become the border between India and China. It was a surprising statement because at that time, the Chinese troops had not marched further than Chamdo, still several weeks away from Lhasa, and several months from the McMahon Line.

Nehru says: "I think it may be taken for granted that China will take possession, in a political sense at least, of the whole of Tibet." He further admits that for the Tibetan people the "autonomy can obviously not be anything like the autonomy, verging on independence, which Tibet has enjoyed during the last forty years or so."

It is beyond comprehension how Nehru, who wanted to be the hero of the oppressed nations, could at the same time accept that a nation 'verging on independence', should lose its independence before his eyes, and he could so easily accept it as a fait accompli. Another point made by Nehru is that "it is exceedingly unlikely that we may have to face any real military invasion [of India] from the Chinese side, whether in peace or in war, in the foreseeable future."

It is not clear what was meant by 'real' invasion, however Nehru came to the conclusion that China would not take the risk to have too many new enemies; for that would weaken China. He was proved wrong. Nehru's Note concludes: "We cannot save Tibet".

Regarding the Tibetan Appeal to the UN, Nehru finally decided to do as little as possible: "It will not take us or Tibet very far. It will only hasten the downfall of Tibet." The facts showed that Tibet was an independent nation, it was clear that China, as the aggressor, was in the wrong and that it was India's moral duty to defend this position, but under the pretext that it would not 'take us very far', the moral stand was dropped and Tibet abandoned to its fate.

All this shows that India had no Tibet Policy.

What should a Tibet Policy be today?

Does Delhi have a Tibet Policy today? If it does not have one, what shape should a Tibet Policy take? To answer this, it is important to have a look at what are India's present interests in Tibet?

They are, of course, of different nature; first and foremost are the strategic interests flowing from the long common (and disputed) border with China. But they are also diplomatic (visa issue), economic (border trade), cultural and civilisational. The presence of the Dalai Lama and more than a lakh of his countrymen and women is an important factor to be taken into account. After defining these interests, a formal (or informal) policy should accordingly be drafted.

The Strategic Interests

Let us have a look at strategic interests as many other issues flow from this core subject. There is currently an argument in India that the country is not prepared for a war. This is an undisputable fact. A few months back a Weekly magazine published a cover story arguing: "Fifty years after its only defeat, the Indian Army is still unprepared for a battle with its scheming adversary, China. Low on equipment and lacking in infrastructure, the bloated war machine is in urgent need of an overhaul."

Though Defence Minister A.K. Antony affirmed that no infiltration takes place across the LAC in Arunachal Pradesh, he recently admitted: "there have been instances of a few Tibetan herb collectors inadvertently crossing over into Indian territory in the last two years." It is common knowledge that the Chinese are masters at testing the ground by sending herders or herb collectors to scout areas that they 'perceive' as theirs.

Behind this new Tibet Policy should be that fact that it is not necessary for India to always be in denial mode. It does not help to engage China.

Does it Mean that 1962 can Repeat Itself?

Take the roads for example: in January 2008, during a visit to Itanagar and Tawang, the Prime Minister announced a Rs 24,000 crores package for the State. The priority was given to the roads (in particular, the construction of a Trans-Arunachal Highway). With the road being enlarged between the plains of Assam and Tawang (en route to the Tibet border), one finds today the messiest imaginable road site; it has become the favorite topic of local jokes. There are however differences between 1962 and 2012: the Indian leadership did not then dare to use the Air Force; it will not be the case today. A full squadron of Sukhoi-30 aircraft have now been deployed at Tezpur air base in Assam (another squadron has been brought to Chabua in Upper Assam). Further, the IAF is planning to open six Advanced Landing Grounds, as well as several helipads in areas close to the border. This may take some time, but the process has started.

Were India attacked today, it will not remain a localized conflict like in 1962; any Chinese misadventure would trigger an 'all-out' conflict, and India would certainly not hesitate to attack the PLA infrastructure in the Nyingchi Prefecture, north of the McMahon line and elsewhere in Tibet. It has been in the public domain that two new infantry divisions are being raised and that the Government is looking for a place in the Northeast to set up the headquarters of a Mountain Strike Corps.

This should be one more deterrent factor for China. Another crucial issue is the support of the local population in Arunachal and Ladakh. In 1962, some villages fully supported the invading Chinese troops. How else could the PLA have built a road from

Bumla, the border pass, to Tawang in 18 days? It is not difficult to imagine the staggering amount of accurate intelligence required for this feat.

An important question is "what will China gain from a misadventure on India's territoory, apart from a hypothetical Asian supremacy?" It is clear that China cannot militarily 'take back' Tawang. The PLA could at the most occupy a few 'disputed pockets' like Samdorong Chu valley, north of Tawang or Demchok in Ladakh, but in the process, Beijing would lose India's present goodwill and the international respect it earns with its 'peaceful rise' policy as well as its integration into the world scene as a responsible State.

Further, it should not be difficult for India to get logistic support from inside Tibet and eventually support a military rebellion; at least a civil disobedience could be organized. Let us not forget that an alien PLA has already to deal with a resentful local population on the Tibetan plateau. The recent immolations of monks and nuns in Eastern Tibet are a proof of this. The launch of the Agni-V long range missile also adds to the deterrence. It has already made Chinese policy makers ponder. The People's Daily stated that it reflects India's "intention of seeking regional balance of power".

If Beijing wants again to 'teach a lesson' to India, it will indeed be a Himalayan task, and what will Beijing gain in the bargain? China can nevertheless use some asymmetric types of warfare, cyber-warfare is one of them.

Traditionally, the Himalayan frontier has been a frontier between India and Tibet; the 1914 border agreement (i.e. the McMahon Line) delineates the frontier in the North-East. This is not acceptable to Beijing which denies the existence of the McMahon Line. It is the main reason why the border talks have today come to a standstill. Presuming that the next generation of Chinese leaders would attempt a 1962-like adventure against India, the Tibet factor would become crucial. The Indian Government could for example immediately recognize the Central Tibetan Administration in Dharamsala as the legitimate exiled government of Tibet.

A Tibet Policy should be based on deterrence, as India can't match today with China in terms of infrastructure and armed forces. Some of the developments mentioned above should be part of this policy of deterrence.

Diplomatic Contacts between Dharamsala and Delhi

A few years ago, the diplomatic contacts between Dharamsala and Delhi were enhanced when the post of the Dalai Lama's Liaison Officer (an officer of the Indian Ministry of External Affairs) was upgraded to the rank of Director and a post of Deputy Liaison Officer was created. In the recent years, successive Foreign Secretaries have visited Dharamsala and called not only on the Dalai Lama, but also on the Kalon Tripa (Prime Minister), the elected head of the Central Tibetan Administration.

However, there is still a feeling that "we should not upset the Chinese" and often ministers are 'shy' to meet the Dalai Lama and the Kalon Tripa. Officials contacts should be upgraded at the ministerial, if not prime-ministerial levels. It could be explained to the Chinese ambassador that it is nothing against the People's Republic of China, but the mere fact that the Dalai Lama is an 'honoured guest' and one and half lakh of his countrymen/women live in India, requires some coordination meetings from time to time.

Further, India should continue to insist to reopen its Consulate General in Lhasa. It would be an important step to restore the traditional relations. But when the question came to open a Consulate in Lhasa, some Chinese India experts objected. Zhao Gancheng, director of South Asia Studies at the Shanghai Institute for International Studies criticized India's proposal saying that the move was motivated by political, rather than economic interests: "The Indian government hopes to closely watch, observe, and infiltrate the Tibetan area after the opening of a Lhasa consulate,... The issue regarding Tibet is an internal affair and we won't tolerate any external forces imposing a negative impact on the situation in Tibet."

In this case, why to have a Nepali Consulate in Lhasa? Has (and had) Nepal closer contacts with Tibet than India? Zhao

Gancheng, who, by the way is often invited by Indian think-tanks, seems unaware of the traditional bonds between Tibet and India. The Indian presence on the Roof of the World is older than the British 'imperialist' (for the Chinese) inroads in Tibet.

One of the best proofs is the collections of thousands of 700-year old Sanskrit manuscripts found in Tibetan monasteries by the scholar Mahapandit Rahul Sankrityayan when he visited Tibet in the 1930's. Such examples could be multiplied.

If the Indian Government had wanted "to watch, observe, and infiltrate" Tibet, they could have done it long ago, with or without a Consulate General in Lhasa. Regarding the visa issue, if China continues to issue visas on stapled paper for the residents of J&K or Arunachal Pradesh, India should simply reciprocate for Tibetans, Uyghurs and Mongols from Inner Mongolia.

Trade between India and Tibet

Trade has, for centuries, been a traditional link between Tibet and India. Even when the Government of India decided to 'bury' Tibet as a de facto Independent nation in 1954, an agreement on 'Trade and Intercourse' between Tibet and India was signed (it is remembered as the Panchsheel Agreement). Inter alia, it says:

The High Contracting Parties mutually agree to establish Trade Agencies:

(1) The Government of India agrees that the Government of China may establish Trade Agencies at New Delhi, Calcutta and Kalimpong.

(2) The Government of China agrees that the Government of India may establish Trade Agencies at Yatung, Gyantse and Gartok.

The Trade Agencies of both Parties shall be accorded the same status and same treatment. Indians and Chinese traders were allowed to use the following places, (1) Yatung, (2) Gyantse and (3) Phari as trademarts. Further the Government of India agreed that trade may be carried on in India, in places like (1) Kalimpong, (2) Siliguri and (3) Calcutta.

The Chinese Government of China specified (1) Gartok, (2) Taklakot, (3) Gyanima-Khargo, (4) Gyaniina-Chaltra, (5) Ramura,

(6) Dongbra, (7) Puling-Sumdo, (8) Nabra, (9) Shangtse and (10) Tashigong as markets for Indian traders in Tibet.

Traders and pilgrims were allowed to use the following passes and routes: (1) Shipki pass (Himachal), (2) Mana pass (Uttarakhand), (3) Niti pass (Uttarakhand), (4) Kungri Bingri pass, (5) Darma pass (Uttarakhand), and (6) Lipulekh pass (Uttarakhand)

Unfortunately, after the 1962 conflict, all these trade marts and passes were closed. Since then, a series of border trade agreements were signed to reopen Lipulekh-la in Uttarakhand (1991), Shipki-la in Himachal Pradesh (1991).

In 2003 a Memorandum on Expanding Border Trade was signed between India and China; it was agreed to reopen Nathu-la as a border pass. Article II says: "The two sides agree to use Nathu-la as the pass for entry and exit of persons, means of transport and commodities engaged in border trade. Each side shall establish checkpoints at appropriate locations to monitor and manage their entry and exit through the Nathu-la Pass."

A recent report of the Institute of Peace and Conflict Studies explains: "Border trade markets [are] scheduled to be opened from Monday to Thursday every week. A permit fee of Rs. 50 each would be levied for every vehicle entering Sikkim side from China. Similarly, a fee of 5 Yuan (Rs. 25 approximately) would be levied for every vehicle crossing over to the Chinese side up to the trade mart point at Renqinggang.

Unfortunately, business is not flourishing as yet. On April 21, 2011, iSikkim reported: "The fifth edition of Indo-China trade through the Nathu-la border in 2010 recorded absolute zero import. In 2009 also the Nathu-la border trade closed for the season recording zero import. As per the official record, [year] 2010 saw exports worth a little over Rs 4 crore."

The Sikkimese publication quoted Kesang Diki, the Tibetan Autonomous Region's in-charge, affirming that the reason for zero import was the non-feasible list of items. She requested the Indian Government to expand the trade list and cater to today's market demands. Many feel that most of the items listed in the schedule are obsolete and do not have a commercial value; interestingly both the Tibetan and the Sikkimese traders agree on this. It is worth noticing that a few hundred kilometers westwards the trade is with Nepal is blooming.

The website China Tibet Online affirms that the "total volume of cross-border petty trade between Tibet and Nepal has increased remarkably in the first quarter of 2011". Like for India, Europe and the United States, the trade is heavily tilting in China's favour, but the Nepalis do not seem to mind too much.

A new Tibet Policy should take into account this important traditional bilateral activity and if there is a political will, the situation could greatly improve, with both side benefiting from it. Further, new traditional land ports such as between Walong-Rima in the Lohit Valley, Bumla in the Tawang district or Demchok in Ladakh could be opened, once the security concerns are taken care of. The softening of the borders would be one of the measures to bring more understanding on both sides of the frontier.

Pilgrimage

The Panchsheel Agreement mentions that as both India and China were "desirous of promoting trade and cultural intercourse between Tibet Region of China and India", (1) pilgrims from India of Lamaist, Hindu and Buddhists faiths may visit the Kailash and Manasarovar lake while pilgrims from Tibet may visit Banaras, Sarnath, Gaya and Sanchi. Today the immediate need is to open a new route for the Kailash-Manasarovar yatra. Demchok should be easier than the present one through Uttarakhand. Unfortunately, the Chinese side seems overcautious about the project.

In a longer term, if the security risks can be sorted out, the old Tsari pilgrimage around the Dakpa Sheri, the Pure Crystal Mountain in Tsari region of Southern Tibet could be reopened for the Buddhist populations of Arunachal Pradesh. It would, of course, raise the problem of visas as the Chinese authorities still claim the Indian State as part of 'Southern Tibet'. A special agreement would be required for this pilgrimage which occurs every 12 years, as part of it is located south of the McMahon Line. However, if allowed, the sacred yatra could greatly help to 'soften' the border. Year 2016, is the next date for the Tsari pilgrimage.

Buddhist Studies

As part of a global Tibet Policy, India should take the lead in promoting Buddhism and Buddhist studies. In this context, the Global Buddhist Congregation (GBC), organized by the Ashoka Mission in November 2011 was a good exercise. Some 900 monks and nuns from over 40 countries attended the event in Delhi. China, as usual, objected to the function. Beijing was particularly incensed by the invitation sent to the Dalai Lama to address the valedictory function. China even threatened to call off the 15th round of border talks between the Special Representatives if India refused to yield and cancel the Conference. Beijing also objected to the Prime Minister and the President of India attending the opening ceremony of the Congregation.

Eventually, India partially backed out with the Prime Minister and the President suddenly becoming 'busy', but the program with the Dalai Lama was reconfirmed. The External Affairs ministry issued a bland statement "We are looking forward to the 15th round of Special Representatives' talks in the near future and the two sides remain in touch to find convenient dates for the meeting."

The Ministry explained to China that the Congregation was of a religious nature and not a political event; further it had no power to cancel it. The Conference came at a time when Beijing had been trying to take on the leadership of the Buddhist world movement through its involvement in projects as in Lumbini and Nalanda and later a Buddhist Conference in Honk Kong.

One could think that the atheist regime in Beijing does not believe in Buddhism, but on the contrary, Beijing recently seems to embrace the philosophy taught by the Great Gautama, for political purposes at least.

The Economist reported that China plans to invest $3 billion in Lumbini, the birthplace of the Buddha. The magazine explains: "After Prachanda, the leader of Nepal's Maoists, stepped down as Prime Minister in 2009, he met representatives of the Asia Pacific Exchange and Cooperation Foundation (APECF) several times. In July, the Chinese media reported that the Hong Kong-based foundation which is widely thought to have China's backing had signed an agreement with UNIDO, the UN's industrial development organization, to invest $3 billion in Lumbini."

The objective is to make Lumbini a 'Mecca for Buddhists' (under China's sponsorship). Unfortunately for Beijing, the dynamic 82-year old Lama Lobzang from Ladakah and his colleagues from the Himalayan belt decided to celebrate the 2600th anniversary of the Enlightenment of the Buddha and to do it in India.

The Global Buddhist Conference eventually resolved to "preserve and conserve sacred sites and holy relics worldwide, particularly those that are historically connected to the life and times of Buddha such as Lumbini in Nepal, and Bodhgaya, Sarnath and Kushinagar in India". It was stated that Buddhism can help the human civilization which "today faces many challenges such as conflict, violence, extremism, discrimination, injustice, inequality, materialism, environmental degradation, natural disasters" and that solutions "to these issues of global concern can be found within the principles and values contained in Buddha's teachings."

India should certainly have a say in most of these issues whereas Buddhist ethics cannot flourish in China where the individual liberties are still very restricted under an authoritarian regime. India should give a lead to the Buddhist world in which Tibet and the Dalai Lama (representing the true Nalanda tradition) have a significant role to play. Once again, Indian leaders should not be shy to attend these types of religious functions.

Tibetan Studies

Tibetan studies is also a field where India has traditionally been present as most of the Tibetan literature originated from India. Unfortunately, here also it is China which invests in this field. Traditionally, scholars, pundits, lamas from India and Tibet have criss-crossed the Himalayas. For centuries, vast amounts of knowledge have freely been exchanged between the subcontinent and the Land of Snows over the Himalayan passes.

Today the situation has changed. From August 1 to 4, 2012, the 5th Beijing International Seminar on Tibetan Studies was held in the Chinese capital under the auspices of the China Tibetology Research Center. It is said it attracted 246 scholars from 21 countries and regions including Mongolia, India, Japan, France, Australia and the United States.

According to the organizers, the Seminar on Tibetan Studies was aimed at 'preserving culture and serving society'. The topics of discussion focused on social development in Tibet. The China Daily quoted Lhagpa Phuntshoks, the Director-General of the China Tibetology Research Center who stated during his opening speech: "Tibetan studies are expanding in China, with the government investing heavily in the protection of traditional heritage, printing of historic texts in the Tibetan language and the cultivation of young researchers". Sitar, the Vice-president of the China Association for Preservation and Development of Tibetan Culture declared that "China has been steadily endeavoring to preserve the Tibetan language, cultural relics, folk arts such as the Epic of King Gesar, and the religious practice. It is for this purpose that we organized a panel on Development, Sustainability and Livelihood Security in Tibetan-inhabited Areas."

The question is why should China have the monopoly of Tibet studies? Delhi, with the help and support of institutions in the Himalayan regions as well as Dharamsala, should revive Tibetan studies in a big way.

Further, why not open Chairs on Tibetan history, culture and politics in some of the main Indian Universities; particularly in J&K, Himachal Pradesh, Uttarakhand, Sikkim and Arunachal Pradesh? The age-old intellectual, spiritual and also environmental relations between India (particularly the Himalayan belt) and Tibet should flourish again. The People's Republic of China can keep the monopoly on Tibetan studies. A new Tibet Policy should promote the traditional links and help reestablish them through regular conferences/seminars and exchanges.

A GREATER TRANS-HIMALAYAN COOPERATION

Sowa Rigpa System of Medicine

There are different fields through which the Himalayans have a deeper and closer cooperation with the Tibetan civilization. One of them is Tibetan medicine. In August 2010, the Indian Parliament officially recognised the Tibetan system of medicine, known as Sowa Rigpa.

The Parliament adopted a bill to add the Sowa-Rigpa system of medicine practiced in sub-Himalayan region, as one of the Indian systems. While replying to a debate on the Indian Medicine Central Council (Amendment) Bill, 2010, Health Minister Ghulam Nabi Azad said: "It would be the endeavour of the government to bring to mainstream Sowa-Rigpa system of medicine in regions where it is prevalent."

Mr. Azad assured the Members that the Bill will provide protection and preservation of this ancient system of medicine and help its propagation and development. It will also facilitate the setting up of a regulatory mechanism in the field of education and practice. Further the government would set up a Pharmacopoeia Commission for Indian Systems of Medicine, including Sowa-Rigpa. The Rajya Sabha had passed the Bill on August 25.

The Sowa-Rigpa system of medicine is practiced in Himalayan belt and other parts of the country besides Nepal, Tibet, Baltistan, Mongolia and Japan. The practice and research in this field should be further supported.

BHOTI LANGUAGE

Language is one of man's best mediums of communication. It is also a reflection of history, culture, religion and politics of a nation or a region. One of the richest and less known languages of India is the Bhoti language. It is widely used in Ladakh, Kinnaur, Lahul, Spiti, Sikkim, Arunachal Pradesh, but also in Bhutan, Nepal and Baltistan. Bhoti language is closely linked with Tibetan, using the same scripts. Bhoti is the language of the Buddhists of the Himalayan belt. It is the language of the pundits, scholars and saints who criss-crossed the Himalayas generations after generations. It is also the language for the Himalayans people struggling to preserve their identity, in a global world.

In the same way that Sowa Rigpa has been acknowledged by the Government of India as one of the indigenous systems of medicine, Bhoti language should be recognized as one of the

Indian languages. The time has come to introduce a bill for its inclusion in the eighth schedule of Indian constitution. It will go a long way to acknowledge the century-old link between the people of the Himalayan belt and Tibet.

Right now, Bhoti language is preserved at a slow pace. For example in Ladakh, winter classes in Bhoti are organized in some villages, but only middle aged people usually attend. One step forward would be to start classes at the primary school level. In an online debate on the subject, a participant wrote: "There is still immense appreciation and interest for Bhoti language among the local people of Lahul & Spiti, Ladakh. We still organize sessions in winters to keep the traditions of the oral songs and verses alive. People take interest, but mostly middle aged, learned persons, government employees. Every winter we put up notices indicating the timings of such sessions. People from Tod, Garh, Khoksar and Myad valley are often more interested. But it is not taught in schools for the younger generation. In Spiti the enthusiasm is much more as the community is more homogenous and they have been able to introduce Bhoti in schools. Many of us have tried to document the lyrics in Bhoti and learn the script because, if we write them down in Hindi, we don't do justice to the unique pronunciations. The SC/ST Commission and the Himalayan Buddhist Culture Association are taking some initiative in promoting the language."

Ultimately, if the Himalayans can find their own roots and reestablish their link with the Tibetan civilization, they can participate in the preservation of an endanger culture.

Environment

Environment is a field where the Himalayans should be able to 'share' more and should be encouraged to do so. After all, they have a common ecological past and future. In this context, an interesting event was organized in Simla in October 2009. The Chief ministers of Himachal Pradesh, Jammu and Kashmir, Uttarakhand, Arunachal Pradesh and Sikkim issued a detailed action plan known as 'Simla Declaration'. Union Minister of State for Environment and Forest, Jairam Ramesh, presided over the

Chief Ministers' meet. Experts from the five Himalayan States discussed the impact of climatic change in the Himalayan region and its relation with the people living in mountains.

The declaration states: "The mountain people have traditionally lived a low energy, low consumption, and low waste life styles. It is very important to learn from these, and emulate this in a larger scale in view of the necessity of reducing the global emission of green house gasses."

Adding: "Himalaya, which provides life-sustaining 'eco-system services' to a large part of south-Asia, is one such region. While the impacts of climate change on the Himalayan ecosystems like accelerated glacial melt and distorted rainfall patterns have been studied in depth, preparation to tackle these impacts, both at the national and state levels seem to lack vision and are generally based upon the same paradigm of unsustainable development that has brought this world to the current state of crisis."

The Chief Ministers of Himalayan States decided in Simla to adopt a common strategy to combat climate change. A trans-Himalayan organization in the line of the International Centre for Integrated Mountain Development (ICIMOD), but purely Indian should be established, collaborating with Tibetan experts in the field of environment.

ICIMOD is a "regional intergovernmental learning and knowledge sharing centre serving the eight regional member countries of the Hindu Kush Himalayas – Afghanistan, Bangladesh, Bhutan, China, India, Myanmar, Nepal, and Pakistan." It is based in Kathmandu. ICIMOD's strategic framework stresses: "Globalization and climate change have an increasing influence on the stability of fragile mountain ecosystems and the livelihoods of mountain people. ICIMOD aims to assist mountain people to understand these changes, adapt to them, and make the most of new opportunities, while addressing upstream-downstream issues."

A similar organization should be instituted for the Indian Himalayas in close collaboration with ICIMOD. It will be one more occasion to share similar problems on both sides of the Himalayas.

THE TIBETANS IN INDIA

Regarding the third aspect of a new Tibet Policy, i.e. a greater security for the Tibetan refugees living in India, it is enough to cite a few possibilities:

- Long term residential permits could be given to the Tibetans settled in India for a long time.
- Possibility to apply to OCI scheme under the Ministry of Home Affairs.
- A long-term solution for people living in the Himalayan States having difficulty to acquire land and build up assets on these lands.
- The Special Frontier Forces, the Tibetan Force fighting under India's colours should be given proper recognition, first of all in terms of decorations and awards. India should not be ashamed to employ Tibetans jawans
- The Special Frontier Forces should train a few jawans for the new Olympics Games in shooting, wrestling or other disciplines where Tibetans excel. An Olympic medal would be a great boost to the Tibetan community in exile and will prove to China that India attaches a great importance to the Tibetan presence in India.
- Facilitate admission of Tibetan students in Indian educational institutions under a special quota.

All these different aspects should form part of a Tibet Policy whose objectives would be to reestablish the century old economic, cultural and religious links between India and Tibet and at the same time make the Indo-Tibet (now Indo-China) borders softer, even if it takes time to return to the 1950s open frontiers.

INDIA NEEDS TO RE-VISIT ITS TIBET POLICY

The continuing border incursions by the Chinese PLA into the Indian borders with growing frequency, Chinese cartographic aggression as a part of well-calibrated strategy and openly showing areas of other neighbouring countries including India as parts of China in the passports issued by China, denying Indian military officers posted in J&K to be included in the delegations, declaring the visit of Indian PM to Arunachal Pradesh as illegal, etc. are factors that demand a change in India's policy towards Tibet. Their aggressiveness has crossed all limits as they are indulging in highly provocative acts of stopping the Indian patrols from covering their area. These constitute a direct challenge to India's sovereignty. In addition, the continuing human rights violations in Tibet resulting in Tibetans resorting to extreme step of committing suicide, which have crossed 100 in the last four years, themselves provide sufficient ground for India to change its policy towards Tibet.

A look at the history of Tibet too would reveal that the China invaded Tibet and has virtually converted it into its colony. Since the Chinese Revolution of 1911, when the Chinese forces were withdrawn from Tibet, Tibet had enjoyed de facto independence and had opposed Chinese attempts to reassert control. Even prior to 1911, Tibet had only acknowledged suzerainty (and not sovereignty) of the Manchu Emperors and their control fluctuated between military presence to a nominal link. It is interesting to note that in history there were periods when China was under the suzerainty of the Tibetan Emperor. The Tibetan Emperor Trisong Detsan (755-797 A.D.) invaded parts of China including Chengan (now Xian) and forced China to pay tribute to Tibet and accept Tibetan suzerainty. In 1821 a treaty between Tibet and China was concluded that accepted that both the nations were independent.

The British, noting the situation, had always been treating Tibet as an autonomous region under the nominal Chinese suzerainty. British made several attempts after 1911 to bring China and Tibet together to accept this situation but the attempts always broke down on the issue of boundary between China and Tibet and not between Tibet and India. Eventually, the British presented the Chinese government in 1921 with a declaration to the effect that they did not feel justified in withholding any longer their recognition of the status of Tibet as an autonomous state under the suzerainty of China, and that they intended dealing on that basis with Tibet in the future. The British, after 1921, promised support to the Tibetan government in maintaining the latter's practical autonomy which was considered important to the security of India and to the tranquillity of India's north-eastern frontier. The above policy was clearly mentioned in the memorandum issued by the British government on 23rd June 1943. The British PM Antony Eden on November 5, 1945 reiterated this in writing to the Chinese foreign minister Dr. TV Soong.

After 1947, the Indian authorities too continued with this policy. When China invaded Tibet in 1950, Sardar Patel then Deputy PM of India, in a note to the then secretary general in the external affairs ministry, Sir Girja Shankar Bajpai noting the implications of the Chinese moves in Tibet stated that the Chinese invasion had completely changed the security calculations and clearly pointed out that a serious danger was developing in the north and north east. He also agreed with the latter that 'a reconsideration of our military position and a redisposition of our forces were inescapable.' Sardar Patel later sent this note to the then Indian PM J L Nehru outlining the need for taking suitable action for India's defence. He clearly spelt out the strategic implications in the following lines-

"We have also to take note of a thoroughly unscrupulous, unreliable and determined power practically at our doors. The invasion of Tibet in my judgment, entitles us to treat them with a certain amount of hostility, let alone a great deal of circumspection. In these circumstances, one thing, to my mind, is quite clear; and, that is, that we cannot be friendly with China and must think in terms of defence against a determined, calculating, unscrupulous, ruthless, and unprincipled and prejudiced combination of powers, of which the Chinese will be the spearhead." He certainly had Pakistan in mind when he talked of combination of powers. In the detailed note to Bajpai, he had mentioned that the threat from the West and North West had not reduced. How accurate his assessment was can be seen in the present context.

Unfortunately India's policy of non-interference allowed the Chinese government to impose 17-Point Agreement on Tibet under duress. The immediate consequence of this was that the Indo-Tibetan border became Sino-Indian border – a situation the British had tried to avoid at all costs. The trade agreement signed in 1954 was based on Panchsheel principles and that in effect buried the de facto independent Tibet nation. After this, India in the hope of managing China, signed a number of agreements that showed that India had accepted Tibet as an autonomous region of China. These included Agreement on Maintenance of Peace and Tranquillity along the Line of Actual Control in the India-China Border of 1993, Agreement between China and India on the Confidence Building Measures in the Military Field along the Line of Actual Control in the India- China Border Areas of 1996, Declaration on Principles for Relations and Comprehensive Cooperation of People's Republic of China and Republic of India of 2003 and Agreement between the Government of Republic of India and the Government of the People's Republic of China on Political Parameters and Guiding Principles for the Settlement of India-China Boundary Question of 2005. The text of these high sounding agreements would reflect that both sides would not do anything that would increase tension on the border and that both sides are sincere in resolving the issue through peaceful means. However, the Chinese actions have been contrary to the contents of agreements.

In addition to the lack of sincerity on the part of the Chinese in making these agreements, these agreements could not be implemented as there was no agreement on the length of the Sino-Indian border. While China does not include the area of J&K and considers Arunachal Pradesh as part of Tibet, India considers the entire length of the border between Tibet and India as Sino-Indian border. With this ambiguity, there are bound to be problems in the resolution of the issue. However, these agreements placed India in a disadvantageous position. India in these agreements accepted the Tibetan Autonomous Region as a part of China without obtaining any commitment from China on the issue of J&K or Arunachal Pradesh. Even after 2003 agreement, which agreed to the establishment of a trading mart in Nathula in Sikkim, Chinese maps continued to show Sikkim as an independent nation. Whenever, this issue was raised, the Chinese authorities brushed it aside by saying that they had inherited this from history and there was no need to give importance to the issue.

Basic issue is not what China is projecting through various statements and agreements but it is the intention of China towards

India, which needs to be analysed in the light of its activities. Several experts have pointed out that China has encircled India by developing its strategic relations in our neighbourhood and desires to keep India under pressure so that it may it may not emerge as a strong nation. The Chinese activities certainly reveal this intention. China in the name of "Four Modernization" focussed on developing its armed forces and building infrastructure along the border. The recent aggressiveness shown in all the bordering areas reflects the intents of grabbing all the disputed areas along the Chinese borders. Its continued assistance in nuclear and missile fields to Pakistan is certainly affecting India's security and this cannot be regarded as a friendly act.

On the other hand some writers point out that Xi Jinping the Chinese President has told the Indian PM that China wants to settle the boundary question soon and therefore India should give some time more to China. Chinese President Xi Jinping in the "Five Point" proposal had committed that both sides would accommodate each other's core concerns and would reconcile bilateral disagreements amicably is underlined by them. To strengthen their argument they highlight that the fact that China had settled the boundary disputes with 12 other nations and there was give and take. Hence they argue that there is a possibility that China with the changed leadership may make serious efforts to resolve the boundary dispute with India.

On balance when the Chinese motives are analysed in the backdrop of continued anti-India activities, the view of the first category of experts appears to be correct. The Chinese leaders in the past had also made statements indicating their desire to amicably settle the issue. Late Sri Brijesh Mishra as the Indian envoy was told by Mao himself that the two countries should continue to fight. Deng also told the then Indian PM Rajiv Gandhi that the two countries should forge closer relations. Even Hu Jintao had expressed similar views. However the Chinese activities reflect that they have different plans and the Chinese continue with their intrusions without paying any attention to the Indian core concerns. The talks of the Chinese leaders when seen in the light of their activities only reveal their duplicitous nature.

The justification for the change in the policy towards Tibet is in fact provided by the Chinese themselves. Notwithstanding so many agreements, if the Chinese authorities are not considering the J&K as a part of India, India is fully justified in not treating the Tibet Autonomous Region as part of China. What India needs to discuss is the return of the territory illegally occupied by China in J&K. Rest is the border between India and Tibet, which should be discussed with the latter. India should declare that the length of India-China border is only limited to the J&K part that touches China. India at the same time stop policy of accommodating Chinese wishes by not sending officers from J&K or Arunachal Pradesh. Such acts actually go against our national interests by giving the impression that India is prepared to accept such demands. This does not mean that India and China would go to war but would establish that India can react against unjust demands of China. India –China trade, which is highly in favour of China, is yet another leverage against China and can be effectively used. The India-China trade deficit increased by 34% against India in the first five months of this year over the last year. The Chinese PM had recently come to India with a large delegation of the Chinese companies. The Chinese companies should be placed in the category of companies from the countries of concern and should not be given facilities to operate.

In addition, the continued human rights violations in Tibet demand suitable response from India. India being the neighbouring country cannot turn a blind eye to the happenings in Tibet. In fact this in itself is a sufficient reason for changing our policy towards Tibet. The Tibetans today remain marginalised. China has settled Hans by giving them incentives, with the result that in Lhasa and other urban centres Hans are in majority. The Asia Watch Report of 1990 had pointed out that in Amdo (Qinghai), Kham (Sichuan) and Lhasa Hans had outstripped the locals. The Tibet Youth Congress has also noted that recently that about 2 million Tibetans have been relocated since 2006. The unemployment among the Tibetans is increasing. The Tibetans cannot join as guides for tourists as the fluency in Mandarin is essential. In addition, as the locals have been moved to rural areas, they are not in a position to take advantage of the flourishing tourism in Tibet. Recently,

Tibetans in Canada had protested against the Chinese policy of removing the Tibetans from urban areas and settling them in rural areas.

However, what is hurting the Tibetans most is the attack on religion of Tibetans. Dalai Lama, who is the spiritual head of Tibetans, is being demonised by the Chinese authorities. The real Panchen Lama, Gedhun Cheokyi Nyima, was imprisoned along with his family in 1995 and they selected their own man as Panchen Lama. In addition laws have been imposed which say that no one with criminal cases can join monasteries. The Chinese slap charges on all those who are considered to be anti-Chinese. And by the State Administration for Religious Affairs bill of 2007, all Lamas who wish to re-incarnate are required to obtain permission from the Government and that re-incarnation has to take place only in China.

The Chinese authorities are getting concerned about their vulnerabilities and therefore are trying to project that they intend to take necessary steps by changing their policies. The Chinese are aware that much of the economic development of China is due to the exploitation of natural resources of Tibet and they need them. Recent comments of Professor Jin Wei in Yazhou Zhoukan (Asia Weekly), a Chinese weekly in Hong Kong on June 9, 2013, and the reported proposals for new approach suggest that the current hard-line policy on Tibet is being questioned. The Chinese authorities may also be worried about the continued latent militancy in Tibet and suicides by Tibetans.

In sum, the security and foreign policies should be dictated by the strategic vision. The border incidents should not be treated as localized affairs. By saying this, Indian leadership is encouraging China to continue with their intrusions. The security establishment of the country and experts have been demanding a change in the policy to protect our national interests. It is well known that there are no permanent friends and no perennial enemies, what is permanent are our national interests. Tibet is not merely a strategic card against China but also the responsibility of India to support Tibetans against the continued human rights violations.

TIME FOR TRANSFORMING INDIA'S POLICY ON TIBET

As India enters the 65th year of its existence as a sovereign nation, it is time to take a pause to reflect on the policies of the past, to revisit our triumphs, our failures and to reflect on challenges met and opportunities lost.

The macro picture that emerges is of great success. Following a traumatic and violent partition, and burdened with a colonial economy drained by 200 years of exploitation, India in 1947 faced an uncertain future. In contrast the India by 2011 boasts of a strong demographically young society and a $4 trillion economy set on the path of irreversible growth. It is taken for granted that India will be a major player in the new global balance of power.

And yet, as we celebrate success, we need to introspect and identify the areas where we missed the mark. If I am asked to name a single issue on which India failed to measure up to its challenges I will, without hesitation, say it was Tibet. The Tibet issue is a perfect illustration of Murphy's Law: if something can go wrong, it will! Many will question this conclusion as wisdom by hind sight. Yes it is. And such wisdom by hind sight is important because it insures that the errors of judgment of the past will not be repeated.

What Went Wrong With India's Tibet Policy?

So what went wrong with our Tibet policy? Ten points, according to me:-

1. India's assumption that China was interested in larger issues like joining India in creating an Asian renaissance turned out to be entirely erroneous.
2. Under a policy described by former Foreign Secretary Mr. Jagat Mehta as "Unilateral friendliness" with China, India naively believed the false assurances of the Chinese leaders that the Chinese maps of our northern borders were cartographic errors. This would be rectified soon. They were never corrected.
3. Equally naively India believed the Chinese assurances regarding the safety of the Dalai Lama and the Welfare of the Tibetan People. This was never carried out.

4. In subsequent negotiations with China on the border issue, we were wrong in taking a rigid, legalistic posture and asserting territorial claims for which there was insufficient evidence. The jury is still out on the assertion of Mr. A.G. Noorani that all our claims were not entirely founded by empirical evidences.
5. The Tibetan issue reflects a major systemic failure in the Indian system. There were voices within the cabinet that were urging caution in dealing with China – amongst them two Home Ministers; Sardar Patel and Pandit Govind Ballabh Pant and Finance Minister Morarji Desai. Their advice was ignored. India's national interests would have been better protected if Pandit Nehru had taken his cabinet colleagues to his meeting with Chou En Lai in February 1960. Also ignored was the professional advice of the Foreign Service establishment, including Sir G.S. Bajpai, then Secretary General in the MEA and younger Foreign Service officers like Sumal Sinha, Mr. V.V. Paranjpe, Mr. P.K. Banerjee and Mr. Arvind Deo who incidentally served as India's Counsel General in Lhasa.

   Sadly, the Prime Minister relied on a group of political appointees like Sardar K.M. Panikkar and Mr. Raghavan, who failed in offering their independent assessment of what was happening in Tibet to the PM. Mr. Panikkar in fact was informed in advance of the Chinese plans to quote unquote "Liberate" Tibet but did not apparently report this for fear that it would affect India's ambitions to play a mediating role in the aftermath of the Korean war.
6. India failed to demand reciprocity before accepting the Chinese demands to support its "One China" policy and its sovereignty over Tibet and Taiwan. Had reciprocities been applied in the beginning, China might have refrained from questioning India's sovereignty in J&K and Arunachal Pradesh.
7. The Chinese have been relentlessly pursuing their goal of integrating Tibet with mainland China by rail, road and air. Let us be clear, they have every night to do so. India,

in contrast has lagged behind in integrating the border areas adjoining Tibet.

8. There is growing evidence to suggest that China is seriously proceeding to construct a series of dams on the Brahmaputra or the Yarlung – Tsangpo. This will have catastrophic consequences on the North East of India and Bangladesh. India's concerns on this issue have been muted and ineffective.
9. The frantic pace of development activities in Tibet is having its effects on the environment, with consequences not only for Tibet, but the entire South Asian region and parts of South East Asia. It will affect the glaciers, the rivers which supply water to the region and the seismic safety of the fragile Himalayan eco system. I am not aware if this has been seriously discussed by India, either bilaterally or internationality.
10. And finally, the conclusion is inescapable that we have failed the people of Tibet time and again, in their greatest hour of need. India was a silent witness to the brutal takeover of Tibet, the systematic suppression of the cultural and religious rights of the Tibetans, the savage attacks on Buddhist monks and nuns, the pillaging and destruction of their monasteries and the demographic manipulation under which Tibetans may well became a minority in their own homeland.In 1950, when PLA troops entered Lhasa, not only did India do nothing, it dissuaded the UN and other countries that were willing to come to the rescue of the Tibetans. In 1951, when the so-called 17 point agreement was forced on the hapless government of the Dalai Lama, India did not protest.

In 1954, India signed an agreement with China under which it surrendered all its rights and responsibilities in Tibet and withdrew its garrisons from Yatung and Shigatse. That the 1954 agreement was signed in the name of the Buddhist principles of the Pancha shila made it a tragic mockery of the Tibetan people.

Let me make one point clear, if there was a failure of India's Tibet policy, it was a bipartisan failure. Every government of India, whether led by the Congress or the BJP, has been complicit in evading India's historic responsibilities in Tibet. The formulation of the 1954 agreement has been repeated as a Mantra in joint statements issued during Mr. Rajiv Gandhi's visit to China in 1988, Mr. A.B. Vajyapee's visit in 2003, and during the Indian visits of Wen Jia Bao and Hu Jin Tao in 2005 and 2006.

It is worth noting that the standard formulation on Tibet was absent, for the first time, in the joint statement issued after Wen Jia Bao's visit during December 2010.

If this is a signal of change in our China policy, it is to be welcomed.

Can Anything Be Done?

If, as our scholars conclude, India has irrevocably surrendered its 'Tibet Card' and formally accepted Chinese sovereignty over Tibet, is there nothing that can be done for the Tibetan people by India or the international Community?

I am not so pessimistic. There is growing body of opinion that in a global and interdependent world, the concept of state sovereignty is no longer absolute. The talk is increasingly about a "responsible sovereignty" or "shared sovereignty". No state in the world today can claim the absolute, sovereign right to deny basic human rights and freedom to its own citizens. In extreme circumstances, and subject to transparent and credible safeguards, the international community can also exercise the Right to Protect (R2P) to affected groups.

Admittedly, this is still a grey area in international law but this is increasingly acceptable internationally. I am not suggesting that the R2P should be applied to the Tibetans in China. It is nevertheless a useful reminder to China a great nation and civilization that it must act as a responsible global citizen and show sensitivity to the rights of its own Tibetan people.

Secondly, India has never hesitated to express concerns over the plight of people who happen to be the citizens of another state. Mahatma Gandhi wrote letters to President Roosevelt about the status of Blacks in America. India took the leadership in opposing Apartheid in South Africa. India continues to voice its anxiety about the treatment of the Tamil citizens in Sri Lanka. These are but a few examples.

A NEW OPPORTUNITY FOR INDIA

India must seize the opportunity that has opened up today to review and recalibrate its policy on Tibet. The decision of the Dalai Lama to abdicate his political responsibilities and hand them over to a democratically elected 'Kalon Tripa' is a momentous development in the history of Tibet. It reflects the profound wisdom and foresight of the Dalai Lama.

Felicitations are due to the new Kalon Tripa, Dr. Lobsang Sangay. I have followed his articles, speeches and interviews with great interest and admiration. It is also fortunate that the Tibetans today have in addition to their supreme spiritual guide, the Dalai Lama, two young leaders from the next generation: the 17th Karmapa and the Kalon Tripa, Dr. Lobsang Sangay.

Let me conclude by offering a few suggestions for the action India needs to take as a part of a bold new policy on Tibet.

1. Removal of restrictions on the activities and movements of the Dalai Lama and the Karmapa. All directives in place must be withdrawn which require political leaders and senior officials not to be seen in public with the Dalai Lama and the Karmapa. It is an affront to India's sovereignty that such restrictions are in force to accommodate the wishes of another country. The Dalai Lama and the Karmapa deserve our deepest respect as internationally acclaimed sprintual leaders.There should also be an end to the suspicions and reservations that a section of our establishment has against the Dalai Lama and the Karmapa. There were powerful voices in the Indian establishment in the 1950s and 1960s that the Dalai Lama should be sent back to Tibet. There are segments of our establishment today that are keen to accord the same treatment to the Karmapa. I am pleased that the external affairs department prevailed in offering asylum to the Karmapa when he turned up in Dharamsala a decade ago. I am convinced that it was the right thing to do.

2. India must identify completely with efforts to preserve Tibetan culture and Tibetan Buddhism. When Buddhism was virtually wiped out from India, the land of its origin, the Tibetans undertook to nurture this rich heritage over the centuries. The time has come for India to reciprocate this gesture.I hope that the Dalai Lama can be persuaded to take the leadership in bringing the scattered schools of Buddhism in India under a common umbrella. On a personal note, as a Vice President of the Maha Bodhi Society of India, I am keen on seeing this success.

   I would also like to see the Dalai Lama being closely associated with the Nalanda University Project. It is hard to appreciate that he is being kept at arm's length fearing the reactions of another country.

3. It is time to remove the refugee tag from the Tibetans who have opted to make India their home. Those who are inclined to be Indian citizens must be granted citizenship without going through harassing procedures. Tibetans must be given the same privileges as the citizens of Nepal and Bhutan. Young Tibetans of Indian origin should be encouraged to form Indo-Tibet friendship societies or associations which will promote the awareness of Tibet among the Indian public.

4. Reciprocity must be the guiding principle hereafter in India's response to Chinese demands on the status of Tibet.

5. India must not hesitate to express concern over the violation of the human, cultural and religious rights of the Tibetan people, not only in the Tibetan Autonomous Region, but in other states with significant Tibetan population. This should not be seen as a challenge to China's sovereignty but as a part of India's continuing advocacy of the rights of vulnerable communities across the world.

6. India must publicly and vehemently oppose the construction of dams on the Brahmaputra / Yarlang Tsangpo which would divert its waters away from India and Bangladesh. This should be taken up by India both bilaterally and at appropriate global forums.

7. India must be equally firmly in expressing concern over the ecological damage caused by the unrestricted development projects in Tibet. It is the source of 10 major rivers and numerous glaciers which provide sustenance to two million people in Asia.

INDIA REVEALS FLAWED TIBET POLICY

The recent decision by India's ruling United Progressive Alliance government to bar ministers from attending a felicitation ceremony for the Dalai Lama is an indication not only of the blunders committed by the government in its foreign policy decision-making, but more perilously it exposes the flawed nature of India's policy towards Tibet.

India has so far failed to understand the nuances in Chinese diplomatic practice and negotiating tactics. It has time and again fallen into the Chinese trap, sacrificing its national interests in the process.

Clearly, China is tackling its Tibet problem at two levels. One, it is involving the Dalai Lama's representatives in fruitless talks on the resolution of the Tibetan problem, while also disparaging him as a "splittist" who aims to disintegrate China. Two, it is arm-twisting India on the border dispute by raising the Tawang district issue and asking India to remove its army bunkers from its outposts at Batang La near the India-Bhutan-China tri-junction, while at the same time mesmerizing the Indian leadership with rhetoric on India-China joint leadership in bringing about an Asian renaissance.

China's Tibet policy forms the linchpin of its nationalist project. Its sovereignty over Tibet has significant ramifications not only for its national integrity but also for stability in its other minority areas, particularly Xinjiang. If Tibet falls from China's grip, Xinjiang would follow suit. The bottom line of China's Tibet policy thus has been the maintenance of its sovereignty over Tibet through military and economic means, whereby the region is fully integrated with the mainland and Tibetans are reduced to a minority in their own province.

More importantly, China's Tibet policy has significant external security ramifications owing to the entanglement of the Tibet issue in the Sino-Indian border dispute. India inherited the British policy of sustaining Tibet as a buffer zone and Tibet's de facto independent status under Chinese suzerainty suited its national security interests. In the post-1949 period, when the People's Republic of China came into being, India urged China to let Tibet be an autonomous region, as this would be in line with its historical status, its religious, cultural and political identity, and minimize China's military presence in the region.

However, the entry of 20,000 PLA (People's Liberation Army) troops in 1950-51 into Tibet ended its independent status. The Chinese occupation of Tibet brought to the fore the issue of India-China border. During his visit to China in 1954, Jawaharlal Nehru raised the issue of inaccurate border alignment in some Chinese maps to which Chinese premier Zhou Enlai replied that those maps were reproductions of the old Kuomintang maps and that the Chinese government had no time to revise them.

Ironically, these two developments formed the undercurrent of the Hindi-Chini Bhai Bhai era (India and China are brothers)when India signed the agreement with China on trade and intercourse between India and Tibet on April 29, 1954. Under the agreement, India gave up all extra-territorial rights and privileges that it had inherited from the British Indian government and recognized Tibet as part of China.

The first official Chinese statement on the Sino-Indian border dispute came on January 23, 1959, in response to Nehru's letter of December 14, 1958, in which he had drawn Chinese attention to the incorrect Sino-Indian border alignment shown in Chinese maps. Zhou Enlai wrote saying that the Sino-Indian border was never delimited and that China had never recognized the McMahon Line.

It may be recalled that the British had delineated the McMahon line as the boundary between India and Tibet following a tripartite agreement among the British India, Tibet and China in 1914 but the treaty was not ratified by China. After the India-China 1962 war China went on to claim about 90,000 square kilometers of Indian territory in the eastern sector and 38,000 square kilometres in the Aksai Chin area. China's Tibet policy thus had brought to the fore a serious border dispute between India and China, and it has remained intractable till date.

Indeed, China's claim over Tawang (Arunachal Pradesh) on the basis of old Tibetan religious and monastic links is a reminder of the fact that the Tibetan issue is far from over. In fact, the 11th round of the meeting between the special representatives of the two countries in September 2007 ended on an inconclusive note partly because of the Tawang issue.

The former Chinese ambassador to New Delhi, Zhou Gang, said that as the Chinese people would never accept the "McMahon line", India would have to make substantial adjustments in the Eastern sector by giving Tawang to China.

India's policy towards Tibet has suffered because of its many dilemmas. In the 1950s, though India opposed China's invasion of Tibet, it refused to sponsor a Tibetan appeal to the United Nations, turned down US proposals for cooperation in support of the Tibetan resistance and persuaded the young Dalai Lama not to flee abroad but to reach an agreement with the Chinese government.

All this forced the Dalai Lama to sign a 17-point agreement with Beijing in May 1951. This Indian policy stemmed from the need to preserve Tibet as an autonomous region within China, while simultaneously advancing ties with Beijing. Consequently, India signed the 1954 agreement with China on Tibet, in which it virtually surrendered its Tibetan card. The 1956 uprising in Tibet exposed the insincerity of the Chinese towards granting autonomy to Tibet and in an effort to retrieve the lost ground India granted asylum to the Dalai Lama in 1959.

But Beijing saw the granting of asylum to Dalai Lama and enabling him to mobilize international support as an anti-China policy. Consequently, in all subsequent India-China joint statements, it ensured the insertion of a clause on India's acceptance of Tibet as a part of China.

By repeatedly reiterating over the years that Tibet is a part of China, India diluted its leverage not only in shoring up the Tibetan cause but also in its border negotiations with China. At the same time, China continues to fear that India might use the Tibetan card at some point in the future. Despite these Chinese fears, India has steadfastly avoided using the Tibetan card as a bargaining strategy.

Given its tradition of pursuing an independent foreign policy, it is incomprehensible why India is buckling down under Chinese pressure on Tibet. It is well known that given the present dynamics of India-China relations with greater synergy as the goal, New Delhi is not likely to take up the Tibetan cause actively.

But at the same time, it is well within the parameters of Indian foreign policy to regard the Dalai Lama as Tibet's spiritual leader. When China hosted the World Buddhist Forum, no eyebrows were raised though the event had significant political import. India, being the land of Buddha, should take the initiative to felicitate the Dalai Lama. After all, the Dalai Lama is not demanding independence but is only legitimately demanding the preservation of Tibetan identity, religion and culture within Chinese frontiers.

India lacks the political will to creatively use the Tibetan card and is losing an important leverage in its negotiations with China. India has the Tibet card if it chooses to use. The very presence of the Dalai Lama in India along with 120,000 Tibetan refugees spread across 35 settlements is leverage for India.

Further, the Dalai Lama recognizes the 1914 Simla agreement, in which case the Chinese claims on Tawang on the basis of history do not hold ground. In any case, historically, the Tawang tract did not belong to China. The Chinese side in their dialog with the Tibetan Task Force have tried to persuade the Tibetans to accept Arunachal Pradesh as Chinese territory, to which the Tibetans have firmly refused.

Interestingly, while the Chinese are trying to solve the border dispute with India through special representatives group meetings, they are also simultaneously holding talks with the Tibetans on the Tibet issue.

This indicates entanglement of the Tibetan issue with the India-China border dispute. Therefore, the problem of Tibet including the fate of Tibetan refugees in India and the border dispute cannot be solved effectively without a tripartite participation of India, China and Tibet.

India should explore ways to involve the Tibetans in the border resolution. In fact, an effective solution to the India-China border dispute would depend on involving the Tibetans as representatives in the ongoing border negotiations. It may be similar to the Sino-Japanese history issue where a joint committee has been set up to resolve the history question. India-China-Tibet need a joint historical research to resolve the "leftover" of history.

INDIA SHOULD REVISIT ITS TIBET POLICY

The Indian government's response to the protests in Tibet has been to merely state its "distress" about the situation and reaffirm its position that Tibet is an "internal" affair of China. New Delhi had assured Beijing that its position on the Tibet issue is "clear and consistent" and that this "would not change in the future." The Indian position is based on its traditional opposition to separatist movements and to foreign intervention in support of such movements. Also, given the present dynamics of India-China relations with greater synergy as the goal, New Delhi does not favour supporting the Tibetan cause. However, protests by Tibetans have implications for India as the Tibet issue is entangled with the India-China border dispute.

The Tibet issue is rooted in the histories of the three countries – India, China and Tibet. Tibet has existed throughout history as a distinct civilization with rich culture, language, religion, polity and identity. Through the centuries India and Tibet have maintained strong religious and trade ties, and have shared a peaceful border. But the advent of British power in the Indian sub-continent altered the nature of this relationship.

The British Raj's policy towards Tibet was shaped by the Great Game and the need to prevent Russia from posing a threat to India. It was against this backdrop that the Raj called for the tripartite Simla conference in October 1913, which was attended by representatives from British India (Henry McMahon), Republican China (Chen Yifan) and Tibet (Lonchen Shatra). The goal was to settle the boundary between British India and Tibet on the one hand and between Tibet and China on the other. The result was the Simla Agreement of 1914, which the Chinese representative initialled but only under British pressure. The Agreement divided Tibet into Inner and Outer Tibet. China was given sovereignty over Inner Tibet but only suzerain control over Outer Tibet. And the boundary between India and Tibet was demarcated, with the Raj retaining trading and extra-territorial rights in Outer Tibet.

Independent India inherited this arrangement, which boiled down to sustaining Tibet as a buffer zone with de facto independent status under Chinese suzerainty. In the post-1949 period, when the People's Republic of China came into being, India urged China to let Tibet continue as an autonomous region in line with its historical status, religious, cultural and political identity. However, the entry of 20,000 PLA troops in 1950-51 into Tibet ended its independent status and eventually brought to the fore the India-China border issue.

During his 1954 visit to China, Jawaharlal Nehru had raised the issue of inaccurate border alignment as depicted in some Chinese maps. Premier Zhou Enlai responded that these maps were reproductions of old Kuomintang maps and that his government has had no time to revise them. However, Nehru's December 14, 1958 letter, in which he had once again raised the issue of Chinese maps depicting the border alignment inaccurately, elicited a different response from Zhou. The Chinese Premier wrote back on January 23, 1959 stating that the Sino-Indian border was never delimited and that China has never recognised the McMahon Line.

After the 1962 India-China war, China began to claim some 90,000 square kilometres of Indian territory in the eastern sector and 38,000 square kilometres in the Aksai Chin area. These claims flow directly from China's control over Tibet and its felt need to consolidate its rule over this rebellious territory.

Between 1947 and 1954, India's position on Tibet was based on recognising it as an independent nation. Tibet represented itself as an independent country at the Asian Relations Conference held in New Delhi in March-April 1947. But India subsequently gave up this position on April 29, 1954, when it signed an agreement with China on trade and intercourse between India and Tibet.

Under the terms of the agreement, India gave up all extra-territorial rights and privileges that it had inherited from the British Raj and recognised Tibet as part of China. This, in effect, was a unilateral concession without the Indian government gaining anything in return.

In subsequent decades, New Delhi has repeatedly reiterated that Tibet is a part of China, in spite of the latter's encroachment into and extravagant claims over Indian territory, the border war it imposed on India in 1962, and the unresolved border dispute at the centre of which lies Tibet. In effect, such reiteration has meant the dilution of a bargaining card in the border negotiations. In 2003, the Vajpayee government went further than any other government before by stating that the "Tibetan Autonomous Region of China is part of the territory of China." This has two critical implications for Indian security. First, it excluded Inner Tibet (present day Sichuan, Yunnan and Qinghai provinces) from the geographical notion of Tibet, thus recognising Inner Tibet as Chinese land. Second, it provided China a greater opening to advance its claims on Arunachal Pradesh. For, Outer Tibet or the Tibetan Autonomous Region (TAR), according to the Chinese definition, includes Arunachal Pradesh, which it refers to as its 'southern state'.

India has consistently failed to understand nuances in Chinese diplomatic practice and negotiating tactics. China is tackling the Tibet problem at two levels. One, it is involving the Dalai Lama's representatives in fruitless talks, while also disparaging him as a 'splittist' who aims to disintegrate China. Two, it is arm-twisting India by repeatedly claiming that Arunachal Pradesh is part of China. Here, it is worth noting that at the sixth round of talks with Tibetan representatives Chinese negotiators had conveyed that the Dalai Lama should accept Arunachal Pradesh as part of China, which the Dalai Lama has refused to accept. China is not seriously considering a resolution to the Tibet issue or the border dispute with India. It is simply buying time till the Dalai Lama passes away, after which, it hopes, the Tibetan movement would fizzle out. This would also further weaken India's bargaining position on the border negotiations while at the same time gaining for itself greater manoeuvrability.

The presence of the Dalai Lama in India along with 120,000 Tibetan refugees spread across 35 settlements is leverage for India. But India has so far steadfastly avoided using the Tibetan card. Given the intricate linkage between the Tibet issue and the border dispute, India needs to revise its policy on Tibet. Its present policy of appeasement and unilateral concessions has not stopped China from claiming Indian territory. Chinese maps continue to show Arunachal Pradesh as part of China, and Jammu and Kashmir as falling outside India. Some Chinese maps still do not represent Beijing's revised position on Sikkim.

The latest unrest among Tibetans provides an opportunity for India to revisit and revise its Tibet policy. First, India should make it clear to the Chinese government that developments in Tibet are a concern for India and that it cannot remain unaffected by developments there. Second, on the border issue, instead of merely restating that all of Arunachal Pradesh is an integral part of its territory, India should make it very clear that these are non-negotiable. Third, upholding its democratic principles as well as its cultural affinity with the Tibetans, India should impress upon the Chinese that while it does not support political activity by Tibetans in its soil, it also cannot suppress peaceful demonstrations by them. Fourth, India should move away from its 'over-cautious' and diffident policy on Tibet and adopt a more independent stand that takes into account its national interests.

CENTRAL GOVERNMENT'S POLICY AND DALAI LAMA

Starting from the point of maintaining the unification of the motherland and national unity, the central government adopted an attitude of patient waiting towards the Dalai Lama after he fled abroad. His position as a vice-chairman of the NPC Standing Committee was preserved until 1964. However, surrounded by foreign anti-China forces and Tibetan separatists, the Dalai Lama completely renounced the patriotic stand which he once expressed and engaged in numerous activities to split the motherland.

Publicly advocating that "Tibet is an independent state." In June 1959, the Dalai Lama issued a statement in Mussoorie, India which read "Tibet had actually been independent." In March 1991, during his visit to Britain, the Dalai Lama told the press that Tibet "is the biggest occupied country in the world today." He proclaimed on many occasions that "the task of realizing the independence of Tibet has fallen upon all Tibetans in and outside Tibet."

Setting up the "government in exile." In the early 1960s, the Dalai clique convened the "people's congress of Tibet" in Dharamsala, India, which established the so-called "Tibetan government in exile." A so-called "constitution" was promulgated, which states that "the Dalai Lama is the head of state," "the ministers shall be appointed by the Dalai Lama" and "all work of the government shall not be approved without the consent of the Dalai Lama." The 1991 revised "constitution" of the Dalai clique still stipulates that the Dalai is "the head of the state." The Dalai Lama and his so-called "government in exile" kept levying an "independence tax" on Tibetans residing abroad, established "offices" in some countries, published magazines and books advocating "Tibetan independence" and engaged in political activities for "Tibetan independence."

Reorganizing the armed rebel forces. In September 1960, the Dalai clique re-organized the "religion guards of the four rivers and six ranges" in Mustang, Nepal, which carried on military harassment activities along the Chinese border for ten years. Its first commander-in-chief Anzhugcang Goinbo Zhaxi wrote in his memoirs *Four Rivers and Six Ranges* that "a series of attacks were organized on Chinese outposts" and "sometimes, 100 or 200 Tibetan guerrillas went as far as 100 miles into the area occupied by the Chinese." The Dalai Lama wrote articles praising Goinbo Zhaxi.

Spreading rumors and calumnies and plotting riots. Ignoring facts, the Dalai Lama fabricated numerous lies to sow dissension among the various nationalities and incite the Tibetan people to oppose the central government during his 30-year self-exile abroad. He said that "the 17-Article Agreement was imposed on Tibet under armed force"; "the Hans have massacred 1.2 million Tibetans"; "owing to Han immigration, the Tibetans have become a minority in Tibet"; "the Communists in Tibet force women to practice birth control and abortion"; the government opposes religious freedom and persecutes religious people; traditional

Tibetan culture and art are in danger of extinction; the natural resources in Tibet have been seriously depleted; there is severe environmental pollution in Tibet, etc. The riots in Lhasa from September 1987 to March 1989 were incited by the Dalai clique and plotted by rebels who were sent back to Tibet. The riots incurred severe losses to the lives and property of Tibetans.

The Dalai's words and deeds have showed that he is no longer only a religious leader as he claims. On the contrary, he has become the political leader engaged in long-term divisive activities abroad.

'TIBETAN INDEPEDENCE' BROOKS NO DISCUSSION

The central government has adopted a consistent policy towards the Dalai Lama. It urges him to renounce separatism and return to the stand of patriotism and unity. On December 28, 1978, the Chinese leader Deng Xiaoping said to AP correspondents that "the Dalai Lama may return, but only as a Chinese citizen"; "we have but one demand — patriotism. And we say that anyone is welcome, whether he embraces patriotism early or late." This indicates the central government's attitude of welcoming the Dalai Lama back to the motherland.

The Dalai Lama sent representatives to Beijing to contact the central government on February 28, 1979. On March 12, Deng Xiaoping met the Dalai Lama's representatives and said to them, "The Dalai Lama is welcome to come back. He can go out again after his return." With regard to the central government's negotiation with the side of the Dalai Lama, Deng pointed out, "Now, whether the dialogue to discuss and settle problems will be between the central government and Tibet as a state or Tibet as a part of China? This is a practical question." "Essentially Tibet is a part of China. This is the criterion for judging right or wrong." The central government did everything possible to persuade the Dalai Lama and his followers, through negotiations, to give up their separatism and return to the motherland. The central government leaders have since 1980 met a number of delegations sent back by the Dalai Lama and reiterated on many occasions the central government's policy towards the Dalai Lama.

To satisfy the desire of both local and overseas Tibetans for visits and contacts, the central government has formulated and practiced the policy of free movement in and out of the country. It has also made clear that all patriots belong to one big family, whether they rally to the common cause now or later, and bygones can be bygones. From August 1979 to September 1980, central government departments concerned received three visiting delegations and two groups of relatives sent by the Dalai Lama. Most of the Dalai Lama's kin residing abroad have made return visits to China. Since 1979, Tibet and other Tibetan-inhabited areas have received some 8,000 overseas Tibetans who came to visit relatives or for sightseeing, and helped settle nearly 2,000 Tibetan compatriots.

Regretfully, the Dalai Lama did not draw on the good will of the central government. Instead, he further intensified his separatist activities. At a meeting of the Human Rights Subcommittee of the US Congress held in September 1987, the Dalai Lama put forward a "five-point proposal" regarding the so-called status of Tibet. He continued to advocate "Tibetan Independence," and instigate and plot a number of riots in Lhasa. In June 1988, the Dalai Lama raised a so-called "Strasbourg proposal" for the solution of the Tibet issue. On the premise that Tibet "had always been" an independent state, the proposal interpreted the issue of a regional national autonomy within a country as a relationship between a suzerain and a vassal state, and between a protector and a protected state, thus denying China's sovereignty over Tibet and advocating the independence of Tibet in a disguised way. The central government naturally rejected the proposal, because it was a conspiracy the imperialists once hatched in order to carve up China. The Chinese government solemnly declared, "China's sovereignty over Tibet brooks no denial. Of Tibet there could be no independence, nor semi-independence, nor independence in disguise." Nevertheless, the central government still hopes that the Dalai Lama would rein in at the brink of the precipice and change his mind. In early 1989, the 10th Bainqen Lama passed away. Taking into account the historical religious ties between various generations of the Dalai Lama and the Bainqen Lama as teacher and student, the Buddhist Association of China, with the approval of the central government, invited the Dalai Lama to come back to attend the Bainqen Lama's memorial ceremonies. President Zhao Puchu of the association handed a letter of invitation to a personal representative of the Dalai Lama, providing the Dalai Lama with a good opportunity to meet with people in the Buddhist circles in China after 30 years of exile. But the Dalai Lama rejected the invitation.

As 1989 witnessed a new international anti-China wave, the Nobel Peace Prize Committee in Norway, with clearly political motives, awarded the 1989 Nobel Peace Prize to the Dalai Lama, giving its strong support to the Dalai Lama and the Tibetan separatists. Since then, the Dalai Lama has travelled the world, advocating Tibet's separation from China.

The Dalai Lama simultaneously intensified his efforts to incite and plot riots in Tibet. On January 19, 1990, he said over the BBC: If the Beijing government fails to hold talks with him on his plan of Tibet's autonomy within a year, he will have to change his stand of compromise with China; many young Tibetans stand for the use of force. On April 4, 1991, the Dalai Lama said in the Tibetan language program of the Voice of America, "All matters shall be further strengthened for Tibet's independence." Again on October 10 the same year, he tried instigation in a similar program, "At present, so large a number of Hans are pouring into Tibet that many young Tibetans cannot find jobs. This adds a further element of instability in the Tibetan society. Therefore, new riots are quite possible."

It is because the Dalai Lama sticks to his position of "Tibetan independence" and continues his efforts to split the motherland in and outside China that contacts between the central government and the representatives of the Dalai Lama have yielded no results.

In an interview with Xinhua News Agency reporters on May 19, 1991, on the eve of the 40th anniversary of Tibet's peaceful liberation, Premier Li Peng of the State Council of the People's Republic of China pointed out, "The central government's policy towards the Dalai Lama has been consistent and remains unchanged. We have only one fundamental principle, namely, Tibet is an inalienable part of China. On this fundamental issue there is no room for haggling. The central government has always expressed its willingness to have contact with the Dalai Lama, but he must stop activities to split the motherland and change his position for 'Tibetan independence.' All matters except 'Tibetan independence' can be discussed."

The central government is willing to contact and negotiate with the Dalai Lama; the door remains open. The central government's policy towards the Dalai Lama is also clear. To be responsible for the history, the Chinese nation and its 1.1 billion people, including the Tibetan people, the central government will make not the slightest concession on the fundamental issue of maintaining the motherland's unification. Any activity attempting to realize "Tibetan independence" and split the motherland by relying on foreign forces is an ignominious move betraying the motherland and the whole Chinese nation including the Tibetan nationality. The central government resolutely denounces this kind of action and will never allow it to succeed. The central government will continue to implement a series of special policies and preferential measures to promote the construction and development of Tibet so as to enhance national unity, construct a prosperous economy, enrich culture and improve the people's livelihood. Any activity sabotaging stability and unity in Tibet and any unlawful deed creating disturbance and inciting riots runs against the basic interests of the Tibetan people and will be cracked down on relentlessly.

So long as the Dalai Lama can give up his divisive stand and admit that Tibet is an inalienable part of China, the central government is willing to hold talks at any time with him. The Dalai Lama is warmly welcome to return to the embrace of the motherland at an early date and do some work that is conducive to maintaining the motherland's unification, the national unity, as well as the affluent and happy lives of the Tibetan people.

6

The Tibet Factor in India-China Relations

INTRODUCTION

For thousands of years, Tibet was the buffer that kept India and China geographically apart and therefore at peace. It has only been for the last six decades or so, after China invaded and occupied Tibet in 1950, that India and China have come to share a common border, and with it the inherent issues of border security, such as the delineation and demarcation of the border and the movement of people and flow of trade across it. However, in the absence of any extensive historical experience of relations with each other, each country has a poor understanding of the psyche and system of the other. This was a critical lacuna when the two countries began to interact after India's independence in 1947 and the Communist Revolution in China in 1949. Both were then governed by proud nationalist leaders who were imbued with an exalted sense of the greatness, destiny and mission of their respective nations, but who also had deeply ingrained grievances arising out of the humiliations they suffered under colonial rule. Given the vanities, egos and different ways of thinking of the leaders of India and China, the likelihood of misperceptions and misunderstandings was built into the situation.

SINO-INDIAN RELATIONS AND TIBET PRE-1950

Before the mid-20th century, India-China relations were minimal. There was some overland and seaborne trade, as well as occasional exchanges of pilgrims and scholars. The experience of the Indians and the Chinese of the outside world was completely different. India did not—indeed could not—keep out foreign influences and ideas. Macedonians, Turks, Afghans, Persians, Mongols and assorted tribes from the Eurasian heartland who invaded India over the centuries made a profound and lasting impact on the country. The old order was not swept away. Rather, a new composite culture and society emerged as, over time, the invaders settled down in the hospitable climes of the plains of India. Here they lived in peace and prospered, eventually becoming indistinguishable from, indeed a part of, the local population. That was not the experience of the Chinese, who remained self-assured that they were the "Middle Kingdom" and all others barbarians.

A DIPLOMATIC GIMMICK OR STRATEGIC SURRENDER?

The year 2014 marks the 60th anniversary of the Panchsheel Agreement between India and China and the Governments declared year 2014 as 'India—China Year of Friendly Exchanges'. For the Tibetans, each such 'celebration' or the reiteration of the so-called Panchsheel principles in every Sino-Indian Joint communiqué is a haunting reminder of their national tragedy.

With the signing on April 29, 1954, the much trumpeted Panchsheel Agreement, which Acharya J B Kriplani referred as 'born in sin', Tibet's political fate was sealed off as the 'Tibet Region of China'. The treaty was the first ever International treaty that recognizes China's Sovereignty over Tibet. Much to everyone's chagrin, the Government of Tibet in Lhasa and the Tibetan people whose fate was decided through this contentious treaty were not even consulted or informed. Indeed, this was an additional injustice to the Tibetans who were passing through the most critical phase of their history.

No wonder, Indian Intelligence Chief B.N. Mullick found the Tibetan Diaspora in Kalimpong shocked and anguished. In his book, "My years with Nehru", Mr. Mullick stated, "The Sino-Indian Treaty of 1954 caused a terrible shock to the Tibetans. They had already been upset by the unilateral Indian acceptance of the

Chinese suzerainty over Tibet which, according to them, allowed China to commit aggression against that country."

Many political analysts wonder, if Prime Minister Nehru was against inheriting the British imperialist's extraterritorial rights and colonial legacy in Tibet, why then accept the British imperialist concept of Chinese suzerainty over Tibet?

Meanwhile, the Independent India's continuous diplomatic vacillations finally culminated into the recognition of Tibet as a part of China in a bid to secure peace and security across Himalayas, thus sealing the fate of Tibet for eternity.

Consequently, as India forfeit all its rights and properties in Tibet; downgrading the Indian Mission in Lhasa to a Consulate General and its gradual closure along with its Trade Agents in Yatung, Gyantse and Gartok etc., surrendering of its 12 Rest Houses and the Postal, Telegraph, Public telephone services, hospitals and withdrawal of the military escorts etc, India failed to obtain any quid pro quo in the clear demarcation of the Indo-Tibetan border. And as if that were not enough, the Indian Government agreed upon opening a Chinese Consulate General in Bombay.

It's another story that barely a month after signing of the Panchsheel treaty, Indian officials and traders in Tibet were unscrupulously harassed and intimidated and eventually coaxed to leave Tibet unceremoniously. This ludicrous harassment campaign involves diverting flashflood and damaging Indian Trade Agent etc, practice of shooting near the Site in order to threaten the lives of the officials and the border incursions in Bara Hoti and other border areas besides the occupation of Aksai Chin.

In July 1954, following the destruction of the Indian Trade Agency buildings in an unprecedented flash flood in Gyantse, Tibet (eyewitnesses suspect Chinese forces of destroying the embankment to let the flash floods into the Agency premises), the Chinese Government had created incessant obstacles in the smooth and timely renovation of the Trade Agent. Later the laborers working on the site of renovation were harassed. Further inconveniences from the Chinese officials included denying accommodation for the official, restriction on the hiring of private trucks or import of India's own trucks during the renovation. Provisions of transport and other support from the local Chinese authorities are a far cry.

To add to the Agency's woe, Chinese Government launched military firing practice over the Agency site. The shooting practice is believed to be a strategy of harassing the Indian officials.

Eventually, China even restricted the movements of the Trade Agent officials and their families inside Tibet. And the mail services of the Agency too were suspended. Furthermore, in the pretext of registration of arms, the Chinese even confiscated the arms possessed by the Agency and the Indian nationals.

The harassment of the Indian traders in Tibet included locking of their shops and confiscation of goods without valid causes. And many others were prosecuted and detained on sheer unfounded suspicion. Indian pilgrims to Mt Kailash were also detained for many weeks and their movements restricted.

Subsequently, the Chinese Government also prevented the Indian Government from evacuating the Indian nationals from Tibet. The Chinese Government refused to accept Indian Government's evacuation of Ladakhi Lamas and the Kashmiri Muslims to India stating that they are Tibetan citizens from times immemorial.

The Indian Government lodged constant protest over the unhelpful and unfriendly attitude of the local Chinese authorities towards Indian officials and national but to no avail. Such ghastly actions by China are hardly in conformity with principles of non-aggression and friendly co-existence enshrined in the Panchsheel treaty.

Meanwhile Chinese Government launched series of hostile propaganda against India in its official 'Lhasa Daily' newspaper accusing the Indian troops based in Gyantse of harassing local Tibetans. The Indian troops were alleged to be seizing food grains and fodders and forcing the local Tibetans to supply transport, firewood, servants, etc in return for nothing. They were also accused of forcing locals to do corvee work, and also destroying crops and colluding with the Tibetan traitor Phala etc. The Indian doctors were also alleged to be charging exorbitant fee from the local Tibetans and the Indian traders purportedly exploiting the Tibetans.

Indian Government denied the allegations as sheer fabrication.

Yet, amid all these developments, curiously enough, unlike India, a small Himalayan nation of Nepal continue to retain its Consulate General in Lhasa to this day.

It was even more appalling to find that the Indian Government was supplying rice and other commodities to the occupying Chinese PLA soldiers in Tibet during the critical period. And in the Indian parliament many lawmakers were alarmed to find the Government "Feeding the enemy?"

In his recent article titled, "60 years on: Unforgiving Legacy of the Panchsheel Agreement", former Special Director of The Intelligence Bureau, Mr. R N Ravi aptly asked, "Why did India go for the Panchsheel Agreement giving away all its geopolitical and geostrategic interests and assets in Tibet accrued over centuries and so crucial to its national security, even without settling the border?"

Later, Prime Minister Nehru was vehemently criticized for naively assuming that the signing of the agreement indirectly symbolizes China's acceptance of the Sino-India frontiers and that he had secured peace in the Himalayas.

Studies show that many Indian foreign ministry officials including Secretary General Girja Sharkar Bajpai did stress on the quid pro quo and in his notes to Ambassador Panikkar on 21st November 1951, Mr. Bajpai emphasized that the recognition of the Sino-India border should be a part of general settlement and that there was no question of surrendering the advantages accrued from the Simla Convention without getting a firm assurance from the Chinese on the McMahon Line and the other sectors. Mr. Bajpai further warned that there was also no question of withdrawing the garrisons in Gyantse and Yatung without securing such an assurance.

Nonetheless, many geo-strategists deemed those as the best period for India to resolve Sino-Indo border crisis with China conclusively.

The First Foreign Secretary of India, Mr. K.P.S. Menon (Senior) justifying Indian Government's stand, clarified in his book, 'Twilight in China' that "Critics of the Government of India have often denounced its alleged inaction on that occasion (Chinese invasion of Tibet). They even say that India gave away Tibet to China. As if Tibet had been India's to be given away!" In that case, it could also be argued that India had no business to define the status of Tibet and that too against the wishes of the Tibetan people. Especially when Prime Minister Nehru had already asserted in the Indian Parliament on 1st November 1950 that 'according to any principles they (China) proclaim and the principles I uphold, the last voice in regard to Tibet should be the voice of the people of Tibet and of nobody else'.

Perhaps, such cold political response to the Tibetan tragedy by Nehru could not have been out of his displeasure over Lhasa Government's cynical demand of the return of 'lost' territories of Darjeeling, Kalimpong, Arunachal Pradesh and certain parts of Ladakh instead of responding promptly to the Independent India's call for ratifying the Simla Convention.

Mr. Claude Arpi, Strategic Analyst and Tibet expert, in his study titled, "The Evolution of Nehru's Policy on Tibet: 1947-1954" published in year 2000, argued that this historical blunder of claiming 'lost' territory would have incalculable consequences for Tibet and for India. Mr. Arpi stressed, "This was in fact one of the most preposterous actions of the Tibetan Government. It was not without reason that Jawaharlal Nehru and other Indian officials were very displeased with the Tibetans. This certainly marks a decisive turn in Nehru's view on Tibet." Mr. B.N. Mullick, the IB Chief, summed up Nehru's feeling when he wrote "this ill-advised claim [to lost Tibetan territories], made by the Tibetan Government resulted in the temporary loss of a certain amount of Indian sympathy for Tibet."

Strategist Mr. Mohan Guruswamy, in his article titled, "Sino-Indian Ties: 20th Century Borders for Stable 21st Century Relations" and many other articles, charged Dalai Lama of staking claim to 'Tibetan territory' in the Indian Himalayas, and wrote, "In 1947 the Dalai Lama (the same gentleman who is now in Dharamshala) sent the newly independent India a note laying claim to some districts in NEFA/Arunachal).

It must be clarified that Dalai Lama did not sent the note of territorial claims to the Indian Government. Mr. Guruswamy fails to notice that Dalai Lama was just 12 years old in 1947 and that Tibet was ruled by the Regent Tagra Rinpoche in 1947. All the decisions were made by the Regent in consultation with the Kashag and the Assembly then.

Dalai Lama was called upon to assume the full political power of Tibet only on 17th November 1950 when he was barely 15 years old (16, according to Tibetan tradition). In fact when the Kashag (The Cabinet) approached Dalai Lama with a request to assume the responsibility of the leader of Tibet, Dalai Lama, in his Autobiography 'My Land and My People' wrote, "This filled me with anxiety. I was only sixteen. I was far from having finished my religious education. I knew nothing about the world and had no experience of politics, and yet I was old enough to know how ignorant I was and how much I had still to learn. I protested at first that I was too young, for eighteen was the accepted age for a Dalai Lama to take over active control from his Regent."

Later, however during an interview with Mr. Claude Arpi in March 1997, when Mr. Arpi asked Dalai Lama if the Kashag had committed a great mistake by refusing to ratify the Simla Convention and bargaining instead for the return of some 'lost territories'? Dalai Lama did acknowledge the blunder and said, "Yes, it is my strong feeling. At that time the Tibetan Government should have sent a strong delegation to celebrate the Independence of India. Of course that was a big mistake". He further clarified that although in 1914 at the Simla Convention the border was already demarcated and the [Convention] was signed, the Tibetan officials did not know the Government's decision.

However, Tibetan Government was among the many nations that had sent the message of Congratulations to the new Independent India.

Mr. Huge E Richardson, British India's last and Independent India's first Representative in Lhasa, who was witness to the unfolding events, in his book, "Tibet and its History" referred to this unpleasant Tibetan request explaining, "The request to India was that counterpart of the message conveyed to the Chinese Government by the goodwill mission in 1946, in which they (Tibetan Government) asked in equally wide terms, for the return of all Tibetan territories still in Chinese hands".

Mr. Richardson however, revealed that Tibetan Government did contemplate signing a new treaty with the Indian Government but "they were dissuaded by the consideration that negotiations of that sort would have given an opportunity for renewed Chinese pressure on Tibet at a time when the Indian Government was not yet securely in the saddle."

When we realize the backdrop of unfolding political complexities of the time, we would comprehend Lhasa's lackluster reaction to the Indian overture. Tibet in the 1940s was passing through one of the most volatile phase of its history when its Government is bogged down in various political quagmire; Regent Reting conspiracy, Panchen Lama imbroglio, The neutrality during the World War-II pitting Tibet against British, American and China on the issue of allowing passage for the weapons through Tibet, indifference to the Tibetan Goodwill Mission by Britain and United States, Chiang Kaishek's Nationalist Party's political hijacking and maneuvering of the Tibetan Goodwill Mission in Nanjing Assembly, Ma Pufang's threat of further invasion of Tibet from the east and Chinese Communist Party's alarming rise in the east etc.

Eventually, after few months of initial dithering, formal agreement was signed and direct diplomatic and trade relations established between Tibet and India in accordance with its extraterritorial rights derived from the Simla Convention; maintaining an Indian Mission in Lhasa, Trade Agencies, maintaining Military escorts, Rest Houses, Postal, Telegraph, Public telephone services and Hospitals etc.

The signing of the fresh agreement and establishing a diplomatic relation between the two nations however did not clear the initial trepidations. Mr. Richardson stated that the Tibetans continued to be anxious over Indian Government's attitude towards the status of Tibet. He elaborated, "Although the new Government of India continued, as its predecessor has done, to deal with Tibet on the basis of its de facto independence, by supplying arms and ammunition and maintaining direct diplomatic contacts, the nature of their relations seemed to be misinterpreted in certain pronouncements by Nehru. On more than one occasion he referred publicly to a general recognition of Chinese suzerainty over Tibet. He qualified that statement by describing the suzerainty as 'vague and shadowy'. Nevertheless, the Tibetans were concerned at his disregard for the obligation, which he had inherited under Simla declaration of 1914, not to accord recognition of Chinese suzerainty over Tibet, of any sort whatsoever." "By gratuitously stressing Chinese suzerainty the Indian Prime Minister appeared to serve notice on the Communists that in their designs on Tibet they need not fear any serious opposition from India", he added.

Meanwhile China's incessant deception and subsequent 1962 attack shocked and shattered Prime Minister Nehru so much that in a broadcast to the nation on October 20, 1962, he confessed, "Perhaps there are not many instances in history where one country (referring to India) has gone out of her way to be friendly and cooperative with the government and people of another country (referring to China) and to plead their cause in the councils of the world, and then that country returns evil for good."

And the Indian Parliament on November 14 1962 adopted a unanimously Resolution affirming, "The firm resolve of the Indian people to drive out the aggressor from the sacred soil of India, however long and hard the struggle may be"

Despite all the brouhaha over the Chinese betrayal and vengeance and all, the subsequent Indian Governments, even after Nehru's tragic death, continue to follow Nehru's India policy on Tibet which he announced in the Indian Parliament on 27th April 1959. Mr. Nehru affirmed, "I stated some time ago that our broad policy (on Tibet) was governed by three factors: (1) the preservation of the security and integrity of India; (2) our desire to maintain friendly relations with China; and (3) our deep sympathy for the people of Tibet. We shall continue to follow that policy because we think that is a correct policy not only for the present but even more so for the future." The policies also entail that the Tibetans in India will be restricted from carrying out anti-Chinese political activities. And that Tibet will be regarded as an internal matter of China.

Over the years, another strange justification over India's restrained political approach to the Tibetan issue is that "if India does anything more to help Tibet, it will upset the Chinese and the fate of Tibet would only worsen". Like many other weird arguments, this too would be repeated ritualistically for many decades to the great dismay of the Tibetans.

Consequently, the challenge for the Government of India's policy on Tibet and the Tibetans is to maintain a balance between the three core principles of 1) the preservation of the security and integrity of India; (2) to maintain friendly relations with China; and (3) to accord deep sympathy for the people of Tibet.

But many believe that the balance has been severely tilted in favour of China to the detriment of India and Tibet's national interest. Compromising principles for the sake of cordial bilateral relation and economic gains is one thing, but compromising national security and long-term interest is anything but Realpolitik.

Indeed, India's humanitarian support to the exiled Tibetans is overwhelming and unparallel in the history of a national struggle and the Tibetan people are highly indebted for the same. But the Tibetan people will be most contented the day India intensify its political support to the Tibetans in tune with its own national and strategic interest. After all, Tibetan struggle is a political and a national struggle and not merely Humanitarian.

Furthermore, Tibet is a lever that India can utilize to further its national interest vis-à-vis China. And on every occasion, Tibetans in India have never failed to demonstrate their utmost loyalty, dedication and love for this country. However it would be morally wrong and practically inconceivable if it employs the leverage against the Tibetan people and their Interest. Thus far, such strategy had always boomeranged in the diplomatic sphere.

While it is indisputable that a policy of a country is driven more by a national interest and pragmatism than principles and emotions, it is imperative that those policies be primarily based on reality and facts rather than false expectations and gimmicks.

And many strategists believe that it is in the national interest; territorial integrity, security, strategic, democratic and in the long term interest of India to adopt more assertive and pragmatic policy vis-à-vis China and effectively neutralize its half a century-long containment policies and campaign.

Thus far, Panchsheel and other appeasements have seriously failed to build a genuine friendly neighborhood with China. Therefore, stakes are definitely high and the task daunting but it's inevitable that the coming Government should revamp its policy on China as a key priority.

BETWEEN TIBET AND CHINA, INDIA PLAYS DELICATE BALANCING ACT

For more than 50 years, India has been a sometimes gracious, sometimes uneasy and occasionally hostile host to tens of thousands of Tibetans who fled their homeland and settled here after claiming religious and political persecution by the Chinese government.

Last week, India played all three roles, as President Hu Jintao of China met with Prime Minister Manmohan Singh and other emerging market leaders in New Delhi. After a Tibetan set himself on fire during a planned protest in central Delhi, the Indian authorities put Tibetan communities under a virtual lock down and jailed hundreds of Tibetans.

For India, which has been sometimes criticized for an ostrich-like "non-alignment" approach to foreign policy, the situation represents an unusually sophisticated balancing act. India has allowed generations of Tibetans to build a miniature Tibet within the country, and officials express sympathy for the Tibetan cause. But maintaining a growing economic relationship with China is vital, analysts and political experts say.

"We need to handle the matter delicately," said Muchukund Dubey, former foreign secretary of India and president of the Council for Social Development, a New Delhi-based research group. That delicacy involves abiding by very specific rules about what Tibetans can do in India, despite India's democratic roots. Tibetans "have every right to organize themselves, but they cannot indulge in political activities," Mr. Dubey said. The Tibetan man's self-immolation was certainly political, he said, as well as "embarrassing" to the government of India.

Associated Press 23-year-old Dalai Lama, bespectacled, astride a white horse crosses the Zsagola pass in Southern Tibet along with his escape party on March 21, 1959, after fleeing Lhasa. Pursued by Red Chinese troops, the Dalai Lama was on the fourth day of his flight to India, in this file photo.

Political experts in India have been openly critical of China's handling of Tibetans' quest for autonomous rule and their desire to preserve an independent culture, while pragmatic about the need to forge good relations with China.

"There is definitely a need for the Chinese government to recognize the policy failure" in Tibet, said Manoranjan Mohanty, chairman of the Institute of Chinese studies, an academic group in New Delhi. The Indian government often raises this issue during private talks with Chinese officials, he said. But India is "also concerned about $70 billion worth of trade we have with China," Mr. Mohanty said. "The target is to increase it to $100 billion by 2015."

Since the Dalai Lama first fled China in 1959 to India after a failed Tibetan uprising, India has maintained a nuanced position. "The Indian government, while sympathetic to the case of the Dalai Lama, contends that Tibet legally is a part of China," an article from The New York Times in September 1959 reported. Flash forward to 2006, the last time Indian and Chinese heads of state made a joint statement about Tibet: "The Indian side reiterates that it has recognized the Tibet Autonomous Region as part of the territory of the People's Republic of China, and that it does not allow Tibetans to engage in anti-China political activities in India. The Chinese side expresses its appreciation for the Indian position," it said.

India's uneasy hospitality does not come without some advantages for India, political analysts say. India has informally agreed with China not to allow its officials to meet with the Dalai Lama or share a stage with him, but that is sometimes broached. "Whenever there is a problem between India and China, India plays the 'Tibet card,'" said Srikanth Kondapalli, the chairman for

East Asian Studies at Jawaharlal Nehru University. "When China indulges in anti-Indian activities, the Indian foreign secretaries meet the Dalai Lama," he said.

In July of 2010, India's foreign secretary, Nirupma Rao, met with the Dalai Lama at his residence. The substance of their discussions was not disclosed, but they happened a week after India's national security adviser, Shiv Shankar Menon, met officials in Beijing to talk about, among other things,

China's plans to build nuclear reactors for Pakistan.

West Bengal's governor breached the agreement not to share a stage with the religious leader last December, attending an event with the Dalai Lama, a move that was interpreted by political analysts as a push back against increasing pressure from China to restrict the Dalai Lama's activities in India.

About 100,000 Tibetans now live in India, mostly in close-knit communities in Delhi, Dharamsala and other areas in northern India. Many consider themselves to be temporary refugees, biding their time before an autonomous homeland is returned them, even if they have lived in India for many years.

They are granted the right to work, health care and education in India, but not to vote. They are promised protection from repatriation and can own land in specific areas, a privilege not extended to other foreigners. The Central Tibetan Administration, based in Dharamsala, is considered by Tibetans to be a fully fledged government. It holds elections and a finance and health department, a planning commission and an attorney general. Still, the Indian government considers it a "non-governmental organization," or NGO, the same designation given to charities.

Some of the young Tibetan students arrested during last week's protests said they had left Tibet as children, without their parents, and spent most of their lives in India. While Tibetan student groups sometimes recruit their Indian counterparts, discussion of Tibet's struggle is somewhat limited –the country's largest English-language newspapers carried pictures of the Tibetan who had set himself alight on Monday in Delhi, but thoughtful political analysis of the situation was sparse. From a purely populist point of view, on Wednesday, when the man who self-immolated died in Delhi, "Rihanna & Ashton Kutcher" was trending on Twitter in India, but "FreeTibet" was not.

Last week's crackdown on Tibetan protests is hardly unusual. In March 2008, about 100 Tibetans, mostly monks and nuns, attempted a march from Dharamsala to the Tibetan capital of Lhasa to protest China's hosting of the Olympics. The Indian authorities quickly quashed the march, issuing a restraining order against the marchers and then arrested them.

Chinese officials thanked India for cracking down on Tibetan protesters last week. The "Chinese side appreciates effective and concrete measures taken by the government of India," in curbing protests, Luo Zhaohui, director general of the Chinese Department of Asian Affairs, said.

While Indian officials and policy experts acknowledge the situation is far from perfect, India is still playing the leading global role in aiding the Tibetans, they say. "We open our hospitals and our schools to them," Mr. Dubey, the former foreign secretary said. "Is any other nation doing any better for the Tibetans?"

7

Tibet and China: History of a Complex Relationship

INTRODUCTION

For at least 1500 years, the nation of Tibet has had a complex relationship with its large and powerful neighbor to the east, China. The political history of Tibet and China reveals that the relationship has not always been as one-sided as it now appears.

Indeed, as with China's relations with the Mongols and the Japanese, the balance of power between China and Tibet has shifted back and forth over the centuries.

Early Interactions

The first known interaction between the two states came in 640 A.D., when the Tibetan King Songtsan Gampo married the Princess Wencheng, a niece of the Tang Emperor Taizong. He also married a Nepalese princess.

Both wives were Buddhists, and this may have been the origin of Tibetan Buddhism. The faith grew when an influx of Central Asian Buddhists flooded Tibet early in the eighth century, fleeing from advancing armies of Arab and Kazakh Muslims.

During his reign, Songtsan Gampo added parts of the Yarlung River Valley to the Kingdom of Tibet; his descendants would also conquer the vast region that is now the Chinese provinces of Qinghai, Gansu, and Xinjiang between 663 and 692. Control of these border regions would change hands back and forth for centuries to come.

In 692, the Chinese retook their western lands from the Tibetans after defeating them at Kashgar. The Tibetan king then allied himself with the enemies of China, the Arabs and eastern Turks.

Chinese power waxed strong in the early decades of the eighth century. Imperial forces under General Gao Xianzhi conquered much of Central Asia, until their defeat by the Arabs and Karluks at theBattle of Talas River in 751. China's power quickly waned, and Tibet resumed control of much of Central Asia.

The ascendant Tibetans pressed their advantage, conquering much of northern India and even seizing the Tang Chinese capital city of Chang'an (now Xian) in 763.

Tibet and China signed a peace treaty in 821 or 822, which delineated the border between the two empires. The Tibetan Empire would concentrate on its Central Asian holdings for the next several decades, before splitting into several small, fractious kingdoms.

TIBET AND THE MONGOLS

Canny politicians, the Tibetans befriended Genghis Khan just as the Mongol leader was conquering the known world in the early 13th century. As a result, though the Tibetans paid tribute to the Mongols after the Hordes had conquered China, they were allowed much greater autonomy than the other Mongol-conquered lands.

Over time, Tibet came to be considered one of the thirteen provinces of the Mongolian-ruled nation ofYuan China. During this period, the Tibetans gained a high degree of influence over the Mongols at court.

The great Tibetan spiritual leader, Sakya Pandita, became the Mongol's representative to Tibet. Sakya's nephew, Chana Dorje, married one of the Mongol Emperor Kublai Khan's daughters. The Tibetans transmitted their Buddhist faith to the eastern Mongols; Kublai Khan himself studied Tibetan beliefs with the great teacher Drogon Chogyal Phagpa.

Independent Tibet

When the Mongols' Yuan Empire fell in 1368 to the ethnic-Han Chinese Ming, Tibet reasserted its independence and refused to pay tribute to the new Emperor. In 1474, the abbot of an important Tibetan Buddhist monastery, Gendun Drup, passed away. A child who born two years later was found to be a reincarnation of the abbot, and was raised to be the next leader of that sect, Gendun Gyatso.

After their lifetimes, the two men were called the First and Second Dalai Lamas.

Their sect, the Gelug or "Yellow Hats," became the dominant form of Tibetan Buddhism. The Third Dalai Lama, Sonam Gyatso (1543-1588), was the first to be so named during his life. He was responsible for converting the Mongols to Gelug Tibetan Buddhism, and it was the Mongol ruler Altan Khan who probably gave the title "Dalai Lama" to Sonam Gyatso.

While the newly-named Dalai Lama consolidated the power of his spiritual position, though, the Gtsang-pa Dynasty assumed the royal throne of Tibet in 1562. The Kings would rule the secular side of Tibetan life for the next 80 years.

The Fourth Dalai Lama, Yonten Gyatso (1589-1616), was a Mongolian prince and the grandson of Altan Khan.

During the 1630s, China was embroiled in power struggles between the Mongols, Han Chinese of the fading Ming Dynasty, and the Manchu people of north-eastern China (Manchuria). The Manchus would eventually defeat the Han in 1644, and establish China's final imperial dynasty, the Qing (1644-1912). Tibet got drawn into this turmoil when the Mongol warlord Ligdan Khan, a Kagyu Tibetan Buddhist, decided to invade Tibet and destroy the Yellow Hats in 1634. Ligdan Khan died on the way, but his follower Tsogt Taij took up the cause.

The great general Gushi Khan, of the Oirad Mongols, fought against Tsogt Taij and defeated him in 1637. The Khan killed the Gtsang-pa Prince of Tsang, as well. With support from Gushi Khan, the Fifth Dalai Lama, Lobsang Gyatso, was able to seize both spiritual and temporal power over all of Tibet in 1642.

THE DALAI LAMA RISES TO POWER

The Potala Palace in Lhasa was constructed as a symbol of this new synthesis of power. The Dalai Lama made a state visit to the Qing Dynasty's second Emperor, Shunzhi, in 1653. The two leaders greeted one another as equals; the Dalai Lama did not kowtow. Each man bestowed honors and titles upon the other, and the Dalai Lama was recognized as the spiritual authority of the Qing Empire.

According to Tibet, the "priest/patron" relationship established at this time between the Dalai Lama and Qing China continued throughout the Qing Era, but it had no bearing on Tibet's status as an independent nation. China, naturally, disagrees.

Lobsang Gyatso died in 1682, but his Prime Minister concealed the Dalai Lama's passing until 1696 so that the Potala Palace could be finished and the power of the Dalai Lama's office consolidated.

The Maverick Dalai Lama

In 1697, fifteen years after the death of Lobsang Gyatso, the Sixth Dalai Lama was finally enthroned. Tsangyang Gyatso (1683-1706) was a maverick who rejected the monastic life, growing his hair long, drinking wine, and enjoying female company. He also wrote great poetry, some of which is still recited today in Tibet.

The Dalai Lama's unconventional lifestyle prompted Lobsang Khan of the Khoshud Mongols to depose him in 1705. Lobsang Khan seized control of Tibet, named himself King, sent Tsangyang Gyatso to Beijing (he "mysteriously" died on the way), and installed a pretender Dalai Lama.

The Dzungar Mongol Invasion

King Lobsang would rule for 12 years, until the Dzungar Mongols invaded and took power. They killed the pretender to the Dalai Lama's throne, to the joy of the Tibetan people, but then began to loot monasteries around Lhasa.

This vandalism brought a quick response from the Qing Emperor Kangxi, who sent troops to Tibet. The Dzungars destroyed the Imperial Chinese battalion near Lhasa in 1718.

In 1720, the angry Kangxi sent another, larger force to Tibet, which crushed the Dzungars. The Qing army also brought the proper Seventh Dalai Lama, Kelzang Gyatso (1708-1757) to Lhasa.

The Border Between China and Tibet

China took advantage of this period of instability in Tibet to seize the regions of Amdo and Kham, making them into the Chinese province of Qinghai in 1724. Three years later, the Chinese and Tibetans signed a treaty that laid out the boundary line between the two nations. It would remain in force until 1910.

Qing China had its hands full trying to control Tibet. The Emperor sent a commissioner to Lhasa, but he was killed in 1750. The Imperial Army then defeated the rebels, but the Emperor recognized that he would have to rule through the Dalai Lama rather than directly. Day-to-day decisions would be made on the local level.

Era of Turmoil Begins

In 1788, the Regent of Nepal sent Gurkha forces to invade Tibet. The Qing Emperor responded in strength, and the Nepalese retreated. The Gurkhas returned three years later, plundering and destroying some famous Tibetan monasteries. The Chinese sent a force of 17,000 which, along with Tibetan troops, drove the Gurkhas out of Tibet and south to within 20 miles of Kathmandu.

Despite this sort of assistance from the Chinese Empire, the people of Tibet chafed under increasingly meddlesome Qing rule. Between 1804, when the Eighth Dalai Lama died, and 1895, when the Thirteenth Dalai Lama assumed the throne, none of the incumbent incarnations of the Dalai Lama lived to see their nineteenth birthdays. If the Chinese found a certain incarnation too hard to control, they would poison him. If the Tibetans thought an incarnation was controlled by the Chinese, then they would poison him themselves.

TIBET AND THE GREAT GAME

Throughout this period, Russia and Britain were engaged in the "Great Game," a struggle for influence and control in Central Asia.

Russia pushed south of its borders, seeking access to warm-water sea ports and a buffer zone between Russia proper and the advancing British. The British pushed northward from India, trying to expand their empire and protect the Raj, the "Crown Jewel of the British Empire," from the expansionist Russians.

Tibet was an important playing piece in this game. Qing Chinese power waned throughout the eighteenth century, as evidenced by its defeat in the Opium Wars with Britain (1839-1842 and 1856-1860), as well as the Taiping Rebellion (1850-1864) and the Boxer Rebellion (1899-1901).

The actual relationship between China and Tibet had been unclear since the early days of the Qing Dynasty, and China's losses at home made the status of Tibet even more uncertain. The ambiguity of control over Tibet lead to problems. In 1893, the British in India concluded a trade and border treaty with Beijing concerning the boundary between Sikkim and Tibet.

However, the Tibetans flatly rejected the treaty terms. The British invaded Tibet in 1903 with 10,000 men, and took Lhasa the following year. Thereupon, they concluded another treaty with the Tibetans, as well as Chinese, Nepalese and Bhutanese representatives, which gave the British themselves some control over Tibet's affairs.

Thubten Gyatso's Balancing Act

The 13th Dalai Lama, Thubten Gyatso, fled the country in 1904 at the urging of his Russian disciple, Agvan Dorzhiev. He went first to Mongolia, then made his way to Beijing. The Chinese declared that the Dalai Lama had been deposed as soon as he left Tibet, and claimed full sovereignty over not only Tibet but also Nepal and Bhutan. The Dalai Lama went to Beijing to discuss the situation with the Emperor Guangxu, but he flatly refused to kowtow to the Emperor.

Thubten Gyatso stayed in the Chinese capital from 1906 to 1908. He returned to Lhasa in 1909, disappointed by Chinese policies towards Tibet. China sent a force of 6,000 troops into Tibet, and the Dalai Lama fled to Darjeeling, India later that same year. The Chinese Revolution swept away the Qing Dynasty in

1911, and the Tibetans promptly expelled all Chinese troops from Lhasa. The Dalai Lama returned home to Tibet in 1912.

TIBETAN INDEPENDENCE

China's new revolutionary government issued a formal apology to the Dalai Lama for the Qing Dynasty's insults, and offered to reinstate him. Thubten Gyatso refused, stating that he had no interest in the Chinese offer. He then issued a proclamation that was distributed across Tibet, rejecting Chinese control and stating that "We are a small, religious, and independent nation."

The Dalai Lama took control of Tibet's internal and external governance in 1913, negotiating directly with foreign powers, and reforming Tibet's judicial, penal, and educational systems.

The Simla Convention (1914)

Representatives of Great Britain, China, and Tibet met in 1914 to negotiate a treaty marking out the boundary lines between India and its northern neighbors. The Simla Convention granted China secular control over "Inner Tibet," (also known as Qinghai Province) while recognizing the autonomy of "Outer Tibet" under the Dalai Lama's rule. Both China and Britain promised to "respect the territorial integrity of [Tibet], and abstain from interference in the administration of Outer Tibet."

China walked out of the conference without signing the treaty after Britain laid claim to the Tawang area of southern Tibet, which is now part of the Indian state of Arunachal Pradesh. Tibet and Britain both signed the treaty. As a result, China has never agreed to India's rights in northern Arunachal Pradesh (Tawang), and the two nations went to war over the area in 1962. The boundary dispute still has not been resolved.

China also claims sovereignty over all of Tibet, while the Tibetan government-in-exile points to the Chinese failure to sign the Simla Convention as proof that both Inner and Outer Tibet legally remain under the Dalai Lama's jurisdiction.

The Issue Rests

Soon, China would be too distracted to concern itself with the issue of Tibet. Japan had invaded Manchuria in 1910, and would advance south and east across large swaths of Chinese territory through 1945.

The new government of the Republic of China would hold nominal power over the majority of Chinese territory for only four years before war broke out between numerous armed factions. Indeed, the span of Chinese history from 1916 to 1938 came to be called the "Warlord Era," as the different military factions sought to fill the power vacuum left by the collapse of the Qing Dynasty.

China would see near-continuous civil war up to the Communist victory in 1949, and this era of conflict was exacerbated by the Japanese Occupation and World War II. Under such circumstances, the Chinese showed little interest in Tibet. The 13th Dalai Lama ruled independent Tibet in peace until his death in 1933.

The 14th Dalai Lama

Following Thubten Gyatso's death, the new reincarnation of the Dalai Lama was born in Amdo in 1935. Tenzin Gyatso, the current Dalai Lama, was taken to Lhasa in 1937 to begin training for his duties as the leader of Tibet. He would remain there until 1959, when the Chinese forced him into exile in India.

People's Republic of China Invades Tibet

In 1950, the People's Liberation Army (PLA) of the newly-formed People's Republic of China invaded Tibet. With stability reestablished in Beijing for the first time in decades, Mao Zedong sought to assert China's right to rule over Tibet as well. The PLA inflicted a swift and total defeat on Tibet's small army, and China drafted the "Seventeen Point Agreement" incorporating Tibet as an autonomous region of the People's Republic of China. Representatives of the Dalai Lama's government signed the agreement under protest, and the Tibetans repudiated the agreement nine years later.

Collectivization and Revolt

The Mao government of the PRC immediately initiated land redistribution in Tibet. Landholdings of the monasteries and nobility were seized for redistribution to the peasants. The communist forces hoped to destroy the power base of the wealthy and of Buddhism within Tibetan society. In reaction, a uprising led by the monks broke out in June of 1956, and continued through 1959. The poorly-armed Tibetans used guerrilla war tactics in an attempt to drive out the Chinese.

The PLA responded by razing entire villages and monasteries to the ground. The Chinese even threatened to blow up the Potala Palace and kill the Dalai Lama, but this threat was not carried out. Three years of bitter fighting left 86,000 Tibetans dead, according to the Dalai Lama's government in exile.

FLIGHT OF THE DALAI LAMA

On March 1, 1959, the Dalai Lama received an odd invitation to attend a theater performance at PLA headquarters near Lhasa.

The Dalai Lama demurred, and the performance date was postponed until March 10. On March 9, PLA officers notified the Dalai Lama's bodyguards that they would not accompany the Tibetan leader to the performance, nor were they to notify the Tibetan people that he was leaving the palace. (Ordinarily, the people of Lhasa would line the streets to greet the Dalai Lama each time he ventured out.) The guards immediately publicized this rather ham-handed attempted abduction, and the following day an estimated crowd of 300,000 Tibetans surrounded Potala Palace to protect their leader.

The PLA moved artillery into range of major monasteries and the Dalai Lama's summer palace, Norbulingka. Both sides began to dig in, although the Tibetan army was much smaller than its adversary, and poorly armed. Tibetan troops were able to secure a route for the Dalai Lama to escape into India on March 17. Actual fighting began on March 19, and lasted only two days before the Tibetan troops were defeated.

AFTERMATH OF THE 1959 TIBETAN UPRISING

Much of Lhasa lay in ruins on March 20, 1959. An estimated 800 artillery shells had pummeled Norbulingka, and Lhasa's three largest monasteries were essentially leveled. The Chinese rounded up thousands of monks, executing many of them. Monasteries and temples all over Lhasa were ransacked.

The remaining members of the Dalai Lama's bodyguard were publicly executed by firing squad. By the time of the 1964 census, 300,000 Tibetans had gone "missing" in the previous five years, either secretly imprisoned, killed, or in exile.

In the days after the 1959 Uprising, the Chinese government revoked most aspects of Tibet's autonomy, and initiated resettlement and land distribution across the country. The Dalai Lama has remained in exile ever since. China's central government, in a bid to dilute the Tibetan population and provide jobs for Han Chinese, initiated a "Western China Development Program" in 1978.

As many as 300,000 Han now live in Tibet, 2/3 of them in the capital city. The Tibetan population of Lhasa, in contrast, is only 100,000. Ethnic Chinese hold the vast majority of government posts.

Return of the Panchen Lama

Beijing allowed the Panchen Lama, Tibetan Buddhism's second-in-command, to return to Tibet in 1989. He immediately gave a speech before a crowd of 30,000 of the faithful, decrying the harm being done to Tibet under the PRC. He died five days later at the age of 50, allegedly of a massive heart attack.

Deaths at Drapchi Prison, 1998

On May 1, 1998, the Chinese officials at Drapchi Prison in Tibet ordered hundreds of prisoners, both criminals and political detainees, to participate in a Chinese flag-raising ceremony. Some of the prisoners began to shout anti-Chinese and pro-Dalai Lama slogans, and prison guards fired shots into the air before returning all the prisoners to their cells.

The prisoners were then severely beaten with belt buckles, rifle butts, and plastic batons, and some were put into solitary confinement for months at a time, according to one young nun who was released from the prison a year later. Three days later, the prison administration decided to hold the flag-raising ceremony again.

Once more, some of the prisoners began to shout slogans. Prison official reacted with even more brutality, and five nuns, three monks, and one male criminal were killed by the guards. One man was shot; the rest were beaten to death.

2008 Uprising

On March 10, 2008, Tibetans marked the 49th anniversary of the 1959 uprising by peacefully protesting for the release of imprisoned monks and nuns. Chinese police then broke up the protest with tear gas and gunfire. The protest resumed for several more days, finally turning into a riot. Tibetan anger was fueled by reports that imprisoned monks and nuns were being mistreated or killed in prison as a reaction to the street demonstrations.

Furious Tibetans ransacked and burned the shops of ethnic Chinese immigrants in Lhasa and other cities. The official Chinese media states that 18 people were killed by the rioters. China immediately cut off access to Tibet for foreign media and tourists.

The unrest spread to neighbouring Qinghai (Inner Tibet), Gansu, and Sichuan Provinces. The Chinese government cracked down hard, mobilizing as many as 5,000 troops. Reports indicate that the military killed between 80 and 140 people, and arrested more than 2,300 Tibetans. The unrest came at a sensitive time for China, which was gearing up for the 2008 Summer Olympics in Beijing.

The situation in Tibet caused increased international scrutiny of Beijing's entire human rights record, leading some foreign leaders to boycott the Olympic Opening Ceremonies. Olympic torch-bearers around the world were met by thousands of human rights protestors.

Conclusion

Tibet and China have had a long relationship, fraught with difficulty and change. At times, the two nations have worked closely together. At other times, they have been at war.

Today, the nation of Tibet does not exist; not one foreign government officially recognizes the Tibetan government-in-exile. The past teaches us, however, that the geopolitical situation is nothing if not fluid. It is impossible to predict where Tibet and China will stand, relative to one another, one hundred years from now.

HOW HAVE IMPERIALISTS INSTIGATED TIBETAN INDEPENDENCE?

There was no such word as "independence" in the Tibetan vocabulary at the beginning of the 20th century. After the British imperialists started the Opium War of aggression against China in 1840, China was reduced from an independent sovereign country to a semi-colonial country. Imperialist forces took advantage of a weak Qing Dynasty and began plotting to carve up China, Tibet included.

In order to bring Tibet into its sphere of influence, British aggressors invaded China's Tibet twice in 1888 and 1903. The Tibetan army and civilians rose to resist but were defeated. In the second aggressive war against Tibet, the British army occupied Lhasa, and the 13th Dalai Lama was forced to flee from the city. The invaders compelled the Tibetan local government officials to sign the Lhasa Convention. But because the Ministry of External Affairs of the Qing government believed the Lhasa Convention would do damage to national sovereignty, the high commissioner stationed in Tibet by the Qing government refused to sign it, leaving it ineffectual.

After their failure to assume full control of Tibet through direct military incursion, the imperialists changed their tack and began plotting to separate Tibet from China. On August 31, 1907, Britain and Russia signed the Convention Between Great Britain and Russia, which changed China's sovereignty over Tibet into "suzerainty." This marked the first time Chin's sovereignty over Tibet was altered into "suzerainty" in international documents.

The year following the 1911 Revolution, Britain took advantage of the political chaos in China after the collapse of the Qing Dynasty and the new birth of the Republic of China, and put before the Chinese Ministry of Foreign Affairs a five-point demand, indicating the denial of China's sovereignty over Tibet. When the Chinese government rejected the British demand, the British blocked all the roads leading from India to Tibet. In 1913 the British government inveigled the Tibetan authorities into declaring independence and proposed that "Britain be the weaponry supplier after total independence of Tibet;" "Tibet accept British envoys' supervision of Tibetan financial and military affairs in return for Britain's support of Tibetan independence;" "Britain be responsible for resisting the army of the Republic of China when it reaches Tibet;" "Tibet adopt an open policy and allow freedom of movement of the British." However, Britain's schemes failed.

In 1913, taking advantage of the fact that Yuan Shikai, who had usurped the presidency of the Republic of China, was eager to get foreign diplomatic recognition and international loans, the British government forced the Beijing government to participate in a tripartite conference of China, Britain and Tibet, namely the Simla Conference held at the behest of the British government. Before the conference, Charles Bell political officer sent to Sikkim by the British-Indian government, privately met with Lon-chen Shatra, the representative of the Tibetan local government to the conference. Bell trumpeted to Lon-chen Shatra that "suzerainty" implied "independence." In his book Tibet: *Past and Present*, Bell wrote, "When I met Lon-chen Shatra in Gyantse, I advised him to bring down all the documents which he could collect bearing on the Tibetan relationship to China in the past, and on the former's claims to the various provinces and districts which had from time to time been occupied by China." Stirred up by the British, the Tibetan representative raised the slogan of "Tibetan independence" for the first time. He also claimed "Tibetan territory includes Qinghai, Litang, Batang and Dajianlu." When these demands were rejected by the representative of the Chinese government, the British delegate introduced the pre-arranged "compromise" scheme, which divided China's Tibetan-inhabited areas into "inner Tibet" and "outer Tibet." "Inner Tibet," including Tibetan-inhabited areas in Qinghai, Gansu, Sichuan and Yunnan provinces, would be under the jurisdiction of the Chinese government. With regard to "outer Tibet," including Tibet and west Xikang, the Chinese government was requested to "recognize the autonomy of outer Tibet" and "refrain from interfering in its internal affairs;" "however, China may still send its high commissioner to Lhasa and maintain an escort army of no more than 300 soldiers." The essence of this "compromise" scheme was to change China's sovereignty over Tibet into "suzerainty," and separate Tibet from the authority of the Chinese government under the pretext of "autonomy." Naturally these unreasonable demands were strongly opposed by the Chinese people. On July 3, 1914, the Chinese government representative Chen Yifan upon instruction refused to sign the Simla Convention. In his statement, Chen said, "Government of China refuses to recognize any agreement which His Majesty's Government and Tibet might conclude independently either now or in the future." The Chinese government also sent a note to the British government, reiterating its position. Therefore, the conference broke down.

In the summer of 1942, the Tibetan local government, with the support of the British representative, suddenly announced the establishment of a "foreign affairs bureau," and openly carried out "Tibetan independence" activities. These actions, as soon as they were made public, were condemned unanimously by the Chinese people. The national government also issued a stern warning. Under this pressure, the Tibetan local government had no choice but to withdraw its decision and reported the change to the national government. At the "Asian Relations Conference" held in New Delhi in March 1947, the British imperialists plotted behind the curtains to invite Tibetan representatives and even identified Tibet as an independent country on the map of Asia in the conference hall and in the array of national flags. The organizers were forced to rectify this after the Chinese delegation made serious protests.

Around the end of 1949, the American Lowell Thomas roamed Tibet in the guise of a "radio commentator" to explore the "possibility of aid that Washington could give Tibet." He wrote in a US newspaper: " The United States is ready to recognize Tibet as an independent and free country." In the first half of 1950, a load of American weaponry was shipped into Tibet through Calcutta in order to help resist the PLA's entry into Tibet. On November 1 of the same year, US Secretary of State Dean Acheson openly slandered China's liberation of its own territory of Tibet as "invasion." In the same month the United States prodded some other countries to propose a motion at the United Nations for intervention in China's Tibet. The scheme was unsuccessful in face of the stern stand of the Chinese government and the opposition of some countries.

Historical facts over more than a century clearly demonstrate that so-called "Tibetan independence" was, in reality, cooked up by old and new imperialists out of their crave to wrest Tibet from China. The 14th Dalai Lama in his early years pointed out, "It was the imperialists who, taking advantage of the Tibetan people's antipathy to the Qing Dynasty and the reactionary Kuomintang government, attempted by enticement, deception and instigation to get the Tibetan people to separate from the motherland and come under their oppression and enslavement."

HOW DOES THE 1959 ARMED REBELLION OCCUR?

Before peaceful liberation in 1951, Tibet was under a feudal serfdom characterized by the dictatorship of upper-class monks and nobles. The broad masses of serfs in Tibet eagerly wanted to break the shackles of serfdom. After the peaceful liberation, many enlightened people of the upper and middle classes also realized that if the old system was not reformed, the Tibetan people would never attain prosperity. In light of Tibetan history and the region's special situation, the central people's government adopted a very circumspect attitude toward the reform of the social system in Tibet. The 17-Article Agreement stipulated that the central government would not use coercion to implement such reform and that it was to be carried out by the Tibetan local government on its own. During his visit to India in January 1957, Premier Zhou Enlai of the State Council handed a letter from Chairman Mao Zedong to the Dalai Lama and Bainqen Lama and the accompanying Tibetan local government senior officials. The letter informed them of the decision of the central authorities that reform would not be conducted during the Second Five-Year Plan period (1958-62); whether reform should be conducted after six years would still be decided by Tibet according to its own situation and conditions then.

However, some members of the Tibetan ruling class were hostile to reform and wanted to preserve the serfdom forever so as to maintain their own vested interests. They deliberately violated and sabotaged the 17-Article Agreement and intensified their efforts to split the motherland. Between March and April 1952, Sicab Lukangwa and Losang Zhaxi of the Tibetan local government gave secret support to the illicit organization "the people's conference" to oppose the 17-Article Agreement and create disturbance in Lhasa, demanding that the PLA "pull out of Tibet." In 1955, Galoin Surkang Wangqen Geleg of the Tibetan local government and others secretly plotted an armed rebellion in the Tibetan-inhabited area of Xikang Province. Rebellion broke out in that area in 1956 and the rebels besieged the local government institutions and massacred hundreds of government staff as well as common people. In May 1957, with the support of Galoins Neuxar Tubdain Tarba and Xainga Gyurme Doje, a rebel organization named "four rivers and six ranges" and later the rebel armed forces named "religion guards" were founded. They raised the slogan of "Tibetan Independence" and "opposition to reform" and further intensified their rebellious activities. The armed rebels harassed Qamdo, Dengqen, Heihe and Shannan. They killed cadres, disrupted communication lines, and attacked institutions and army troops stationed there by the central authorities. They looted, cruelly persecuted people and raped women. A merchant named Dongda Bazha in Nedong County was captured together with his wife because he refused to take part in the rebellion. The rebels tied up the couple and lashed them before killing the husband and raping his wife. The then Tibetan local government admitted that many Tibetan people lodged complaints against the rebels with it. In August 1958 alone, there were more than 70 complaints.

The central people's government, in the spirit of national unity, repeatedly urged the Tibetan local government to punish the rebels to maintain public order. Meanwhile, it told the Galoins of the Tibetan local government, "The central government will not change its decision on postponing reform in Tibet and in the future, when the reform is conducted, the policy to be followed will still be one of peaceful reform." However, the reactionary clique of the upper social strata in Tibet took the extreme forbearance of the central government as a sign of weakness and easiness to bully. They declared, "For nine years, the Hans have not dared to touch our most glorious and sacrosanct system. When we attacked them, they could only parry our blows without being able to strike back. So long as we transfer a large number of troops to Lhasa from outside, the Hans will surely flee at the first blow. If they don't run away, we will carry His Holiness the Dalai Lama to Shannan, and gather our strength there to launch a counter-attack and seize back Lhasa. If all these efforts fail, we can go to India."

The armed rebellion in Tibet was supported from the beginning by foreign anti-China forces. In his book*The United States, Tibet and China* American Norman C. Hall reveals that in 1957 the CIA culled six young men from among Tibetans residing abroad and sent them to Guam of the United States to receive training in map-reading, radio transmission, shooting and parachuting. Subsequently, the United States trained 170 "Kamba guerrillas" in batches in Hale Camp, Colorado. The trained "Kamba guerrillas" were air-dropped or sneaked into Tibet to "launch an effective resistance movement" to "oppose the Chinese occupation." An article entitled *The CIA Tibetan Conspiracy* in the Hong Kong-based *Far Eastern Economic Review* disclosed in its September 5 issue of 1975 that in May 1958, two agents trained by the Americans in the first batch brought a transceiver to the headquarter set up by the rebel leader Anzhugcang Goinbo Zhaxi in Shannan to make contact with the CIA. Before long, the United States air-dropped arms and ammunition, including 20 sub-machine guns, two mortars, 100 rifles, 600 hand-grenades, 600 artillery shells and close to 40,000 bullets, to the rebels in the plateau called Chigu Lama Thang. During the same period, the United States clandestinely shipped large amounts of arms and ammunition overland to the rebels entrenched in the Shannan area.

With the collusion of the Tibetan serf-owners bent on retaining serfdom and the foreign anti-China forces, the rebellious activities soon became rampant. The climax was the elaborately planned armed rebellion in Lhasa on March 10, 1959.

On February 7, the Dalai Lama took the initiative and said to Deng Shaodong, deputy commander of the Tibet Military Area Command, and other officers, "I was told that after its return from studies in the hinterland, the Song and Dance Ensemble under the

Tibet Military Area Command has a very good repetoire. I would like to see its show. Please arrange it for me." Deng and the other officers expressed immediate readiness and asked the Dalai Lama to fix the time and place for performance. They also conveyed the Dalai Lama's wish to Surkang and other Galoins of the Tibetan local government and Paglha Tubdain Weidain, adjutant general of the Dalai Lama. On March 8, the Dalai Lama said he would go to the performance in the Tibet Military Area Command Auditorium at 3 pm on March 10. The Tibet Military Area Command carefully prepared for the occasion. But on the evening of March 9, the Miboin (mayor) of Lhasa provoked citizens by saying: tomorrow the Dalai Lama will go to the Military Area Command for a banquet and a performance; the Hans have prepared a plane to kidnap the Dalai Lama to Beijing; every household should send people to Norbu Lingka, the residence of the Dalai Lama, to petition him not to attend the performance in the Military Area Command. The next morning, the rebels coerced more than 2,000 people to mass at Norbu Lingka, spreading the rumor that "the Military Area Command is planning to poison the Dalai Lama" and shouting slogans such as "Tibetan Independence" and "Away with the Hans." The rebels hit and wounded Sampo Cewang Rinzin, a former Galoin of the Tibetan local government and then a deputy commander of the Tibet Military Area Command. They stoned to death Kainqoin Pagbalha Soinam Gyamco, a progressive patriot and member of the Preparatory Committee for the Tibet Autonomous Region. His body was tied to the tail of a horse and dragged through downtown as a warning. Subsequently, the rebel leaders convened the so-called "people's congress" and "people's conference of the independent state of Tibet," intensifying their efforts to organize and expand armed rebellion. They brazenly tore up the 17-Article Agreement and declared "the independence of Tibet," launching a full-scale armed rebellion against the motherland.

Although Norbu Lingka was controlled by the rebels and it was hard to make contact with the Dalai Lama, acting representative of the central government Tan Guansan managed to send three letters to the Dalai Lama on March 10, 11 and 15 through patriots. In them, Tan expressed his understanding of the Dalai Lama's situation as well as his concern for the latter's safety. He pointed out that the rebels were making reckless military provocations and demanded that the Tibetan local government immediately work to stop them. The Dalai Lama penned three letters in reply to Tan on March 11, 12 and 16. In his letters, the Dalai Lama wrote, "Reactionary, evil elements are carrying out activities endangering me under the pretext of ensuring my safety. I am taking measures to calm things down." "The unlawful activities of the reactionary clique cause me endless worry and sorrow.... As to the incidents of yesterday and the day before, which were brought about under the pretext of ensuring my safety and have seriously estranged relations between the central people's government and the local government, I am making every possible effort to deal with them." In the letter of March 16, he said that he had "educated" and "severely criticized" officials of the Tibetan local government. He also expressed the desire to still go to the Military Area Command a few days later. All three letters of the Dalai Lama have been photographed by reporters of the Xinhua News Agency and published, and are still well preserved.

However, on the evening of March 17, Galoins Surkang, Neuxar and Xaisur and other rebel leaders held the Dalai Lama under duress and carried him away from Lhasa to Shannan, the "base" of the armed rebel forces. When the armed rebellion failed, they fled to India.

After the Dalai Lama left Lhasa, about 7,000 rebels gathered to wage a full-scale attack on the Party, government and army institutions before dawn on March 20. The PLA, driven beyond its forbearance, launched under orders a counterattack at 10 am the same day. With the support of patriotic Tibetan monks and lay people, the PLA completely put down the armed rebellion in Lhasa within two days. Before long, the PLA suppressed the armed rebellion in Shannan, where the rebels had been entrenched for a long time. Armed rebel forces who fled to other places were dissolved.

The PLA was highly disciplined in the course of quelling the rebellion and this won the wholehearted support of Buddhist monks and laymen. They took the initiative to help the PLA in putting down the rebellion. Various self-defense, joint-defense, livestock protection and other forms of joint-defense teams sprang up in various places to build roads, provide transport, dispatch mail, serve as guides, boil tea, send water, stand sentry and give first-aid to wounded PLA soldiers, effectively isolating the rebels.

TIBETAN SOVEREIGNTY DEBATE

The Tibetan sovereignty debate refers to two political debates. The first is whether the various territories within the People's Republic of China (PRC) that are claimed as political Tibet should separate and become a new sovereign state. Many of the points in the debate rest on a second debate, about whether Tibet was independent or subordinate to China in certain parts of its recent history.

It is generally agreed that China and Tibet were independent prior to the Yuan Dynasty (1271–1368), and that Tibet has been ruled by the People's Republic of China (PRC) since 1959. The nature of Tibet's relationship to China in the intervening time is a matter of debate. The PRC claims that Tibet has been a part of China since the Yuan Dynasty (1271–1368). The Republic of China (1912–1949) (ROC) claimed that "Tibet was placed under the sovereignty of China" when the Qing Dynasty (1644–1912)expelled Nepal from Tibet in c. 1793. The Tibetan Government in Exile claims that Tibet was an independent state until the PRC invaded Tibet in 1949/50. Western scholars claim that Tibet and China were ruled by the Mongols during the Yuan Dynasty, that Tibet was independent during the Chinese Ming Dynasty (1368–1644). and that Tibet was ruled by China or subordinate to the Qing during much of the Qing Dynasty. Western scholars also claim that Tibet was independent from c. 1912 to 1950, although it had extremely limited international recognition.

VIEW OF THE CHINESE GOVERNMENTS

The government of the People's Republic of China contends that it has had control over Tibet since the Yuan Dynasty(1271–1368).

The government of the Republic of China, which ruled mainland China from 1912 until 1949 and now controls Taiwan, had a cabinet-level Mongolian and Tibetan Affairs Commission in charge of the administration of Tibet and Mongolia regions from 1912. The commission retained its cabinet level status after 1949, but no longer executes that function. On 10 May 1943, Chiang Kai-shek asserted that "Tibet is part of Chinese territory... No foreign nation is allowed to interfere in our domestic affairs". He again declared in 1946 that the Tibetans were Han Chinese. The Republic of China still claims sovereignty over Tibet and Mongolia in its constitution.

In the late 19th century, China adopted the Western model of nation-state diplomacy. As the government of Tibet, China concluded several treaties (1876,1886,1890,1893) with British India touching on the status, boundaries and access to Tibet. Chinese government sources consider this a sign of sovereignty rather than suzerainty. However, by the 20th century British India found the treaties to be ineffective due to China's weakened control over the Tibetan local government.The British invaded Tibet in 1904 and forced the signing of a separate treaty, directly with the Tibetan government in Lhasa. In 1906, an Anglo-Chinese Convention was signed at Peking between Great Britain and China. It incorporated the 1904 Lhasa Convention (with modification), which was attached as Annex. A treaty between Britain and Russia (1907) followed. Article II of this treaty stated that "In conformity with the admitted principle of the suzerainty of China over Tibet, Great Britain and Russia engage not to enter into negotiations with Tibet except through the intermediary of the Chinese Government." China sent troops into Tibet in 1908. The result of the policy of both Great Britain and Russia has been the virtual annexation of Tibet by China. China controlled Tibet up to 1912. Thereafter, Tibet entered the period described commonly as *de facto* independence, though it was not recognized by any country as enjoying *de jure* independence.

More recently the position of the Republic of China with regard to Tibet appeared to have changed as was stated in the following opening speech to the International Symposium on Human Rights in Tibet on 8 September 2007 through the pro-Taiwan independence then ROC President Chen Shui-bian who stated that he considered Tibet and China to be separate.

Legal arguments based on historical status

The position of the People's Republic of China (PRC), which has ruled mainland China since 1949, as well as the official position of the Republic of China (ROC), which ruled mainland China before 1949 and currently controls Taiwan, is that Tibet has been an indivisible part of China *de jure* since the Yuan Dynasty of Mongol-ruled China in the 13th century, comparable to other states such as the Kingdom of Dali and the Tangut Empire that were also incorporated into China at the time.

The PRC contends that, according to international law and the Succession of states theory, all subsequent Chinese governments have succeeded the Yuan Dynasty in exercising de jure sovereignty over Tibet, with the PRC having succeeded the ROC as the legitimate government of all China.

Unique ethnicity

According to the PRC, successive Chinese governments have recognized Tibet as having its own unique culture and language; however, they believe that this situation does not necessarily argue in favour of its independence, because China has over 56 unique ethnic groups and is one of many multi-national states in the world.

De facto independence

The ROC government had no effective control over Tibet from 1912 to 1951; however, in the opinion of the Chinese government, this condition does not represent Tibet's independence as many other parts of China also enjoyed *de facto*independence when the Chinese nation was torn by warlordism, Japanese invasion, and civil war. Goldstein explains what is meant by *de facto* independence in the following statement:

...[Britain] instead adopted a policy based on the idea of *autonomy* for Tibet within the context of Chinese *suzerainty*, that is to say, *de facto* independence for Tibet in the context of token subordination to China. Britain articulated this policy in the Simla Convention of 1914. While at times the Tibetans were fiercely independent-minded, at other times, Tibet indicated its willingness to accept subordinate status as *part of China* provided that Tibetan internal systems were left untouched and China relinquished control over a number of important ethnic Tibetan groups in Kham and Amdo. China insists that during this period the ROC government continued to maintain sovereignty over Tibet. The Provisional Constitution of the Republic of China (1912) stipulated that Tibet was a province of the Republic of China. Provisions concerning Tibet in the Constitution of the Republic of China promulgated later all stress the inseparability of Tibet from Chinese territory, and the Central Government of China exercise of sovereignty in Tibet. In 1927, the Commission in Charge of Mongolian and Tibetan Affairs of the Chinese Government contained members of great influence in the Mongolian and Tibetan areas, such as the 13th Dalai Lama, the 9th Panchen Lama and other Tibetan government representatives. In 1934, on his condolence mission for the demise of the Dalai Lama, the Chinese General Huang Musong posted notices in Chinese and Tibetan throughout Lhasa that alluded to Tibet as an integral part of China while expressing the utmost reverence for the Dalai Lama and the Buddhist religion.

The 9th Panchen Lama traditionally ruled over one-third of Tibet. On 1 February 1925, the Panchen Lama attended the preparatory session of the "National Reconstruction Meeting" (*Shanhou huiyi*) meant to identify ways and means of unifying the Chinese nation, and gave a speech about achieving the unification of five nationalities, including Tibetans, Mongolians and Han Chinese. In 1933, he called upon the Mongols to national unity and to obey the Chinese Government to resist Japanese invasion. In February 1935 the Chinese government appointed Panchen Lama "Special Cultural Commissioner for the Western Regions" and assigned him 500 Chinese troops. He spent much of his time teaching and preaching Buddhist doctrines - including the principles of unity and pacification for the border regions - extensively in inland China, outside of Tibet, from 1924 until 1 December 1937, when he died on his way back to Tibet under the protection of Chinese troops.

During the Sino-Tibetan War, the warlords Ma Bufang and Liu Wenhui jointly attacked and defeated invading Tibetan forces.

The Kuomintang government sought to portray itself as necessary to validate the choice of the Dalai Lama and Panchen Lama. When the current (14th) Dalai Lama was installed in Lhasa, it was with an armed escort of Chinese troops and an attending Chinese minister The Muslim Kuomintang General Bai Chongxi said that the Tibetans suffered under British repression, and he called upon the Republic of China to assist them in expelling the British. According to Yu Shiyu, during China's resistance war against Japanese invasion, Chiang Kai-shek ordered the Chinese Muslim General Ma Bufang, Governor of Qinghai (1937–1949), to repair the Yushu airport in Qinghai Province to deter Tibetan independence. In May 1943, Chiang warned that Tibet must accept and follow the instructions and orders of the Central Government, that they must agree and help to build the Chinese-India [war-supply] road, and that they must maintain direct communications with the Office of the Mongolian and Tibetan Affairs Commission (MTAC) in Lhasa and not through the newly established "Foreign Office" of Tibet. He sternly warned that he would "send an air force to bomb Tibet immediately" should Tibet be found to be collaborating with Japan. Official Communications between Lhasa and Chiang Kai-shek's government was through MTAC, not the "Foreign Office", until July 1949 just before the Communists' final victory in the civil war. The presence of MTAC in Lhasa was viewed by both Nationalist and Communist governments as an assertion of Chinese sovereignty over Tibet. Throughout the Kuomintang years, no country gave Tibet diplomatic recognition.

In 1950 after the People's Liberation Army entered Tibet Nehru stated that India would continue the British policy with regards to Tibet in considering it to be outwardly part of China but internally autonomous.

Foreign interventions

The PRC considers all pro-independence movements aimed at ending Chinese sovereignty in Tibet, including British attempts to establish control in the late 19th century and early 20th century, the CIA's backing of Tibetan insurgents during the 1950s and 1960s, and the Government of Tibet in Exile till the turn of the

21st century, as one long campaign abetted by Western imperialism aimed at destroying Chinese territorial integrity and sovereignty, or destabilizing China. Until 2008 the British position remained the same that China held suzerainty over Tibet but not sovereignty. It was the only state still to hold this view which it revised on 29 October 2008, when the British Foreign Office recognised Chinese sovereignty over Tibet by issuing a statement on its website. The Economist stated that although the Foreign Office's website does not use the word sovereignty, officials at the Foreign Office said "it means that, as far as Britain is concerned, 'Tibet is part of China. Full stop.' " The *New York Times* commented on the American policy during the 1960s saying that it was part of the CIA's efforts to undermine Communist regimes. After the end of the cold war the United States uses the National Endowment for Democracy to primarily support Tibetan independence groups.

VIEW OF THE TIBETAN GOVERNMENT AND SUBSEQUENT GOVERNMENT IN EXILE

Government of Tibet (1912–1951)

A proclamation issued by 13th Dalai Lama in 1913 states, "During the time of Genghis Khan and Altan Khan of the Mongols, theMing dynasty of the Chinese, and the Qing Dynasty of the Manchus, Tibet and China cooperated on the basis of benefactor and priest relationship. [...] the existing relationship between Tibet and China had been that of patron and priest and had not been based on the subordination of one to the other." He condemned that the " Chinese authorities in Szechuan and Yunnan endeavored to colonize our territory Chinese" in 1910–12 and stated that "We are a small, religious, and independent nation".

Tibetan passports

In 2003, an old Tibetan passport was rediscovered in Nepal. Issued by the Kashag to Tibet's finance minister Tsepon Shakabpa for foreign travel, the passport was a single piece of pink paper, complete with photograph. It has a message in hand-written Tibetan and typed English, similar to the message by the nominal issuing officers of today's passports, stating that ""*the bearer of this letter*

– Tsepon Shakabpa, Chief of the Finance Department of the Government of Tibet, is hereby sent to China, the United States of America, the United Kingdom and other countries to explore and review trade possibilities between these countries and Tibet. We shall, therefore, be grateful if all the Governments concerned on his route would kindly give due recognition as such, grant necessary passport, visa, etc. without any hindrance and render assistance in all possible ways to him." The text and the photograph is sealed by a square stamp belonging to the Kashag, and is dated *"26th day of the 8th month of Fire-Pig year (Tibetan)"* (14 October 1947 in the gregorian calendar).

The passport has received visas and entry stamps from several countries and territories, including India, the United States, the United Kingdom, France, Italy, Switzerland, Pakistan, Iraq and Hong Kong, but not China. Some visa do reflect an official status, with mentions such as "Diplomatic courtesy, Service visa, Official gratis, Diplomatic visa, For government official".

However, acceptance of a passport does not indicate recognition of independence, as for example the Republic of China passport is accepted by almost all the countries of the world, even though few of them recognize the ROC as independent.

Tibet Government in exile (post 1959)

In 1959, the 14th Dalai Lama fled Tibet and established a government in exile at Dharamsala in northern India. This group claims sovereignty over various ethnically or historically Tibetan areas now governed by China. Aside from the Tibet Autonomous Region, an area that was administered directly by the Dalai Lama's government until 1951, the group also claims Amdo (Qinghai) and eastern Kham (western Sichuan). About 45 percent of ethnic Tibetans under Chinese rule live in the Tibet Autonomous Region, according to the 2000 census. Prior to 1949, much of Amdo and eastern Kham were governed by local rulers and even warlords.

The view of the current Dalai Lama in 1989 was as follows:

During the 5th Dalai Lama's time [1617–1682], I think it was quite evident that we were a separate sovereign nation with no problems. The 6th Dalai Lama [1683–1706] was spiritually pre-eminent, but politically, he was weak and uninterested. He could not follow the 5th Dalai Lama's path. This was a great failure. So, then the Chinese influence increased. During this time, the Tibetans showed quite a deal of respect to the Chinese. But even during these times, the Tibetans never regarded Tibet as a part of China. All the documents were very clear that China, Mongolia and Tibet were all separate countries. Because the Chinese emperor was powerful and influential, the small nations accepted the Chinese power or influence. You cannot use the previous invasion as evidence that Tibet belongs to China. In the Tibetan mind, regardless of who was in power, whether it was the Manchus [the Qing dynasty], the Mongols [the Yuan dynasty] or the Chinese, the east of Tibet was simply referred to as China. In the Tibetan mind, India and China were treated the same; two separate countries.

The International Commission of Jurists concluded that from 1913 to 1950 Tibet demonstrated the conditions of statehood as generally accepted under international law. In the opinion of the commission, the government of Tibet conducted its own domestic and foreign affairs free from any outside authority, and countries with whom Tibet had foreign relations are shown by official documents to have treated Tibet in practice as an independent State.

The United Nations General Assembly passed resolutions urging respect for the rights of Tibetans in 1959, 1961 and 1965. The 1961 resolution calls for that "principle of self-determination of peoples and nations" applies to the Tibetan people.

The Tibetan Government in Exile views current PRC rule in Tibet as colonial and illegitimate, motivated solely by the natural resources and strategic value of Tibet, and in gross violation of both Tibet's historical status as an independent country and the right of Tibetan people to self-determination. It also points to PRC's autocratic policies,divide-and-rule policies, and what it contends are assimilationist policies, and regard those as an example of ongoing imperialism aimed at destroying Tibet's distinct ethnic makeup, culture, and identity, thereby cementing it as an indivisible part of China. That said, the Dalai Lama stated in 2008 that he wishes only for Tibetan autonomy, and not separation from

China, under certain democratic conditions, like freedom of speech and expression and genuine self-rule.

THIRD-PARTY VIEWS

During the Tang Dynasty of China, Tibet and China frequently warred. Parts of Tibet were temporarily captured by the Chinese and became territories of the Tang dynasty (618–907 AD). Around 650, the Chinese captured Lhasa. In 763, Tibet very briefly took the Chinese capital of Chang'an during the Tang civil war.

Most scholars outside of China say that during the Ming Dynasty (1368–1644), Tibet was independent without even a nominal Ming suzerainty. In contrast since the mid-18th century it is agreed that China had control over Tibet reaching its maximum in the end of the 18th century. Luciano Petech, a scholar of Himalayan history, indicated that Tibet was a Qing protectorate.

The "Patron-Priest" relationship held between the Qing court and the Tibetan lamas has been subjected to varying interpretation. The 13th Dalai Lama, for example, knelt, but did not kowtow, before the Empress Dowager and the young Emperor while he delivered his petition in Beijing. Chinese sources emphasize the submission of kneeling; Tibetan sources emphasize the lack of the kowtow. Titles and commands given to Tibetans by the Chinese, likewise, are variously interpreted. The Qing authorities gave the 13th Dalai Lama the title of "Loyally Submissive Vice-Regent", and ordered to follow Qing's commands and communicate with the Emperor only through the Manchu Amban in Lhasa; but opinions vary as to whether these titles and commands reflected actual political power, or symbolic gestures ignored by Tibetans. Some authors claim that kneeling before the Emperor followed the 17th-century precedent in the case of the 5th Dalai Lama. Other historians indicate that the emperor treated the Dalai Lama as an equal

Tibetologist Melvyn C. Goldstein writes that Britain and Russia formally acknowledged Chinese authority over Tibet in treaties of 1906 and 1907; and that the British invasion of Tibet stirred China into getting more directly involved in Tibetan affairs and working to integrate Tibet with "the rest of China."

The status of Tibet after the Xinhai Revolution ended the Qing Dynasty is also a matter to debate. After the revolution, the Chinese Republic of five races, including Tibetans, was proclaimed. Western powers recognized the Chinese Republic, however the 13th Dalai Lama proclaimed Tibet's independence. Some authors indicate that personal allegiance of the Dalai Lama to the Manchu Emperor came to an end and no new type of allegiance of Tibet to China was established, or that Tibet had relationships with the empire and not with the new nation-state of China. Barnett observes that there is no document before 1950 in which Tibet explicitly recognizes Chinese sovereignty, and considers Tibet's subordination to China during the periods when China had most authority comparable to that of a colony. Tibetologist Elliot Sperling noted that the Tibetan term for China, Rgya-nag, did not mean anything more than a country bordering Tibet from the east, and did not include Tibet. Other Tibetologists write that no country publicly accepts Tibet as an independent state, although there are several instances of government officials appealing to their superiors to do so. Treaties signed by Britain and Russia in the early years of the 20th century, and others signed by Nepal and India in the 1950s, recognized Tibet's political subordination to China. The United States presented a similar viewpoint in 1943. Goldstein also says that a 1943 British official letter "reconfirmed that Britain considered Tibet as part of China."

Thomas Heberer, professor of political science and East Asian studies at the University of Duisburg-Essen, Germany, wrote: "No country in the world has ever recognized the independence of Tibet or declared that Tibet is an 'occupied country'. For all countries in the world, Tibet is Chinese territory." However during the early 1990s governmental bodies, including the European Union and United States Congress, and other international organisations declared that Tibetans lacked the right to self-determination or that it was an occupied territory.

In 2008, European Union leader José Manuel Barroso stated that the EU recognized Tibet as integral part of China: On 1 April 2009, the French Government reaffirmed its position on the Tibet issue.

This lack of legal recognition makes it difficult for international legal experts sympathetic to the Tibetan Government in Exile to argue that Tibet formally established its independence. On the other hand, in 1959 and 1960 the International Commission of Jurists concluded that Tibet had been independent between 1913 and 1950.

HUMAN RIGHTS

Genocide charges

Groups such as the Madrid-based Committee to Support Tibet claim the death toll in Tibet since the 1950 People's Liberation Army invasion of Tibet to be 1,200,000 and have filed official charges of genocide against prominent Chinese leaders and officials. This figure has been disputed by Patrick French, a supporter of the Tibetan cause who was able to view the data and calculations, but rather, concludes a no less devastating death toll of half a million people as a direct result of Chinese policies.

Other rights

The PRC argues that the Tibetan authority under successive Dalai Lamas was also itself a human rights violator. The old society, say the Chinese government and its supporters, was a serfdom and, according to reports of an early English explorer, had remnants of "a very mild form of slavery" prior to the 13th Dalai Lama's reforms of 1913.

Tibetologist Robert Barnett wrote about clerical resistance to the introduction of anything Anti-Buddhist that might disturb the prevailing power structure. Clergy obstructed modernization attempts by the 13th Dalai Lama.

Old Tibet had a long history of persecuting non-Buddhist Christians. In the years 1630 and 1742, Tibetan Christian communities were suppressed by the lamas of the Gelugpa Sect, whose chief lama was the Dalai Lama. Jesuit priests were made prisoners in 1630 or attacked before they reached Tsaparang. Between 1850 and 1880, eleven fathers of the Paris Foreign Mission Society were murdered in Tibet, or killed or injured during their journeys to other missionary outposts in the Sino-Tibetan borderlands. In 1881 Father Brieux was reported to have been murdered on his way to Lhasa. Qing officials later discovered that the murder cases were in fact covertly supported and even orchestrated by local lamaseries and their patrons—the native chieftains. In 1904, Qing official Feng Quan sought to curtail the influence of the Gelugpa Sect and ordered the protection of Western missionaries and their churches. Indignation over Feng Quan and the Christian presence escalated to a climax in March 1905, when thousands of the Batang lamas revolted, killing Feng, his entourage, local Manchu and Han Chinese officials, and the local French Catholic priests. The revolt soon spread to other cities in eastern Tibet, such as Chamdo, Litang and Nyarong, and at one point almost spilled over into neighbouring Sichuan Province. The missionary stations and churches in these areas were burned and destroyed by the angry Gelugpa monks and local chieftains. Dozens of local Westerners, including at least four priests, were killed or fatally wounded. The scale of the rebellion was so tremendous that only when panicked Qing authorities hurriedly sent 2,000 troops from Sichuan to pacify the mobs did the revolt gradually come to an end. The lamasery authorities and local native chieftains' hostility towards the Western missionaries in Tibet lingered through the last throes of the Manchu dynasty and into the Republican period.

Three UN resolutions of 1959, 1961, and 1965 condemned human rights violation in Tibet. These resolutions were passed at a time when the PRC was not permitted to become a member and of course was not allowed to present its singular version of events in the region (however, the Republic of China on Taiwan, which the PRC also tries to claim sovereignty over, was a member of the UN at the time, and it equally claimed sovereignty over Tibet and opposed Tibetan self-determination). Sinologist Grunfeld called the resolutions impractical and justified the PRC in ignoring them.

Grunfeld questioned Human Rights Watch reports on human rights abuses in Tibet, saying they distorted the big picture.

According to Barnett, since Western powers and especially the United States used the Tibet issue in the 1950s and 1960s for cold war political purposes, the PRC is now able to get support from developing countries in defeating the last nine attempts at the United Nations to criticize China. Barnett writes that the position of the Chinese in Tibet would be more accurately characterized as a colonial occupation, and that such an approach might cause developing nations to be more supportive of the Tibetan cause.

The Chinese government ignores the issue of its alleged violations of Tibetan human rights, and prefers to argue that the invasion was about territorial integrity and unity of the State. Furthermore, Tibetan activists inside Tibet have until recently focused on independence, not human rights.

Leaders of the Tibetan Youth Congress which claims 30,000 over members are alleged by China to advocate violence. In 1998, Barnett wrote that India's military includes 10,000 Tibetans, causing China some unease; and that "at least seven bombs exploded in Tibet between 1995 and 1997, one of them laid by a monk, and a significant number of individual Tibetans are known to be actively seeking the taking up of arms; hundreds of Chinese soldiers and police have been beaten during demonstrations in Tibet, and at least one killed in cold blood, probably several more."

Chinadaily.com reported on the discovery of weapons subsequent to the protests by peaceful Buddhists monks on March 14, 2008: "Police in Lhasa seized more than 100 guns, tens of thousands of bullets, several thousand kilograms of explosives and tens of thousands of detonators, acting on reports from lamas and ordinary people."

And on 23 March 2008, there was a bombing incident in the Qambo prefecture.

Self-determination

While the earliest ROC constitutional documents already claim Tibet as part of China, Chinese political leaders also acknowledged the principle of self-determination. For example, at a party conference in 1924, Kuomintang leader Sun Yat-sen issued a statement calling for the right of self-determination of all Chinese ethnic groups: "*The Kuomintang can state with solemnity that it recognizes the right of self-determination of all national minorities in China and it will organize a free and united Chinese republic.*" In 1931, the CCP issued a constitution for the short-lived Chinese Soviet Republic which states that Tibetans and other ethnic minorities, "may either join the Union of Chinese Soviets or secede from it." It is notable that China was in a state of civil war at the time and that the "Chinese Soviets" only represents a faction. Saying that Tibet may secede from the "Chinese Soviets" does not mean that it can secede from China. The quote above is merely a statement of Tibetans' freedom to choose their political orientation. The possibility of complete secession was denied by Communist leader Mao Zedong in 1938: "They must have the right to self-determination and at the same time they should continue to unite with the Chinese people to form one nation". This policy was codified in PRC's first constitution which, in Article 3, reaffirmed China as a "*single* multi-national state," while the "national *autonomous areas* are inalienable parts". The Chinese government insists that the United Nations documents, which codifies the principle of self-determination, provides that the principle shall not be abused in disrupting territorial integrity: "Any attempt aimed at the partial or total disruption of the national unity and the territorial integrity of a country is incompatible with the purposes and principles of the Charter of the United Nations...."

Legitimacy

The PRC also points to what it claims are the autocratic, oppressive and theocratic policies of the government of Tibet before 1959, its toleration of existence of serfdom and slaves, its so-called "renunciation" of (Arunachal Pradesh) and its association with India and other foreign countries, and as such claims the Government of Tibet in Exile has no legitimacy to govern Tibet and no credibility or justification in criticizing PRC's policies.

China claims that the People's Liberation Army's march into Tibet in 1951 was "not without the support of a handful of Tibetan people", including the 10th Panchen Lama. Ian Buruma writes:

...It is often forgotten that many Tibetans, especially educated people in the larger towns, were so keen to modernize their society in the mid-20th century that they saw the Chinese communists as allies against rule by monks and serf-owning landlords. The Dalai

Lama himself, in the early 1950s, was impressed by Chinese reforms and wrote poems praising Chairman Mao.

Instances have been documented when the PRC government gained support from a portion of the Tibetan population, including monastic leaders, monks, nobility and ordinary Tibetans prior to the crackdown in the 1959 uprising. The PRC government and some Tibetan leaders characterize PLA's operation as a peaceful liberation of Tibetans from a "feudal serfdom system."

When Tibet complained to the United Nations through El Salvador about Chinese invasion in November 1950—after China captured Chamdo (or Qamdo) when Tibet failed to respond by the deadline to China's demand for negotiation— members debated about it but refused to admit the "Tibet Question" into the agenda of the U.N. General Assembly. Key stakeholder India told the General Assembly that "the Peking Government had declared that it had not abandoned its intention to settle the difficulties by peaceful means", and that "the Indian Government *was certain* that the Tibet Question could still be settled by peaceful means". The Russian delegate said that "China's sovereignty over Tibet had been recognized for a long time by the United Kingdom, the United States, and the U.S.S.R." The United Nations postponed this matter on the pretext Tibet was officially an "autonomous nationality region belonging to territorial China", and because the outlook of peaceful settlement seemed good.

Subsequently, *The Agreement Between the Central Government and the Local Government of Tibet on Method for the Peaceful Liberation of Tibet*, also known as Seventeen-Point Agreement, was signed between delegates of China and Tibet on 23 May 1951. The Dalai Lama,despite the massive Chinese military presence, had ample time and opportunity to repudiate and denounce the Seventeen-Point Agreement. He was encouraged and instigated to do so with promise of public but not military support by the US, which by now had become hostile to Communist-ruled China.

On May 29, the 10th Panchen Erdeni (i.e. 10th Panchen Lama) and the Panchen Kampus Assembly made a formal statement, expressing their heartfelt support for the agreement. The statement indicated their resolution to guarantee the correct implementation of the agreement and to realize solidarity between the different ethnic groups of China and ethnic solidarity among the Tibetans; and on May 30, the 10th Panchen Erdeni telegrammed the 14th Dalai Lama, expressing his hope for unity and his vow to support the 14th Dalai Lama and the government of Tibet with the implementation of the agreement under the guidance of the Central Government and Chairman Mao.

The Agreement was finally accepted by Tibet's National Assembly, which then advised the Dalai Lama to accept it. Finally, on 24 October 1951, the Dalai Lama dispatched a telegram to Mao Zedong:

The Tibet Local Government as well as the ecclesiastic and secular People unanimously support this agreement, and under the leadership of Chairman Mao and the Central People's Government, will actively support the People's Liberation Army in Tibet to consolidate defence, drive out imperialist influences from Tibet and safeguard the unification of the territory and sovereignty of the Motherland.

On 28 October 1951, the Panchen Rinpoche [i.e. Panchen Lama] made a similar public statement accepting the agreement. He urged the "people of Shigatse to give active support" to carrying out the agreement.

Tsering Shakya writes about the general acceptance of the Tibetans toward the Seventeen-Point Agreement, and its legal significance:

The most vocal supporters of the agreement came from the monastic community...As a result many Tibetans were willing to accept the agreement....Finally there were strong factions in Tibet who felt that the agreement was acceptable...this section was led by the religious community...In the Tibetans' view their independence was not a question of international legal status, but as Dawa Norbu writes, "Our sense of independence was based on the independence of our way of life and culture, which was more real to the unlettered masses than law or history, canons by which the non-Tibetans decide the fate of Tibet...This was the first formal agreement between Tibet and Communist China and it established the legal basis for Chinese rule in Tibet."

On March 28, 1959, premier Zhou Enlai signed the order of the PRC State Council with regard to the uprising in Tibet, accusing the Tibetan government of disrupting the Agreement despite the facts that this was not true. The creation of the TAR finally buried the Agreement that was discarded back in 1959.

On April 18, 1959, the Dalai Lama published a statement in Tezpur, India, which explained the reasons for his escape to India. He pointed out that the 17 Point Agreement was signed under pressure because the Tibetans had no other choice; later the Chinese side permanently violated it. According to Michael Van Walt Van Praag, "treaties and similar agreements concluded under the use or threat of force are invalid under international law ab initio". Therefore, this Agreement is not considered legal by those who consider Tibet as an independent state before its signing; but it is considered legal by those who deny Tibet's independence. In either case the PRC did not abide by the agreement.

TIBETAN INDEPENDENCE MOVEMENT

The Tibetan independence movement is a movement for the independence of Tibet and the political separation of Tibet from the People's Republic of China. It is principally led by the Tibetan diaspora in countries like India and the United States, and by celebrities and Tibetan Buddhists in the United States and Europe. The movement is not supported by the 14th Dalai Lama, who although having advocated it from 1961 to the late 1970s, proposed a sort of high-level autonomy in a speech in Strasbourg in 1988, and has since then restricted his position to either autonomy for the Tibetan people in the Tibet Autonomous Region *within* China, or for the autonomy to extend also to areas of neighbouring Chinese provinces inhabited by Tibetans.

Among other reasons for independence, campaigners assert that Tibet has been historically independent. However, some dispute this claim by using different definitions of "Tibet" and "independence." The campaigners also argue that Tibetans are currently mistreated and denied certain human rights, although the Chinese government disputes this and claims progress in human rights. Various organizations with overlapping campaigns for independence and human rights have sought to pressure various governments to support Tibetan independence or to take punitive action against China for opposing it.

HISTORICAL BACKGROUND

After the Mongol Prince Köden took control of the Kokonor region in 1239, he sent his general Doorda Darqan on a reconnaissance mission into Tibet in 1240. During this expedition the Kadampa monasteries of Rwa-sgreng and Rgyal-lha-khang were burned, and 500 people killed. The death of Ögödei the Mongol Qaghan in 1241 brought Mongol military activity around the world temporarily to a halt. Mongol interests in Tibet resumed in 1244 when Prince Köden sent an invitation to the leader of the Sakya sect, to come to his capital and formally surrender Tibet to the Mongols. The Sakya leader arrived in Kokonor with his two nephews Drogön Chögyal Phagpa ('Phags-pa; 1235–80) and Chana Dorje (Phyag-na Rdo-rje) (1239–67) in 1246. This event marked the incorporation of Tibet into the Mongol Empire.

In 1710, the Qing Dynasty army entered Tibet, in aid of the local and defeated the Mongol and Lha-bzang Khan of Khoshut. Later, the Chinese emperor assigned Dalai Lama and Panchen Lama to be in charge of religious and political matters of Tibet. The Dalai Lama was leader of area around Lhasa, Panchen Lama was leader area of Shigatse Prefecture.

By the early 18th century, the Qing Dynasty sent resident commissioners (*amban*) to Lhasa. Tibetan factions rebelled in 1759 and killed the resident commissioners after the central government decided to reduce the number of soldiers to about 100. The Qing army entered and defeated the rebels and reinstalled the resident commissioner. The number of soldiers in Tibet was kept at about 2,000. The defensive duties were assisted by a local force which was reorganized by the resident commissioner, and the Tibetan government continued to manage day-to-day affairs as before.

In 1904, a British mission, accompanied by a large military escort, invaded Tibet, forcing its way through to Lhasa. 13th Dalai Lama escaped. Britain forced The Great Three Tibetan Temple signing of the Convention Between Great Britain and Tibet. The head of the mission was Colonel Francis Younghusband. The principal motivation for the British mission was a fear, which proved to be unfounded, that Russia was extending its footprint into Tibet and possibly even giving military aid to the Tibetan government. But on his way to Lhasa, Younghusband killed 1,300 Tibetans in Gyangzê (as written in "The Great Game" of Peter Hopkirk), because the natives were in fear of what kind of unequal treaty the British would offer the Tibetans. Some documents claim that 5,000 Tibetans were killed by the British army.

The Anglo-Chinese Convention of 1906 recognized Chinese suzerainty over the region and the Anglo-Russian Convention of 1907, without Lhasa's and Beijing's acknowledgement, recognized the *suzerainty of China over Tibet*. The Qing central government claimed for sovereignty and direct rule over Tibet in 1910. The thirteenth Dalai Lama fled to British India in February 1910. In the same month, the Chinese government issued a proclamation 'deposing' the Dalai Lama and instigating the search for a new incarnation.

The subsequent outbreak of World War I and civil war in China meant that the Chinese factions only controlled part of Tibet. The government of the 13th Dalai Lama controlled Ü-Tsang (Dbus-gtsang) and western Kham, roughly coincident with the borders of the Tibet Autonomous Region today. Eastern Kham, separated by the Yangtze River was under the control of Chinese warlord Liu Wenhui. The situation in Amdo (Qinghai) was more complicated, with the Xining area controlled byChinese Muslim warlord Ma Bufang, who constantly strove to exert control over the rest of Amdo (Qinghai).

The Chinese Muslim General Ma Fuxiang, the chairman of the Mongolian and Tibetan Affairs Commission stated that Tibetwas an integral part of the Republic of China.

Our Party [the Guomindang] takes the development of the weak and small and resistance to the strong and violent as our sole and most urgent task. This is even more true for those groups which are not of our kind. Now the peoples [minzu] of Mongolia and Tibet are closely related to us, and we have great affection for one another: our common existence and common honor already have a history of over a thousand years.... Mongolia and Tibet's life and death are China's life and death. China absolutely cannot cause Mongolia and Tibet to break away from China's territory, and Mongolia and Tibet cannot reject China to become independent. At this time, there is not a single nation on earth except China that will sincerely develop Mongolia and Tibet."

In 1950, the People's Liberation Army of the People's Republic of China entered Tibet, after taking over the rest of China from Republic of China during the five years of civil war. In 1951, the Seventeen Point Agreement for the Peaceful Liberation of Tibet, a treaty signed by representatives of the Dalai Lama and the Panchen Lama, provided for rule by a joint administration under representatives of the central government and the Tibetan government. Most of the population of Tibet at that time were serfs, bound to land owned bylamas. Any attempt at land reform or the redistribution of wealth would have proved unpopular with the established landowners. This agreement was initially put into effect in Tibet proper. However, Eastern Kham and Amdo were outside the administration of the government of Tibet, and were thus treated like any other Chinese province with land reform implemented in full. As a result, a rebellion broke out in these regions in June 1956. The rebellion eventually spread to Lhasa, but was crushed by 1959. The 14th Dalai Lama and other government principals fled to exile in India.

Beginning in the 1950s the Central Intelligence Agency trained Tibetans as paramilitaries.

CIA AND MI6 ACTIVITIES IN TIBET (1950-1970)

Agents of Western governments had infiltrated Tibet by the mid-1950s, a few years after Tibet was annexed by the People's Republic of China. British MI6 agent Sydney Wignall, in his recent autobiography, reveals that he travelled to Tibet with John Harrop in 1955 posing as mountaineers. Captured by the Chinese authority, Wignell recalled that he was surprised to find two CIA agents were already under Chinese detention.

Clandestine military involvement by the U.S. began following the series of uprisings in the eastern Tibetan region of Kham in

1956. Several small groups of Khampa fighters were trained by the CIA camp and then airdropped back into Tibet with supplies. In 1958, with the rebellion in Kham ongoing, two of these fighters, Athar and Lhotse, attempted to meet with the Dalai Lama to determine whether he would cooperate with their activities. However, their request for an audience was refused by the Lord Chamberlain, Phala Thubten Wonden, who believed such a meeting would be impolitic. According to Tsering Shakya, "Phala never told the Dalai Lama or the Kashagof the arrival of Athar and Lhotse. Nor did he inform the Dalai Lama of American willingness to provide aid".

Following a mass uprising in Lhasa in 1959 during the celebration of the Tibetan New Year and the ensuing Chinese military response, the Dalai Lama went into exile in India. Some sources state that the Dalai Lama's escape was assisted by the CIA.

After 1959, the CIA trained Tibetan guerrillas and provided funds and weapons for the fight against China. However, assistance was reduced during the course of the 1960s and finally ended whenRichard Nixon decided to seek rapprochement with China in the early 1970s.

Kenneth Conboy and James Morrison, in The CIA's Secret War in Tibet, reveal how the CIA encouraged Tibetan revolt against China – and eventually came to control its fledgling resistance movement. The New York Times reported on October 2, 1998 that the Dalai Lama's administration acknowledged that it received $1.7 million a year in the 1960s from the CIA, but denied reports that the Tibetan leader benefited personally from an annual subsidy of $180,000.

The money allocated for the resistance movement was spent on training volunteers and paying for guerrilla operations against the Chinese, the Tibetan government-in-exile said. The budget figures for the CIA's Tibetan program were as follows:

- Subsidy to the Dalai Lama: US$180,000
- Support of Tibetan guerrillas based in Nepal: US$500,000
- Other costs: US$1.06m
- Total: US$1.73m

Positions on the status of Tibet

The status of Tibet before 1950, especially in the period between 1912 and 1950, is largely in dispute between supporters and opponents of Tibetan independence. According to supporters of Tibetan independence, Tibet was a distinct nation and state independent between the fall of the Mongol Empire in 1368 and subjugation by the Qing Dynasty in 1720; and again between the fall of the Qing Dynasty in 1912 and its incorporation into the PRC in 1951. Moreover, even during the periods of nominal subjugation to the Yuan and Qing, Tibet was largely self-governing. As such, the Central Tibetan Administration (CTA) views current PRC rule in Tibet as illegitimate, motivated solely by the natural resources and strategic value of Tibet, and in violation of both Tibet's historical status as an independent country and the right of the Tibetan people to self-determination. It also points to PRC's autocratic and divide-and-rule policies, and assimilationist policies, regarding those as an example of imperialism bent on destroying Tibet's distinct ethnic makeup, culture, and identity, thereby cementing it as an indivisible part of China. After the fall of the Qing Dynasty, both Mongolia and TIbet declared independence and recognized each other as such.

On the other hand, opponents assert that the PRC rules Tibet legitimately, by saying that Tibet has been part of Chinese history since 7th century as Tibetan Empire has close interaction with the Chinese dynasties through royal marriage. In addition to the *de facto* power that the Chinese has since then, Yuan Dynasty conquest in 13th century and that all subsequent Chinese governments (Ming Dynasty, Qing Dynasty, Republic of China, and People's Republic of China) have been exercising de jure sovereignty power over Tibet.

In addition, as this position argues that no country gave Tibet diplomatic recognition between 1912 and 1950, they say that China, under the Republic of China government, continued to maintain sovereignty over the region, and the leaders of Tibet themselves acknowledged Chinese sovereignty by sending delegates to the following: the Drafting Committee for a new constitution of the Republic of China in 1925, the National Assembly of the Republic of China in 1931, the fourth National Congress of the Kuomintang in 1931, a National Assembly for drafting a new Chinese constitution in 1946, and finally to another National Assembly for drafting a new Chinese constitution in 1948. Finally, some within the PRC considers all movements aimed at ending Chinese sovereignty in Tibet, starting with British attempts in the late 19th and early 20th centuries, to the CTA today, as one long campaign abetted by malicious Western imperialism aimed at destroying Chinese integrity and sovereignty, thereby weakening China's position in the world. The PRC also points to what it calls the autocratic and theocratic policies of the government of Tibet before 1959, as well as its renunciation of South Tibet, claimed by China as a part of historical Tibet occupied by India, as well as the Dalai Lama's association with India, and as such claims the CTA has no moral legitimacy to govern Tibet.

POSITIONS ON TIBET AFTER 1950

Tibetan exiles generally say that the number that have died in the Great Leap Forward, violence, or other unnatural causes since 1950 is approximately 1.2 million. However, this number is controversial, and the government does not agree to it. According to Patrick French, a supporter of the Tibetan cause who was able to view the data and calculations, the estimate is not reliable because the Tibetans were not able to process the data well enough to produce a credible total, with many persons double or triple counted. There were, however, many casualties, perhaps as many as 400,000. This figure is extrapolated from a calculation Warren W. Smith made from census reports of Tibet which show 200,000 "missing" from Tibet. Even anti-Communist resources such as *the Black Book of Communism* expresses doubt at the 1.2 million figure, but does note that according to the Chinese census, the total population of ethnic Tibetans in the PRC was 2.8 million in 1953, but only 2.5 million in 1964. It puts forward a figure of 800,000 deaths and alleges that as many as 10% of Tibetans were interned, with few survivors. Chinese demographers have estimated that 90,000 of the 300,000 "missing" Tibetans fled the region.

The Central Tibetan Administration also says that millions of Chinese immigrants to the TAR are diluting the Tibetans both culturally and through intermarriage. Exile groups say that despite recent attempts to restore the appearance of original Tibetan culture to attract tourism, the traditional Tibetan way of life is now irrevocably changed. It is also reported that when Hu Yaobang, the general secretary of the Communist Party of China, visited Lhasa in 1980 he was unhappy when he found out the region was behind neighbouring provinces. Reforms were instituted, and since then the central government's policy in Tibet has granted most religious freedoms. But monks and nuns are still sometimes imprisoned, and many Tibetans (mostly monks and nuns) continue to flee Tibet yearly. At the same time, many Tibetans believe projects that the PRC implement to benefit Tibet, such as the China Western Development economic plan or the Qinghai-Tibet Railway, are politically motivated actions to consolidate central control over Tibet by facilitating militarization and Han Chinese migration while benefiting few Tibetans; they also believe the money funnelled into cultural restoration projects as being aimed at attracting foreign tourists. They also say that there is still preferential treatment awarded to Han Chinese in the labor market as opposed to Tibetans.

The government of the PRC claims that the population of Tibet in 1737 was about 8 million. It claims that due to the 'backward' rule of the local theocracy, there was rapid decrease in the next two hundred years and the population in 1959 was only about one million. Today, the population of Greater Tibet is 7.3 million, of which 5 million is ethnic Tibetan, according to the 2000 census. According to the PRC the increase is viewed as the result of the abolishment of the theocracy and introduction of a modern, higher standard of living. Based on the census numbers, the PRC also rejects claims that the Tibetans are being swamped by Han Chinese; instead the PRC says that the border for Greater Tibet drawn by the government of Tibet in Exile is so large that it incorporates regions such as Xining that are not traditionally Tibetan in the first place, hence exaggerating the number of non-Tibetans.

The government of the PRC also rejects claims that the lives of Tibetans have deteriorated, pointing to rights enjoyed by the Tibetan language in education and in courts and says that the lives of Tibetans have been improved immensely compared to the Dalai Lama's rule before 1950. Benefits that are commonly quoted include: the GDP of Tibet Autonomous Region (TAR) today is 30 times that before 1950; it has 22,500 km of highways, all built since 1950; all secular education in the region was created after integration into the PRC; there are 25 scientific research institutes, all built by the PRC; infant mortality has dropped from 43% in 1950 to 0.661% in 2000; life expectancy has risen from 35.5 years in 1950 to 67 in 2000; the collection and publishing of the traditional *Epic of King Gesar*, which is the longest epic poem in the world and had only been handed down orally before; allocation of 300 million Renminbi since the 1980s to the maintenance and protection of Tibetan monasteries. The Cultural Revolution and the cultural damage it wrought upon the entire PRC is generally condemned as a nationwide catastrophe, whose main instigators (in the PRC's view, the Gang of Four) have been brought to justice and whose recurrence is unthinkable in an increasingly modernized China. The China Western Development plan is viewed by the PRC as a massive, benevolent, and patriotic undertaking by the eastern coast to help the western parts of China, including Tibet, catch up in prosperity and living standards.

DEVELOPMENT AND INFLUENCE

Organisations which support the Tibetan independence movement include:

- Tibetan Youth Congress - Located at Dharamsala, the seat of the Government of Tibet in Exile in India, claims 30,000 members.
- International Tibet Independence Movement - Located in Indiana, United States. It was formed in March 1995 and is now a 501(c)(3) non-profit organization for informing about Tibetan independence.
- International Tibetan Aid Organization - Located in Amsterdam, Netherlands, this organization was formed in 2004.

However, Tenzin Gyatso, the current Dalai Lama, the spiritual leader of Tibetan Buddhists, is no longer calling for independence.

He has spoken in many international venues, including the United States Congress, and the European Parliament. In 1987, he has also started campaigning for a peaceful resolution to the issue of the status of Tibet, and has since then advocated that Tibet should not become independent, but that it should be given meaningful autonomy within the People's Republic of China.

This approach is known as the "Middle Way". As such India has always been very supportive to the cause of Tibetans though silently and has never placed any obstacles on Tibetan migratión to India by any means and their financial transactions have also been kept unchecked. This has always helped Tibetans to mingle with the world. Off late Tibetans have been given voting rights in India too.

Some organisations either support the "Middle Way" or do not adopt a definitive stance on whether they support independence or greater autonomy. Such organisations include:

- Free Tibet Campaign - Located in London, United Kingdom, formed in 1987, stands for the right of Tibetans to determine their own future and for the future of their own country.
- International Tibet Support Network - Located in London, United Kingdom, established in 2000, umbrella organization for Tibet related organization worldwide.

CELEBRITY SUPPORT AND FREEDOM CONCERTS

The Tibetan independence movement receives considerable publicity from celebrities in the United States and Europe, although much of their support comes under a non-specific banner of "Free Tibet", without specifying whether they support independence for Tibet, or the kind of greater autonomy within China advocated by the Dalai Lama.

The "Free Tibet" movement is fashionable among members of the Hollywood set, such as Richard Gere and Paris Hilton.

British comedian Russell Brand also occasionally mentions his support for the movement on his BBC Radio 2 show. Richard Gere is one of the most outspoken supporters of the movement and is chairman of the Board of Directors for the International Campaign for Tibet. Actress Sharon Stone caused significant controversy when she suggested that the 2008 Sichuan earthquake may have been the result of "bad karma," because the Chinese "are not being nice to the Dalai Lama, who is a good friend of mine."

Steven Seagal has been an active supporter of Tibetan independence for several decades and makes regular donations to various Tibetan charities around the world. He has been recognized by Tibetan Lama Penor Rinpoche as the reincarnation of tulku Chungdrag Dorje, the treasure revealer of Palyul Monastery. He also claims to have the special ability of clairvoyance; in a November 2006 interview, he stated: "I was born very different, clairvoyant and a healer".

The Milerepa Fund is an organisation which organises concerts to give publicity to the Tibetan independence movement. The fund was named after Milarepa, the revered 11th-century Tibetan yogi, who used music to enlighten people. It was originally established to disburse royalties from the Beastie Boys album *Ill Communication* in 1994, to benefit Tibetan monks who were sampled on two songs. The Milarepa Fund organizers also jointed the Beastie Boys as they headlined the 1994 Lollapalooza Tour. Inspired by this tour, they began to organise a concert to promote Tibetan independence, in the style of Live Aid.

Organized in June 1996, the first concert (in San Francisco) opened with Icelandic singer Björk and featured acts such as Radiohead, The Smashing Pumpkins, Cibo Matto, Rage Against the Machine, Red Hot Chili Peppers, and De La Soul. The concerts continued for three more years, which helped to generate publicity for the Tibetan independence movement. It also reportedly led to the growth of Tibetan independence organisations such as Students for a Free Tibet and Free Tibet Campaign worldwide.

Gorillaz, the virtual pop band have shown support through a TV spot showing animated frontman, 2D, meditating with fellow supporters outside of the Chinese embassy, followed by a brief message encouraging people to join the Free Tibet Campaign. In addition, during the holographic performances of "Clint Eastwood", 2D is wearing a shirt saying "FREE TIBET."

PROTESTS AND UPRISINGS IN TIBET SINCE 1950

Protests and uprisings in Tibet against the government of the People's Republic of China have occurred since 1950, and include the 1959 uprising, the 2008 uprising, and the subsequent self-immolation protests.

Over the years the Tibetan government in exile, the Central Tibetan Administration of His Holiness the Dalai Lama (CTA), has shifted the goal of its resistance stance from attempting measured cooperation with autonomy, to demanding full independence, to seeking "genuine autonomy for all Tibetans living in the three traditional provinces of Tibet within the framework of the People's Republic of China". However, not all exiled Tibetans are content with pursuing a moderate path and many expressed their frustration in 2008, against the Dalai Lama's wishes, by agitating for independence.

With the 14th Dalai Lama announcing his retirement from political life just before the April 2011 elections for Prime Minister, who will henceforth be Tibet's political leader, the nature of resistance may be moving into yet another phase, although the three leading candidates currently favour the Middle Way Approach.

Background

Isolated geography has naturally defined Tibet as a unique entity, however, its governance and political status have been in flux for centuries. The minor kingdoms and tribal states of the region were first united under Songtsän Gampo to form the Tibetan Empire in the seventh century C.E. Under the influence of his Chinese bride and first Nepali wife Bhrikuti, the Emperor converted to Buddhism and established it as the religion of Tibet. An influx of Chinese culture, the Indian alphabet, and Buddhist monks followed, combining with the native customs and animistic religionBön to give birth to what has become today's ethnic Tibetan people and Tibetan Buddhism, also known as Lamaism,

After the break-up of the Tibetan Empire in the mid-9th century, central rule was largely nonexistent over the region for 400 years. But Buddhism survived and when the Mongols conquered the region, Buddhism was adopted as the official religion of their empire. In 1271, Kublai Khanestablished the Yuan Dynasty and Tibet remained a semi-autonomous entity within it. From the second half of the 14th century until the early 17th, Tibet was ruled by competing Buddhist schools. However, it was during this period that the Gelug order was founded in 1409 and the institution of the Dalai Lama was established in 1569 with the priest-patron relationship between the Altan Khan and the 3rd Dalai Lama (the first two were bestowed the title retroactively). The Dalai Lamas are said to be the reincarnates of the Bodhisattva of Compassion, Avalokiteœvara.

It was when the 5th Dalai Lama Ngawang Lobsang Gyatso succeeded in establishing Gelug supremacy in Tibet, with the help of the Güshi Khan, that the post took on the dual role of political and religious leadership (however, the 9th-12th Dalai Lamas died before adulthood). After Lobsang Gyatso's mortal passing in 1682, which was kept a secret for 15 years, there was a period of anarchy and invasions that eventually led to the establishment of a Manchu protectorate over Tibet in 1721 that would intensify into a suzerainty in the 1790s in response to attacks by Nepal, be renewed in 1903 when the Brisith invaded, and would last until 1912. Tibet became independent with the demise of the Manchu Dynasty and would remain so until 1950.

Early resistance

In his essay *Hidden Tibet: History of Independence and Occupation* published by the Library of Tibetan Works and Archives at Dharamsala, S.L. Kuzmin, quoting the memoirs of Soviet diplomat A.M. Ledovsky, claims that on January 22, 1950, during his negotiations with Joseph Stalin in Moscow, Mao Zedong asked him to provide an aviation regiment because he was preparing to advance towards Tibet. Stalin approved these preparations and provided military support with Soviet pilots and airfield personnel dressed in Chinese clothes, because this aid was illegal In 1950, the People's Liberation Army of the People's Republic of China (PRC) entered Tibet and the US government made contact with the Dalai Lama's brother Gyalo Thondup who was living in India to offer US help, which was rejected. In May 1951, a delegation representing the Dalai Lama, only 15 years-old at the time, and led by Ngapoi Ngawang Jigmei traveled to Beijing to be presented with the Seventeen Point Agreement for the Peaceful Liberation of Tibet, which established a PRC suzerainty over Tibet: assuming responsibility for Tibet's external affairs while leaving the domestic governance to the Lhasa government and assuring religious freedoms. The treaty was signed by the Lhasa delegation and the 10th Panchen Lama, who had already switched his loyalty to the PRC after flirting with the Kuomintangand conspiring against the central Tibetan government, which still refused to recognize him as the true Panchen Llama. Later there would be much controversy over the validity of the agreement stemming from claims it was signed under threat of arms and disagreements about whether the delegates had the authority to sign.

But at the time, in Lhasa, the Kutra aristocrats mingled with Chinese officials and even prospered from this association. Mixed parties were thrown throughout the year and even by the Dalai Lama himself. The burden on farmers and peasants of supplying the troops with food led to shortages and rising prices, coupled with influenza and smallpox outbreaks, weighted heavy on the majority of Tibetans, who were only marginally surviving before. Protests called "people's assemblies" began in Lhasa, where organizers sent letters of grievances to the government and posted anti-Chinese slogans in public places. The leaders were promptly arrested and the protests stifled. (106-108)

In early 1952, Thondup returned to Lhasa with an economic reform plan that would include lowering taxes and land reform. With the Dalai Lama in agreement, Thondup went about implementing the reforms only to meet with strong resistance from the wealthy old guard who labeled him a radical communist. The label sparked the interests of the Chinese who invited him to Beijing to study, but instead he fled back to India, where he began conspiring with the CIA to form and train a Tibetan insurgency. Again the US tried to convince the Dalai Lama to do the same with an offer of "full aid and assistance", but he refused.

The Dalai Lama saw the need to modernize Tibet and was open to Marxism.

"It was only when I went to China in 1954-55 that I actually studied Marxist ideology and learned the history of the Chinese revolution. Once I understood Marxism, my attitude changed completely. I was so attracted to Marxism, I even expressed my wish to become a Communist Party member. Tibet at the time was very, very backward [...] Marxism talked about self-reliance, without depending on a creator or a God. That was very attractive. [...] I still think that if a genuine communist movement had come to Tibet, there would have been much benefit to the people. Instead the Chinese communists brought Tibet so-called liberation.[...] They started destroying monasteries and killing and arresting lamas." *—14th Dalai Lama*

Indeed, on the Tibetan leader's journey home from his year in China, Khampa and Amdowa clan leaders informed his chief of staff of their plans to rebel against the Chinese in retribution for land confiscation and attacks on monasteries. But all was relatively quiet in Lhasa and in April, 1956 he received a Chinese delegation to inaugurate the Preparatory Committee for the Autonomous Region of Tibet: a 51 man committee composed mostly of Tibetans. Meanwhile, open rebellion began the with the massacre of a Communist garrison in Kham which left an estimated 800 Chinese dead, sparking air strikes that killed more Tibetans. In addition, the CIA met with the Dalai Lama's two brothers Thubten Jigme Norbu and Gyalo Thondup in India and offered to train a pilot group of six Khampas in guerrilla warfare and radio communications in Saipan. They were smuggled out of Tibet and would later be parachuted back in to train others and to report back to the CIA on the insurgency's progress and needs.

According to the Dalai Lama, his visit to India in November 1956, during which he met with Tibetan "freedom fighters" which included two of his elder brothers, "spoiled good relations with China." The exiles encouraged him to stay and join their fight for independence but Indian Prime Minister Jawaharlal Nehru warned him that India could not offer support. Chinese Premier Zhou Enlai, who was also in Delhi, assured him of Mao's decision to postpone for six years further reforms in Tibet. Both Nehru and Enlai counciled the Lama to return to Lhasa.

Although the Chinese let up on reforms, they continued military operations in the areas in rebellion causing thousands of refugees to gather around Lhasa. In July 1957, the Dalai Lama hosted a large ceremony in the Potala Palace, during which he accepted a golden throne and petition from representatives of the Chushi Gangdruk movement and in return gave them a blessing touch on their foreheads, and issued them with a talisman.

They would soon become a 5,000 man strong "Defenders of the Faith Volunteer Army" under the leadership of Gompo Tashi Andrugtsang that would struggle against the Chinese for years. However, in September 1957 when the first two CIA trainees dropped into Tibet to deliver a message from the CIA offering support to the Tibetan leader, it was refused.

The second drop of four men was disastrous: only one managed to escape alive. Meanwhile, by 1958 Gompo's army was doing quite well taking control of large portions of central Tibet.

On March 10, 1959, a huge crowd surrounded the summer palace in response to a rumor that the Chinese communists were planning to arrest the Dalai Lama at a cultural performance in the People's Liberation Army (PLA) camp.

The people were determined not to allow the Dalai Lama to leave Norbulingka palace. A mob riot ensued that at first was directed at Tibetan officials perceived not to be adequately protecting the Dalai Lama but quickly evolved into a full-scale anti-Chinese rebellion.

PLA General Tan considered the Dalai Lama to be in danger and offered him refuge if he could just make it to the Chinese camp. He declined the offer. A week into the fighting, the General ordered two mortar rounds shot toward the palace. At that point, the Dalai Lama decided the time had come to slip out over the mountains, with a very small party, arriving a few days later at the Indian border. He was granted asylum by the Nehru government with the stipulation that he would not engage in politics on Indian soil. Meanwhile Enlai dissolved the Tibetan government and appointed the Preparatory Committee for the Founding of the Tibet Autonomous Region to take its place.

1959 TIBETAN UPRISING

Once in exile, the Dalai Lama's discourse changed from cooperative autonomy to independence. He cited the 17-Point Agreement as proof of Tibet's claim to sovereignty, while at the same time he declared it void because the Chinese had violated it and because, he claimed, it had been signed under duress. He also made clear that he was in favour of economic, social and political reforms, but that the Chinese had not acted in good faith. He closed his first press conference in India in April 1959 by subtly establishing the government-in-exile by declaring, "wherever I am accompanied by my Government, the Tibetan people will recognize such as the Government of Tibet." The UN General Assembly responded by passing three resolutions in the first half of the decade calling for "respect for the fundamental human rights of the Tibetan people and for their distinctive cultural and religious life" and recognising the right of the Tibetan people to self-determination. . The US responded differently.

Already in July 1958, air drops of arms to the Chushi Gandruk had begun, the CIA had relocated Tibetan guerrilla trainees to Camp Hale in Colorado, USA (where a strong Tibetan community still resides today), and parachute dispatch officers had been recruited from among the Montana US Forest Service smoke jumpers (who became known as the "Missoula Mafia"). But according to Thundrop, the Dalai Lama did not know about CIA involvement until he reached India.

As he was announcing his whereabouts, the Khampa rebels were met by massive Chinese forces and were nearly obliterated. While they spent several months regrouping, the US failed to form a coalition of nations willing to recognize the Tibetan government-in-exile or even to find countries who would host the Dalai Lama on a tour to explain his cause.

In autumn, the CIA parachuted four groups of Camp Hale trainees inside Tibet. The first was met by Chinese and the men fled for their lives. Two groups arrived safely and even facilitated successful arms drops, but the Chinese caught on and within a month all but a few of the team members and thousands of Khampa families were massacred. The CIA guerrilla training failed to take into account that the Khampa warriors travelled with family and livestock in tow. The fourth group had about the same luck. They arrived, received arms drops, were joined by two more teams, but in February 1960 the Chinese killed them along with another 4,000 rebel fighters and their parties. One last group was dropped in 1961, but all but one were killed only three months after landing. The survivor was captured and as he says, tortured, until he told the entire story of Colorado. He was released from prison in 1979.

At the proposal of Thundop and Gompo Tashi in early 1960, a Tibetan guerrilla base was established in Mustang, Nepal, where some 2,000 mostly ethnic Khampa amassed in such a disorderly fashion that the first year was a challenge for survival given that the US could not get food supplies to them due to a suspension of overflights stemming from the U-2 incident. By spring 1961, Mustang guerrilla units had begun raids along a 250-mile stretch inside Tibet. In addition, some 12,000 Tibetans eventually joined theSpecial Frontier Force that manned the Sino-Indian border. But as the years passed without any bases established inside Tibet, US enthusiasm over the Mustang fighters dwindled and already sparse and insufficient arms drops ceased in 1965, leaving an aging and barely armed guerrilla force in dire straits. The 25 small teams of Colorado-trained Tibetans who were sent into Tibet from 1964 to 1967 on fact-finding missions had no better luck. Only two were able to operate in-country for more than two months, finding no support from compatriots.

Meanwhile, the CIA provided the government-in-exile money to open offices in Geneva and New York, to arrange for resettlement of Tibetan orphans in Switzerland, and to educate a few dozen Tibetans at Cornell University.

By the time Nixon came to the White House, the CIA had already informed Thundrop that they were terminating support. (296) Years later, he would have this to say about the affair:

"America didn't want to help Tibet. It just wanted to make trouble for China. It had no far-sighted policy for Tibet[...]The Americans promised to help make Tibet an independent country. All those promises were broken...I can't say the CIA help was useful...it really provoked the Chinese [and] led to reprisals. I feel very sorry for this." —Gyalo Thondup

According to author and scholar Carole McGranahan of the University of Colorado, today the history of the Tibetan resistance is purposefully down-played, uncelebrated, and even ignored by the Tibetan government in exile as it does not fit well into the global image it wishes to project and the current official position of seeking a peaceful coexistence with China.

Middle Way Approach

According to the office of the Dalai Lama the essence of the Middle Way Approach seeks coexistence based on equality and mutual co-operation. It is a: "non-partisan and moderate position that safeguards the vital interests of all concerned parties- for Tibetans: the protection and preservation of their culture, religion and national identity; for the Chinese: the security and territorial integrity of the motherland; and for neighbours and other third parties: peaceful borders and international relations."

The seeds of the Middle Way Approach were sewn in the early 1970s in a series of internal government and external consultations. The Dalai Lama was encouraged in 1979 when Deng Xiaoping told his brother Gyalo Thondup that "except independence, all other issues can be resolved through negotiations". The Dalai Lama agreed to pursue negotiations for a mutually beneficial and peaceful resolution rather than fighting to restore independence. He sent three fact finding missions into Tibet and wrote Deng Xiaoping a long personal letter before his representatives travelled to Beijing in 1982 to open negotiations. However, they reported that their Chinese counterparts were not interested in discussing the situation in Tibet, only the personal status and future of the 14th Dalai Lama. Nevertheless, during the 1980s, the Dalai Lama would send 6 delegations to China. In 1987, before the U.S. Congressional Human Rights Caucus the Dalai Lama unveiled the Five Point Peace Plan as a "first step towards a lasting solution".

1. Transformation of the whole of Tibet into a zone of peace;
2. Abandonment of China's population transfer policy which threatens the very existence of the Tibetans as a people;

3. Respect for the Tibetan people's fundamental human rights and democratic freedoms;
4. Restoration and protection of Tibet's natural environment and the abandonment of China's use of Tibet for the production of nuclear weapons and dumping of nuclear waste;
5. Commencement of earnest negotiations on the future status of Tibet and of relations between the Tibetan and Chinese peoples.

The next year, the Dalai Lama addressed the European Parliament and offered what was later called the Strasbourg Proposal 1988, which elaborated on the Middle Way Approach and a vision of reconciliation, resembling what some historians say was a suzeraintyrelationship between China and Tibet. The proposal basically calls for the establishment of a democratic Tibet with complete sovereignty over its domestic affairs and non-political foreign affairs, with China retaining its responsibility for Tibet's foreign policy and maintaining its military presence temporarily.

The periodic meetings between CTA envoys and the Chinese government were, Tundrop felt, "like one hand clapping" and so the CTA suspended them in 1994. They resumed at the pace of one per year between 2002 and 2008. In 2008, at 8th round of talk, CTA envoys presented a document calledMemorandum on Genuine Autonomy for the Tibetan People and a Note in response to Chinese government's statement asking what degree of autonomy is being sought by Tibetans. The Memorandum states that "in order for the Tibetan nationality to develop and flourish with its distinct identity, culture and spiritual tradition through the exercise of self-government on the on the above mentioned 11 basic Tibetan needs, the entire community, comprising all the areas currently designated by the PRC as Tibetan autonomous ares, should be under single administrative entity. It further mentions that "bringing all the Tibetans currently living in designated Tibetan autonomous ares within a single autonomous administrative unit is entirely in accordance with the constitutional (Chinese) principle contained in Article 4, also reflected in the

LRNA (Article 2), that "regional autonomy is practiced in areas where people of minority nationalities live in concentrated communities."

According to CTA, Middle Way Approach enjoys widespread support from the international community as well as Chinese people. In 2008, a group of 29 Chinese dissidents urged Beijing to open direct dialogue with Tibet's exiled spiritual leader, the Dalai Lama. In June 2012, the European parliament in Strasbourg passed a resolution commending the new CTA leadership for its commitment to resolve the issue of Tibet through Middle Way Approach. US President Barack Obama after meeting with Dalai lama on 21 February 2014, issued a statement applauding the Dalai Lama's commitment to non-violence and dialogue with China and his pursuit of Middle Way Approach.

On 5 June 2014, CTA launched an international awareness campaign on Middle Way Approach. According to CTA, the campaign was to counter Chinese government deliberate attempts to spread misinformation on Middle Way Approach. During the campaign, CTA published series of documents, website, documentary film and social media handles.

Criticism

The Middle Way Approach has been criticized by Elliot Sperling as a part of larger "self-delusion" of the CTA. The Tibetan Review points out how the Kashag "effectively edits out even crystal-clear voices for independence".

2008 UPRISINGS

Sporadic and isolated outbursts by Tibetans against the Chinese continued especially during the unrest between September 1987 until March 1989 in the Tibetan areas of the PRC. But it wasn't until 2008 that a large-scale and coordinated uprising erupted coinciding with international protests accompanying the Olympics torch relay that would end in Beijing where the 2008 Summer Olympics were held.

What originally began as an annual observance of Tibetan Uprising Day turned into street protests by large numbers of monks from various monasteries for several days. Crowd control and arrests escalated the tensions eventually setting off a riot by thousands of Tibetans in the Ramoche section of Lhasa on March 14, 2008.

When the police fled the scene, rioters looted and burned more than 1200 Chinese shops, offices, and residences and set fire to nearly 100 vehicles.

In the end, an estimated 22 were dead and 325 injured, mostly Han. Total damage was estimated at $40 million USD. Eventually the paramilitary People's Armed Police were sent in and 50-100 Tibetan rioters were killed before things quieted down. Meanwhile in the Gansu Province, a demonstration by 400 monks were met with force that ignited riots by more than 5000 Tibetans who again burned down the establishments of local Han and Hui people before security forces arrived.

The Tibetan chairman of the TAR government Jampa Phuntsok, who was in Beijing at the time, told the foreign press that security personnel in Lhasa had shown great restraint and did not use lethal force.

However, it was the chairman of the Chinese Communist Party who was dispatched to Tibet to deal with the situation and the Tibetan officials remained in other provinces. Eventually 90 locations erupted in protests. Their common slogans and Tibetan flags indicated desires for independence or autonomy.

Simultaneously, in India a coalition of Tibetan exile organizations- Tibetan Youth Congress (YTC),Tibetan Women's Association, Tibetan political prisoners' movement, Students for a Free Tibetand National Democratic Party of Tibet- calling itself the Tibetan People's Uprising Movement(TPUM) struck out on a "Return March to Tibet" on March 10.

Carrying Tibetan flags and calling for independence, they planned to reach Tibet on foot just in time for the opening of the Olympic Games. Both India and Nepal reminded the Dalai Lama that the Tibetans' welcome in the area was predicated on the agreement of no anti-China political maneuvers from their territories. The Dharamsala government met with the marchers.

When it was clear that the marchers would continue their trek, they were arrested by state authorities in the northern Indian state of Uttarakhand on March 28.

On March 24, 2008 the Olympic Torch Relay began its 137,000 km route. Tibetan exiles and supporters in Paris, London, San Francisco, New Delhi, Islamabad, and Jakarta, Soeul, etc. used the event to stage protests.

In some places they were met by local Chinese and other counter-protesters. The fiasco caused the International Olympics Committee to ban international Torch Relay in the future. The Chinese government blamed the "Dalai clique" for the uprising, the march and the Olympic protests and called TYC a terrorist organization prepared to initiate guerrilla warfare once across the border. The PRC published articles denouncing the various historical plots and activities of the Tibetan exiles as well as US funding to Tibetan activists through the National Endowment for Democracy.

The Dalai Lama denied that his government had anything to do with the Olympic protests and said that he did not advocate a boycott of the games.

He called on demonstrators to refrain from any violence, and gave interviews clarifying that his goals were not currently to seek independence from China. The Dalai Lama threatened to resign over TPUM disobedience to the official policy of non-violence and genuine Tibetan autonomy. His ultimately using Indian state authority to stop the march caused a rift between him and some of his younger followers. In the end, international pressure finally led PRC representatives to renew unofficial talks with their Dharmsala counterparts.

SELF-IMMOLATION PROTESTS

As of June 15, 2012 there have been 38 reported self-immolations by Tibetan monks and nuns in China since February 27, 2009 when Tapey, a young monk from Kirti Monastery set himself on fire in the marketplace in Ngawa City, Ngawa County, Sichuan. Some of the protesters who set themselves on fire were teenagers. Most such incidents have taken place in Sichuan province, especially around the Kirti Monastery in Ngawa City, Ngawa County, Sichuan, others in Gansu and Qinghai provinces and Tibet Autonomous Region.

Self-immolation protests by Tibetans also occurred in India and Kathmandu, Nepal. In 2011 a wave of self-immolations by Tibetans in China, India and Nepal occurred after the Phuntsog self-immolation incident of March 16, 2011 in Ngawa County, Sichuan.

The Dalai Lama has said he does not encourage the protests, but he has praised the courage of those who engage in self-immolation and blamed the self-immolations on "cultural genocide" by the Chinese. Premier Wen Jiabao said that such extreme actions hurt social harmony and that Tibet and the Tibetan areas of Sichuan are integral parts of Chinese territory. According to *The Economist*, the self-immolations have caused the government's attitude to harden.

Self-immolations by Tibetans protesting Chinese domination of Tibet have had a greater impact than earlier protests; despite considerable loss of life during the Tibetan protests in 2008 on the part of both the Tibetan and Han population in Tibet, casualties were simply not reported by the Chinese government. Self-immolations, on the other hand, result in dramatic images of the protester while burning or afterwards which can be easily transmitted over the internet to news media and supporters. Internet access has reached even remote areas in the parts of China where Tibetans live.

New Tibetan leadership

Tenzin Gyatso officially announced retirement from his role as the political leader of the Central Tibetan Administration in March 2011 just before elections were to take place to choose the next prime minister, which would become the highest ranking political office of the CTA. He had talked about doing so at least since 2008. In a press conference in December 2010, he claimed that the "400 year-old tradition" of the Dalai Lama serving as spiritual and political leader had already been terminated because since 2001 the CTA's elected political leadership has been carrying out the administrative responsibilities and therefore he had been in semi-retirement for a decade.

The Chinese government called the retirement a "political show" and said that the CTA is illegal and any moves will not be recognized.

Kate Saunders of the International Campaign for Tibet speculates that governments who have found it politically troublesome for them to deal with the Dalai Lama as a political-religious leader may now be able to forge a formal relationship with him as a purely religious leader. Dr. Lobsang Sangay, a Fulbright scholar and graduate of Harvard Law School who was born in a refugee camp in India in 1968 and who has never set foot in Tibet, was named Prime Minister of the CTA on April 27, 2011.

He has announced that he will spend his five-year tenure in Dharamsala, India, the seat of the CTA. There he will not only assume the administrative responsibilities held by the previous PM, but will succeed the Dalai Lama as the political leader of the Tibetan cause, thus ignoring the PRC insistence that the Dalai Lama be succeeded by means of reincarnation, not another method of selection.

Sangay, who once was a militant of the Tibetan Youth Congress, a group that unequivocally supports Tibetan independence, says he has matured and now supports the Middle Way Approach. Only about 80,000 Tibetans, half of the registered exile population, were eligible to vote because those living in Nepal were prevented by their host country from participating. The 6 million Tibetans inside Tibet and China did not participate. It is unknown if an exile government not led by the Dalai Lama, who was legitimated by religious tradition, will be viable.

Meanwhile the Dalai Lama continues resisting Chinese domination over Tibetan culture and religion despite China's attempts to ensure that after leaving this lifetime Avalokiteshvara reincarnates only with China's approval. One way China has done this is by declaring that the next Dalai Lama must be born in China, thereby excluding anyone born outside their political control. The Dalai Lama has refused to be reborn in China and has suggested that perhaps the bodhisattva of compassion will simply choose not to return to earth after this lifetime.

Secondly, it is traditionally believed that only the Dalai Lamas can recognize the incarnations of the Panchen Lama, who in turn can recognize the incarnations of Avalokiteshvara. In the 11th Panchen Lama controversy, the Dalai Lama recognized Gedhun Choekyi Nyima disappeared from public, along with his family when he was 6 years old, in 1995. The Chinese government says that he is under state protection, but has refused all requests from human rights organizations, including the UN Human Rights Council, to supply any proof of this. The Chinese government subsequently named their own Panchen Lama Gyaincain Norbu, installed at Tashilhunpo Monastery, who was recently appointed to theChinese People's Political Consultative Conference. It will be the PRC's Panchen Lama who will be tasked with recognizing the 15th incarnation of Avalokiteœvara, if the bodhisattva chooses to reincarnate.

8

China Invasion in Tibet

INVASION OF TIBET (1950)

The Invasion of Tibet, sometimes known in Chinese as the peaceful liberation of Qamdo, was a military conflict in 1950 that happened between the People's Republic of China (PRC) and the government of Tibet. It resulted in victory for the PRC, including the capture of the Tibetan Army in Chamdo. Active hostilities occurred from October 6 to October 19th and were limited to a border area controlled by the Government of Tibet northeast of the Gyamo Ngul Chu River and east of the 96th meridian. Negotiations resumed after cessation of military hostilities and led to the occupation of Lhasa by PLA forces in the fall of 1951 and the annexation of all areas under the control of the Government of Tibet by the PRC.

In 1913, shortly after the collapse of the Qing Dynasty, the area comprising the present-day Tibetan Autonomous Region (TAR), became *de facto* independent from the rest of present-day China, with other ethnically Tibetan areas remaining under Nationalist, then Communist control. Both the PRC and their predecessors the Guomindang had always maintained that all of Tibet was a part of China and the PRC had made it a top priority to incorporate Tibet into the PRC, peacefully if possible, and by force if necessary.

After months of failed negotiations, attempts by Tibet to secure foreign support and assistance, and PRC and Tibetan troop buildups, the People's Liberation Army (PLA) crossed the Jinsha River on 6 October, defeating the Tibetan army and capturing the border town of Qamdo by 19 October. The PLA did not go on to annex the whole of Tibet however. Rather, they sent a captured commander, Ngabo, to Lhasa to reiterate terms of negotiation, and waited for Tibetan representatives to respond through delegates to Beijing. Talks ensued and the Tibetan representatives and the PRC Government signed the Seventeen Point Agreement on 23 May 1951, authorizing the PLA presence and Central People's Government rule. The Tibetan government was divided about whether it was better to accept the document as written or to flee into exile. The Dalai Lama chose not to flee into exile, and formally accepted the 17 Point Agreement in October 1951. Shortly afterwards, the PLA peacefully entered Lhasa.

For several years the Tibetan Government remained in place in the areas of Tibet where it had ruled prior to the outbreak of hostilities, except for the area surrounding Chamdo that was occupied by the PLA in 1950, which was placed under the authority of the Chamdo Liberation Committee and outside the Tibetan Government's control. During this time, areas under the Tibetan Government maintained a large degree of autonomy from the Central Government and were generally allowed to maintain the their traditional social structure. In 1956, Tibetan militias in the ethnically Tibetan region of Kham on the border of the TAR, spurred by government experiments in land reform, started fighting against the government. When the fighting spread to Lhasa in 1959, the Dalai Lama fled Tibet. Both he and the PRC government in Tibet subsequently repudiated the 17 Point Agreement and the PRC government in Tibet dissolved the Tibetan Local Government.

Background

In 1913, shortly after the collapse of the Qing Dynasty, most of the area comprising the present-day Tibetan Autonomous Region (TAR) became de-facto independent from the rest of present-day China, with the rest of the present day TAR coming under Tibetan Government rule by 1917. Some border areas with high ethnic Tibetan populations remained under Guomindang or local warlord control. Areas under the control of the Tibet Government are known as "Political Tibet", while all areas with a high ethnic Tibetan population are collectively known as "Ethnic Tibet".

At the time Political Tibet obtained *de-facto* independence, its socio-economic and political systems resembled Medieval Europe. Attempts by the 13th Dalai Lama between 1913 and 1933 to enlarge and modernize the Tibetan military had eventually failed, largely due to opposition from powerful aristocrats and monks. The Tibetan government had little contact with other governments of the world during its period of de-facto independence, with some exceptions, notably India, Great Britain, and the United States.. This left Tibet diplomatically isolated and cut off to the point where it could not make its positions on the issues well known to the international community. Hasty attempts at modernizing and enlarging the military and increasing contact with the outside world began in 1949, but proved mostly unsuccessful on both counts. India did provide some small arms aid and military training, however the PLA remained much larger, better trained, better led, better equipped, and more experienced than the Tibetan army.

At the time of the outbreak of hostilities, the 14th Dalia Lama was 15 years old and had not attained his majority, so Regent Taktra was the acting head of the Tibetan Government. The period of the Dalai Lama's minority is traditionally one of instability and division, and the division and instability were made more intense by the recent Reting conspiracy and a 1947 regency dispute.

The Government of Tibet considered Tibet to be an independent country and in November 1949, it sent a letter to the US State Department and a copy to Mao, and a separate letter to Great Britain, declaring its intent to defend itself "by all possible means" against PRC troop incursions into Tibet. In July 1949, in order to prevent Chinese agitation in Political Tibet, the Government of Tibet had expelled the (Nationalist) Chinese delegation.

Both the PRC and their predecessors the Guomindang had always maintained that Tibet was a part of China. The PRC also had an ideological motivation to liberate the Tibetans from a theocratic Feudal system, although the PRC planned to allow Political Tibet to reform at its own pace and in its own way. In September 1949, shortly before the proclamation of the People's Republic of China, the Chinese Communist Party (CCP) made it a top priority to incorporate Tibet, Taiwan, Hainan Island, and the

Pescadores into the PRC, peacefully if possible, and by force if necessary. Because Tibet was unlikely to voluntarily give up its de facto independence, Mao in December 1949 ordered that preparations be made to annex Political Tibet's province centred at Chamdo, in order to induce the Tibetan Government to negotiate. The PRC had over a million men under arms and had extensive combat experience from the recently concluded Chinese Civil War. The soldiers were well disciplined and well lead.

In February 1950, the Tibetan Government sent a delegation to open a dialogue with the newly declared PRC and to secure assurances that the PRC would respect Tibetan "territorial integrity", among other things. There was a great deal of debate between the Tibetan delegation, India, Britain, and the PRC about the location of the talks, with Tibet favouring Singapore or Hong Kong (not Beijing), Britain favouring India (not Hong Kong or Singapore), India and the PRC favouring Beijing, but India and Britain preferring no talks at all. The Tibetan delegation did eventually meet with the PRC's ambassador Yuan Zhongxian in Delhi. Yuan communicated a 3 point proposal that Tibet be regarded as part of China, that China be responsible for Tibet's defence, and that China be responsible for Tibet's trade and foreign relations. The Tibetan delegate Shakagpa recommended acceptance, with some stipulations about implementation, but the Tibetan government eventually rejected the proposal.

Timeline

The People's Republic of China (PRC) was founded on October 1, 1949. The 10th Panchen Lama expressed support for the new government, and Mao Zedong and China's commander-in-chief Zhu De both agreed with the Lama that Tibet should be "liberated at an early date". The Central Government of China sought negotiations with Tibetan government officials through various channels, but the Tibetan government, led by Regent Dagzha, refused to talk, and instead amassed over 8,000 Tibetan soldiers along the west bank of the Jinsha River. The People's Liberation Army crossed the river on October 7, 1950. Two PLA units quickly surrounded the outnumbered Tibetan forces and by 19 October 1950, 5,000 Tibetan soldiers died in battle, and the Tibetan army had surrendered. After confiscating their weapons, the PLA soldiers gave the prisoners lectures on socialism and a small amount of money, before allowing them to return to their homes. The major town of Qamdo along the bank was under PLA control on October 27.

The PLA then continued on to central Tibet, but halted its advance 200 km to the east of Lhasa, at the line of control of the Tibetan government. Although "the PLA could have gone on to further liberate the whole of Tibet", The Central Government ordered them to stop and heed the policy of "peaceful liberation", and to wait for the Tibetan government delegates to reach Beijing.

Tsering Shakya suggests that by halting the invasion, China wanted to avoid intervention by other powers such as the United States, and that China was also set on winning the hearts and minds of the Tibetan populace. At Qamdo, they treated the local populace well, building roads, and paying locals for their labour. According to Tenzin Gyatso, the current as well as the Dalai Lama of the time, the PLA did not attack civilians: "The Chinese were very disciplined. They were like the British soldiers (in 1904). Even better than the British, because they distributed some money (to villagers and local leaders). So they carefully planned."

The PLA sent released prisoners (among them Ngapoi Ngawang Jigme, a captured governor) to Lhasa to negotiate with the Dalai Lama on the PLA's behalf. The PLA promised that if Tibet was "peacefully liberated", the Tibetan elites would keep their privileges and power. At the same time, Jigme and other released captives testified to their good treatment by the PLA. El Salvador sponsored a complaint by the Tibetan government at the UN, but India and the United Kingdom prevented it from being debated. As the PLA had stopped and was asking for peaceful negotiations instead of entering Lhasa unimpeded, the United Nations dropped the issue from the agenda. The combination of military pressure, reports of good treatment from locals and released prisoners, and the lack of international support convinced the Tibetan representatives to enter negotiations with the PLA.

Despite the Chinese military presence, the Dalai Lama had ample time and opportunity to repudiate and denounce the draft agreement that would affirm Chinese sovereignty over Tibet; indeed, he was instigated to do so with promises of support by the United States. However, he did not, and several months after the start of the negotiations, the Tibetan representatives signed a seventeen-point agreement of May 1951 in Beijing with the PRC's Central People's Government, which affirmed China's sovereignty over Tibet. The agreement was ratified in Lhasa a few months later. Point 15 of the agreement stated that the PRC government would set up a military and administrative committee and a military area headquarters in Tibet that would employ local personnel. PLA troops set up this base in Lhasa in late 1951.

PRC GOVERNMENT PERSPECTIVE

According to the PRC government, a portion of the population in old Tibet were serfs ("*mi ser*"), bound to land often owned by wealthy Tibetan monasteries and Tibetan aristocrats. This however was untrue of eastern and northeastern two-thirds of Tibet where the nomads owned their own land. The PRC government claims that most Tibetans were still serfs in 1951, and have proclaimed that the Tibetan government inhibited the development of Tibet during its self-rule from 1913 to 1959, and opposed any modernization efforts proposed by the PRC government. Announcements were made via Radio Peking on October 25 to state the troops were there to "free Tibetans from imperialist oppression". First generation Communist Party leaders such as Mao Zedong stated that the decision to unite Tibet into the PRC was done to achieve ethnic equality. In July 2001 a monument was established to commemorate the event. Beijing says that Tibet was under an uninterrupted series of PRC governments that has ruled Tibet and China since Kublai Khan. In 2010, celebrations were held on the 60th anniversary of the "peaceful liberation of Qamdo." State media hailed the prefecture's 2010 GDP of 5.8 billion yuan, 140 times the 1958 figure.

International Perspectives

David S G Goodman writes that during the invasion, the Communists mistakenly believed that because the Kuomintang Muslim General Ma Bufang subjected Tibetans to harsh military rule and destroyed Buddhist shrines during the Kuomintang Pacification of Qinghai and Sino-Tibetan War, the Tibetans would welcome them as liberators.

The German Parliament held hearings on Tibet on June 19, 1995, and passed a resolution on June 20, 1996 stating they were "deeply concerned that this independent identity has been threatened by destruction since the Chinese action by brutal force of arms in 1950" and that China had deprived the Tibetans of self-determination.

Robert Webster Ford, a Briton who was present during the Chinese invasion of Tibet in 1950, wrote in 1957 an eye-witness account of how the Chinese treated Tibetans who fought them. (Ford was employed by the Tibetan government when the Tibetan town Chamdo was captured by the PLA in 1950).

There was no sacking of monasteries...the Chinese took great care not to cause offense through ignorance...The Chinese had made it clear that they had no quarrel with the Tibetan religion. Nor with the Tibetan people, who were treated with equal care...

Cleverest of all was the way the Chinese solved their prisoner-of-war problem. They simply had the Tibetan troops lined up and gave them all safe-conduct passes and money and told them to go back to Lhasa with their wives and children. Another newsreel was made of this, and the soldiers did not have to be told to smile. Nor would they need to be told to spread the news of what friendly people the Chinese were...

A Khamba survivor of the garrison of fifty told us..."They are strange people, these Chinese...I cut off eight of their heads with my sword, and they just let me go."

John F. Avedon's *In Exile from the Land of Snows,* however, stipulates that the Chinese occupying forces looted monasteries, initiated public "struggle sessions" (*thamzing*) in which monks and the nobility were beaten and berated, and imposed harsh laws.

Aftermath

Some of the more nationalist elements in the Tibetan government, some operating from self-imposed exile in Kalimpong,

India, started agitating for the a reversal of the Seventeen Point Agreement and the separation of the Central Government from Tibet. However, the rebels were not organized until 1956, when wealthy traders in Lhasa and certain monastery heads became patrons of the separatist cause. Grunfeld identifies a siege of rebel-held Litang Monastery as a precipitous event, although later allegations of state interference in religious affairs outside of those few monasteries that sheltered militants are contradicted by contemporary Tibetan accounts. The rebels received an important boost in recruitment when leftist elements in the Communist Party of China, against the gradualist policy of Mao, started land reform in ethnic Tibetan areas in Sichuan in 1956. By then, U.S. support of the anti-Chinese faction made the movement grow beyond the control of the Dalai Lama, and violence spread to Lhasa in 1959, and the Dalai Lama and some of his government officials. fled to India, where he renounced the Seventeen Point Agreement. Months of fighting around rebel strongholds in southern Tibet had decimated the fighters and, according to the CIA, "the backbone of the rebellion had been smashed." Isolated anti-Chinese attacks continued in Tibet until 1972 when President Nixon pursued a new policy towards China and withdrew military and financial support.

CHINESE INVASION AND DOMINANCE

In 1949 the People's Republic of China began invading, occupying, and colonizing Tibet. China entered into Tibet immediately after the communist victory over the Chinese Nationalists, imposed a treaty of "liberation" on the Tibetans, militarily occupied Tibet's territory, and divided that territory into twelve administrative units. It forcibly repressed Tibetan resistance between 1956 and 1959 and annexed Tibet in 1965. Since then it has engaged in massive colonization of all parts of Tibet. For its part, China claims that Tibet has always been a part of China, that a Tibetan person is a type of Chinese person, and that, therefore, all of the above is an internal affair of the Chinese people. The Chinese government has thus sought to overcome the geographical difference with industrial technology, erase and rewrite Tibet's history, destroy Tibet's language, suppress the culture, eradicate the religion (a priority of communist ideology in general), and replace the Tibetan people with Chinese people.

In China itself, communist leader Mao Zedong's policies caused the death of as many as 60 million Chinese people by war, famine, class struggle, and forced labour in thought-reform labour camps. As many as 1.2 million deaths in Tibet resulted from the same policies, as well as lethal agricultural mismanagement, collectivization, class struggle, cultural destruction, and forced sterilization. However, in the case of Tibet, the special long-term imperative of attempting to remove evidence against and provide justification for the Chinese claim of long-term ownership of the land, its resources, and its people gave these policies an additional edge.

The process of the Chinese takeover since 1949 unfolded in several stages. The first phase of invasion by military force, from 1949 to 1951, led to the imposition of a seventeen-point agreement for the liberation of Tibet and the military takeover of Lhasa. Second, the Chinese military rulers pretended to show support for the existing "local" Tibetan government and culture, from 1951 through 1959, but with gradual infiltration of greater numbers of troops and communist cadres into Tibet. A third phase from 1959 involved violent suppression of government and culture, mass arrests, and formation of a vast network of labour camps, with outright annexation of the whole country from 1959 through 1966. Fourth, violent cultural revolution, from 1966 through 1976, destroyed the remaining monasteries and monuments, killed those resisting the destruction of the "four olds," and sought to eradicate all traces of Tibetan Buddhist culture. A fifth phase of temporary liberalization under Hu Yao Bang was quickly reversed by Chinese leader Deng Xiaoping and led to a mass influx of settlers beginning in the early 1980s. Martial law and renewed suppression took place between 1987 and 1993, with intensified population transfer of Chinese settlers. Finally, from 1993, direct orders of the aging Chinese leadership placed Tibet under the control of an aggressive administrator named Chen Kuei Yuan. Chen proclaimed that the Tibetan identity had to be eradicated in order for remaining Tibetans to develop a Chinese identity. Since Tibetan identity was tied up with Tibetan Buddhism, Tibetan Buddhist culture was in itself seditious, or "splittist," as the Chinese call it.

Chen also was able to use China's growing economic power to invest heavily in internal projects in Tibet, bring in millions more colonists, and he extracted unprecedented amounts of timber, herbs, and minerals from the land. He also toughened up the policies of the People's Liberation Army and the Public Security Bureau.

In 1960 the nongovernmental International Commission of Jurists (ICJ) gave a report titled *Tibet and the Chinese People's Republic* to the United Nations. The report was prepared by the ICJ's Legal Inquiry Committee, composed of eleven international lawyers from around the world. This report accused the Chinese of the crime of genocide in Tibet, after nine years of full occupation, six years before the devastation of the cultural revolution began. The Commission was careful to state that the "genocide" was directed against the Tibetans as a religious group, rather than a racial, "ethnical," or national group.

The report's conclusions reflect the uncertainty felt at that time about Tibetans being a distinct race, ethnicity, or nation. The Commission did state that it considered Tibet a de facto independent state at least from 1913 until 1950. However, the Chinese themselves perceive the Tibetans in terms of race, ethnicity, and even nation. In the Chinese constitution, "national minorities" have certain protections on paper, and smaller minorities living in areas where ethnic Chinese constitute the vast majority of the population receive some of these protections.

In the 2000s, many view the Chinese genocide in Tibet as the result of the territorial ambitions of the PRC leadership. It is seen as stemming from their systematic attempt to expand the traditional territory of China by annexing permanently the vast, approximately 900,000-square-mile territory of traditional Tibet. Tibet represents about 30 percent of China's land surface, while the Tibetans represent.004 percent of China's population. Tibetans were not a minority but an absolute majority in their own historical environment. Chinese government efforts can be seen as aiming at securing permanent control of the Tibetans' land. For this reason, some observers see genocide in Tibet as not merely referring to the matter of religion, that is, of destroying Tibetan Buddhism. Chinese policies have involved the extermination of more than 1 million Tibetans, the forced relocation of millions of Tibetan villagers and nomads, the population transfer of millions of Chinese settlers, and systematic assimilation.

HISTORY OF TIBET BEFORE THE CHINESE INVASION OF 1949

Tibet has a history dating back over 2,000 years. A good starting point in analyzing the country's status is the period referred to as Tibet's "imperial age", when the entire country was first united under one ruler. There is no serious dispute over the existence of Tibet as an independent state during this period. Even China's own historical records and the treaties Tibet and China concluded during that period refer to Tibet as a strong state with whom China was forced to deal on a footing of equality.

At what point in history, then, did Tibet cease to exist as a state to become an integral part of China? Tibet's history is not unlike that of other states. At times, Tibet extended its influence over neighboring countries and peoples and, in other periods, came itself under the influence of powerful foreign rulers-the Mongol Khans, the Gorkhas of Nepal, the Manchu emperors and the British rulers of India.

It should be noted, before examining the relevant history, that international law is a system of law created by states primarily for their own protection. As a result, international law protects the independence of states from attempts to destroy it and, therefore, the presumption is in favor of the continuation of statehood. This means that, whereas an independent state that has existed for centuries, such as Tibet, does not need to prove its continued independence when challenged, a foreign state claiming sovereign rights over it needs to prove those rights by showing at what precise moment and by what legal means they were acquired.

China's present claim to Tibet is based entirely on the influence that Mongol and Manchuk emperors exercised over Tibet in the thirteenth and eighteenth centuries, respectively.

As Genghis Khan's Mongol Empire expanded toward Europe in the west and China in the east in the thirteenth century, the Tibetan leaders of the Sakya school of Tibetan Buddhism concluded an agreement with the Mongol rulers in order to avoid the otherwise inevitable conquest of Tibet. They promised political allegiance and religious blessings and teachings in exchange for patronage and protection. The religious relationship became so important that when Kublai Khan conquered China and established the Yuan dynasty, he invited the Sakya Làma to become the Imperial Preceptor and supreme pontiff of his empire.

The relationship that developed and still exists today between the Mongols and Tibetans is a reflection of the close racial, cultural and especially religious affinity between the two Central Asian peoples. To claim that Tibet became a part of China because both countries were independently subjected to varying degrees of Mongol control, as the PRC does, is absurd. The Mongol Empire was a world empire; no evidence exists to indicate that the Mongols integrated the administration of China and Tibet or appended Tibet to China in any manner. It is like claiming that France should belong to England because both came under Roman domination, or that Burma became a part of India when the British Empire extended its authority over both territories.

This relatively brief period of foreign domination over Tibet occurred 700 years ago. Tibet broke away from the Yuan emperor before China regained its independence from the Mongols with the establishment of the native Ming dynasty. Not until the eighteenth century did Tibet once again come under a degree of foreign influence.

The Ming dynasty, which ruled China from I368 to I644, had few ties to and no authority over Tibet. On the other hand, the Manchus, who conquered China and established the Qing dynasty in the seventeenth century, embraced Tibetan Buddhism as the Mongols had and developed close ties with the Tibetans. The Dalai Lama, who had by then become the spiritual and temporal ruler of Tibet, agreed to become the spiritual guide of the Manchu emperor. He accepted patronage and protection in exchange. This "priest-patron" relationship, which the Dalai Lama also maintained with numerous Mongol Khans and Tibetan nobles, was the only formal tie that existed between the Tibetans and Manchus during the Qing dynasty. It did not, in itself, affect Tibet`s independence.

On the political level, some powerful Manchu emperors succeeded in exerting a degree of influence over Tibet. Thus, between I720 and I792 the Manchu emperors Kangxi, Yong Zhen and Qianlong sent imperial troops into Tibet four times to protect the Dalai Lama and the Tibetan people from foreign invasion or internal unrest. It was these expeditions that provided them with influence in Tibet. The emperor sent representatives to the Tibetan capital, Lhasa, some of whom successfully exercised their influence, in his name, over the Tibetan government, particularly with respect to the conduct of foreign relations. At the height of Manchu power, which lasted a few decades, the situation was not unlike that which can exist between a superpower and a neighboring satellite or protectorate. The subjection of a state to foreign influence and even intervention in foreign or domestic affairs, however significant this may be politically, does not in itself entail the legal extinction of that state. Consequently, although some Manchu emperors exerted considerable influence over Tibet, they did not thereby incorporate Tibet into their empire, much less China.

Manchu influence did not last for very long. It was entirely ineffective by the time the British briefly invaded Tibet in I904, and ceased entirely with the overthrow of the Qing dynasty in I9II, and its replacement in China by a native republican government. Whatever ties existed between the Dalai Lama and the Qing emperor were extinguished with the dissolution of the Manchu Empire.

1911-1950

From 1911 to 1950, Tibet successfully avoided undue foreign influence and behaved, in every respect, as a fully independent state. The 13th Dalai Lama emphasized his country's independent status externally, in formal communications to foreign rulers, and internally, by issuing a proclamation reaffirming Tibet's independence and by strengthening the country's defenses. Tibet remained neutral during the Second World War, despite strong pressure from China and its allies, Britain and the U.S.A. The Tibetan government maintained independent international relations with all neighboring countries, most of whom had diplomatic representatives in Lhasa. The attitude of most foreign governments with whom Tibet maintained relations implied their recognition of Tibet's independent status. The British government bound itself not to recognize Chinese suzerainty or any other rights over Tibet unless China signed the draft Simla Convention of 1914 with Britain and Tibet, which China never did. Nepal's recognition was confirmed by the Nepalese government in 1949, in documents presented to the United Nations in support of that governments application for membership.

The turning point in Tibet's history came in 1949, when the People's Liberation Army of the PRC first crossed into Tibet. After defeating the small Tibetan army, the Chinese government imposed the so-called "I7-Point Agreement for the Peaceful Liberation of Tibet" on the Tibetan government in May 1951. Because it was signed under duress, the agreement was void under international law. The presence of 40,000 troops in Tibet, the threat of an immediate occupation of Lhasa and the prospect of the total obliteration of the Tibetan state left Tibetans little choice. It should be noted that numerous countries made statements in the course of UN General Assembly debates following the invasion of Tibet that reflected their recognition of Tibet's independent status. Thus, for example, the delegate from the Philippines declared: "It is clear that on the eve of the invasion 1950, Tibet was not under the rule of any foreign country." The delegate from Thailand reminded the assembly that the majority of states "refute the contention that Tibet is part of China." The US joined most other UN members in condemning the Chinese "aggression" and "invasion" of Tibet.

In the course of Tibet's 2,000-year history, the country came under a degree of foreign influence only for short periods of time in the thirteenth and eighteenth centuries. Few independent countries today can claim as impressive a record. As the ambassador for Ireland at the UN remarked during the General Assembly debates on the question of Tibet,"[f]or thousands of years, or for a couple of thousand years at any rate, [Tibet] was as free and as fully in control of its own affairs as any nation in this Assembly, and a thousand times more free to look after its own affairs than many of the nations here."

From a legal standpoint, Tibet has to this day not lost its statehood. It is an independent state under illegal occupation. Neither China's military invasion nor the continuing occupation has transferred the sovereignty of Tibet to China. As pointed out earlier, the Chinese government has never claimed to have acquired sovereignty over Tibet by conquest. Indeed, China recognizes that the use or threat of force (outside the exceptional circumstances provided for in the UN Charter), the imposition of an unequal treaty or the continued illegal occupation of a country can never grant an invader legal title to territory. Its claims are based solely on the alleged subjection of Tibet to a few of China's strongest foreign rulers in the thirteenth and eighteenth centuries. If other countries were to make such tenuous claims based on their imperial past, how seriously would they be taken? Are we not, in even considering the merits of China's arguments, accepting the right of powerful modern rulers to invade foreign countries in order to recreate lost empires of their ancestors?

1959 TIBETAN UPRISING

The 1959 Tibetan uprising, or 1959 Tibetan Rebellion began on 10 March 1959, when a revolt erupted in Lhasa, the capital of Tibet, which had been under the effective control of the Communist Party of China since the Seventeen Point Agreement in 1951. Although the 14th Dalai Lama's flight occurred in 1959, armed conflict between Tibetan rebellion forces and the Chinese army started in 1956 in the Kham and Amdo regions, which were subjected to socialist reform. The guerrilla warfare later spread to other areas of Tibet and lasted through 1962.

The anniversary of the uprising is observed by some Tibetan exiles as the Tibetan Uprising Day.

Armed Resistance in East Tibet

In 1951, a seventeen point agreement between the People's Republic of China and representatives of the Dalai Lama was put into effect. Socialist reforms such as redistribution of land were delayed in Tibet proper. However, eastern Kham and Amdo (western Sichuan and Qinghai provinces in the Chinese administrative hierarchy) were outside the administration of the Tibetan government in Lhasa, and were thus treated more like other Chinese provinces, with land redistribution implemented in full. The Khampas and nomads of Amdo traditionally owned their own land. Armed resistance broke out in Amdo and eastern Kham in June 1956.

By 1957, Kham was in chaos. People's Liberation Army reprisals against Khampa resistance fighters such as the Chushi Gangdruk became increasingly brutal. Reportedly, they included beatings, starving prisoners, and the rape of prisoners' wives in front of them until they confessed. Monks and nuns were forced to have sex with each other and forcibly renounce their celibacy vows. After torture, these men and women were often killed. By the late 1950s Tibetan rebels numbered in the tens of thousands. Kham's monastic networks came to be used by guerilla forces to relay messages and hide rebels. Punitive strikes were carried out by the Chinese government against Tibetan villages and monasteries. Tibetan exiles assert that threats to bomb the Potala Palace and the Dalai Lama were made by Chinese military commanders in an attempt to intimidate the guerrilla forces into submission.

Lhasa continued to abide by the seventeen point agreement and sent a delegation to Kham to quell the rebellion. After speaking with the rebel leaders, the delegation instead joined the rebellion. Kham leaders contacted the Central Intelligence Agency (CIA), but the CIA under President Dwight D. Eisenhower insisted it required an official request from Lhasa to support the rebels. Lhasa did not act. Eventually the CIA began to provide covert support for the rebellion without word from Lhasa. By then the rebellion had spread to Lhasa which had filled with refugees from Amdo and Kham. Opposition to the Chinese presence in Tibet grew within the city of Lhasa.

In mid-February 1959 the CCP Central Committee's Administrative Office circulated the Xinhua News Agency internal report on how "the revolts in the Tibetan region have gathered pace and developed into a nearly full-scale rebellion." in a "situation report" for top CCP leaders. When Mao read it on 18 February, he commented:

"The more chaotic [the situation] in Tibet becomes the better; for it will help train our troops and toughen the masses. Furthermore, [the chaos] will provide a sufficient reason to crush the rebellion and carry out reforms in the future."

The next day, the Chinese leader saw a report from the PLA General Staff's Operations Department describing rebellions by Tibetans in Sichuan, Yunnan, Gansu, and Qinghai. He again stressed that "rebellions like these are extremely favorable for us because they will benefit us in helping to train our troops, train the people, and provide a sufficient reason to crush the rebellion and carry out comprehensive reforms in the future."

The PLA used Chinese Muslim soldiers, who formally had served under Ma Bufang to crush the Tibetan revolt in Amdo.

Lhasa Rebellion

On 1 March 1959, an unusual invitation to attend a theatrical performance at the Chinese military headquarters outside Lhasa was extended to the Dalai Lama. The Dalai Lama—at the time studying for his lharampa geshe degree—initially postponed the meeting, but the date was eventually set for 10 March. On 9 March, the head of the Dalai Lama's bodyguard was visited by Chinese army officers. The officers insisted that the Dalai Lama would not be accompanied by his traditional armed escort to the performance, and that no public ceremony for the Dalai Lama's procession from the palace to the camp should take place, counter to tradition.

According to historian Tsering Shakya, the Chinese government was pressuring the Dalai Lama to attend the National People's Congress in April 1959, in order to repair China's image with relation to ethnic minorities after the Khampa's rebellion. On 7 February 1959, a significant day on the Tibetan calendar, the Dalai Lama attended a religious dance, after which the acting representative in Tibet, Tan Guansan, offered the Dalai Lama a chance to see a performance from a dance troupe native to Lhasa at the Norbulingka to celebrate the Dalai Lama's completion of his lharampa geshe degree. According to the Dalai Lama's memoirs, the Dalai Lama agreed, but said that the Norbulingka did not have the facilities, and suggested the new auditorium in the PLA headquarters in Lhasa as a more appropriate venue. Neither the Kashag nor the Dalai Lama's bodyguards were informed of the Dalai Lama's plans until Chinese officials briefed them on 9 March, one day before the performance was scheduled, and insisted that they would handle the Dalai Lama's security. Some members of the Kashag were alarmed that were not also invited to lead a customary armed procession, recalling a prophecy that told that the Dalai Lama should not exit his palace.

According to historian Tsering Shakya, some Tibetan government officials feared that plans were being laid for a Chinese abduction of the Dalai Lama, and spread word to that effect amongst the inhabitants of Lhasa. On 10 March, several thousand Tibetans surrounded the Dalai Lama's palace to prevent him from leaving or being removed. The huge crowd had gathered in response to a rumor that the Chinese communists were planning to arrest the Dalai Lama when he went to a cultural performance at the PLA's headquarters. This marked the beginning of the uprising in Lhasa, though Chinese forces had skirmished with guerrillas outside the city in December of the previous year. Although CCP offcials insisted that the "reactionary upper stratum" in Lhasa was responsible for the rumor, there is no way to identify the precise source. At first, the violence was directed at Tibetan officials perceived not to have protected the Dalai Lama or to be pro-Chinese; attacks on Hans started later. One of the first casualties of mob was a senior lama, Pagbalha Soinam Gyamco, who worked with the PRC as a member of the Preparatory Committee of the Tibetan Autonomous Region, who was killed and his body dragged by a horse in front of the crowd for two kilometres.

On 12 March, protesters appeared in the streets of Lhasa declaring Tibet's independence. Barricades went up on the streets of Lhasa, and Chinese and Tibetan rebel forces began to fortify positions within and around Lhasa in preparation for conflict. A petition of support for the armed rebels outside the city was taken up, and an appeal for assistance was made to the Indian consul.

Chinese and Tibetan troops continued moving into position over the next several days, with Chinese artillery pieces being deployed within range of the Dalai Lama's summer palace, the Norbulingka. On 15 March, preparations for the Dalai Lama's evacuation from the city were set in motion, with Tibetan troops being employed to secure an escape route from Lhasa. On 17 March, two artillery shells landed near the Dalai Lama's palace, triggering his flight into exile. On 19 March the Chinese started to shell the Norbulingka, prompting the full force of the Uprising. Combat lasted only about two days, with Tibetan rebel forces being badly outnumbered and poorly armed. Two American Marxist writers, Stuart and Roma Gelder, visited the Chensel Phodrang palace in the Norbulingka in 1962 and "found its contents meticulously preserved". They did not claim that the Norbulingka had not been damaged.

United States involvement

The United States funded training and arms for the guerrillas in Tibet prior to the uprising and for several years following. From 1959 to 1964, Tibetan guerrillas were secretly trained at Camp Hale by the CIA.

The Tibetan project was codenamed ST Circus, and it was similar to the CIA operation that trained dissident Cubans in what later became the Bay of Pigs Invasion. In all, around 259 Tibetans were trained at Camp Hale. Some were parachuted back into Tibet to link up with local resistance groups (most perished); others were sent overland into Tibet on intelligence gathering missions; and yet others were instrumental in setting up the CIA-funded Tibetan resistance force that operated out of Mustang, in northern Nepal (1959–1974).

Casualties

The Tibetan government-in-exile reports variously, 85,000, 86,000, and 87,000 deaths for Tibetans during the rebellion, attributed to "secret Chinese documents captured by guerrillas". Tibetologist Tom Grunfeld said "the veracity of such a claim is difficult to verify." Warren W. Smith, a broadcaster from Radio Free Asia, writes that the "secret documents" came from a 1960 PLA report captured by guerrillas in 1966, with the figures first published by the TGIE in India in 1990. Smith states that the documents said that 87,000 "enemies were eliminated", but does not take "eliminated" to mean "killed", as the TGIE does. A Tibetan Government in Exile (TGIE) official surnamed Samdup released a report for Asia Watch after three fact-finding missions from 1979 to 1981, stating that a speech by premier Zhou Enlai, published in *Beijing Review* in 1980, confirmed the 87,000 figure. Demographer Yan Hao could find no reference to any such figure in the published speech, and concluded, "If these TGIE sources are not reluctant to fabricate Chinese sources in open publications, how can they expect people to believe in their citations of so-called Chinese secret internal documents and speeches that are never available in originals to independent researchers?"

Adam Jones, a Canadian scholar specializing in genocide, notes that after the 1959 Tibetan uprising, the Chinese authorized struggle sessions against reactionaries, during which "...communist cadres denounced, tortured, and frequently executed enemies of the people." He estimates that these sessions resulted in 92,000 deaths out of a population of about 6 million. These deaths, Jones stresses, may be seen not only as a genocide but also as 'eliticide' – "targeting the better educated and leadership oriented elements among the Tibetan population."

Aftermath

Lhasa's three major monasteries-Sera, Ganden, and Drepung-were seriously damaged by shelling, with Sera and Drepung being damaged nearly beyond repair. According to the TGIE, Members of the Dalai Lama's bodyguard remaining in Lhasa were disarmed and publicly executed, along with Tibetans found to be harbouring weapons in their homes. Thousands of Tibetan monks were executed or arrested, and monasteries and temples around the city were looted or destroyed.

The CIA officer, Bruce Walker, who oversaw the operations of CIA-trained Tibetan agents, was troubled by the hostility from the Tibetans towards his agents: "the radio teams were experiencing major resistance from the population inside Tibet." The CIA trained Tibetans from 1957 to 1972, in the United States, and parachuted them back into Tibet to organise rebellions against the PLA. In one incident, one agent was immediately reported by his own brother and all three agents in the team were arrested. They were not mistreated. After less than a month of propaganda sessions, they were escorted to the Indian border and released.

In April 1959, the-19 year-old 10th Panchen Lama, the second ranking spiritual leader in Tibet, residing in Shigatse, called on Tibetans to support the Chinese government. However, after a tour through Tibet, in May 1962, he met Zhou Enlai to discuss a petition he had begun writing at the end of 1961, criticising the situation in Tibet.

The petition was a 70,000 character document that dealt with the brutal suppression of the Tibetan people during and after the Chinese invasion of Tibet.

In this document, he criticized the suppression that the Chinese authorities had conducted in retaliation for the 1959 Tibetan uprising. But in October 1962, the PRC authorities dealing with the population criticized the petition. Chairman Mao called the petition "... a poisoned arrow shot at the Party by reactionary feudal overlords." In 1967 the Panchen Lama was formally arrested and imprisoned until his release in 1977.

Chinese authorities have interpreted the uprising as a revolt of the Tibetan elite against Communist reforms that were improving the lot of Tibetan serfs. Tibetan and third party sources, on the other hand, have usually interpreted it as a popular uprising against the alien Chinese presence. Historian Tsering Shakya has argued that it was a popular revolt against both the Chinese and the Lhasa government, which was perceived as failing to protect the authority and safety of the Dalai Lama from the Chinese.

In his autobiography 'My Land and My People', the Dalai Lama wrote about the 1959 Tibetan uprising, saying:

"The first thought in the mind of every official within the Palace....was that my life must be saved and I must leave the Palace and the city at once......Everything was uncertain, except the compelling anxiety of all my people to get me away before the orgy of Chinese destruction and massacre began".

THE INVASION AND ILLEGAL ANNEXATION OF TIBET

Treaties in international law are binding on the countries signing them, unless they are imposed by force or a country is coerced into signing the agreement by the threat of force. This is reflected in the Vienna Convention on the Law of Treaties, which is regarded as a reflection of customary international law.

The People's Republic of China (PRC) feels strongly about this principle, particularly as it applies to treaties and other agreements China was pressured to sign by Western powers at a time when China was weak. The PRC is particularly adamant that such "unequal" treaties and other agreements cannot be valid, no matter who signed them or for what reasons.

After the military invasion of Tibet had started and the small Tibetan army was defeated, the PRC imposed a treaty on the Tibetan Government under the terms of which Tibet was declared to be a part of China, albeit enjoying a large degree of autonomy. In the White Paper, China claims this treaty was entered into entirely voluntarily by the Tibetan Government, and that the Dalai Lama, his Government and the Tibetan people as a whole welcomed it.

The facts show a very different story, leading to the conclusion that the so-called "Seventeen-Point Agreement on Measures for the Peaceful Liberation of Tibet" was never validly concluded and was rejected by Tibetans. The Dalai Lama writes that the Tibetan Prime Minister, Lukhangwa, told Chinese General Zhang Jinwu in 1952: "It was absurd to refer to the terms of the Seventeen-Point Agreement. Our people did not accept the agreement and the Chinese themselves had repeatedly broken the terms of it. Their army was still in occupation of eastern Tibet; the area had not been returned to the government of Tibet, as it should have been."

Diplomatic Activity and Military Threats

Soon after the Communist victory over the Guomindang and the founding of the PRC on October 1, 1949, Radio Beijing began to announce that "the People's Liberation Army must liberate all Chinese territories, including Tibet, Xinjiang, Hainan and Taiwan".

Partly in response to this threat, and in order to resolve long-standing border disputes with China, the Foreign Office of the Tibetan Government, on November 2, 1949, wrote to Mao Zedong proposing negotiations to settle all territorial disputes. Copies of this letter were sent to the governments of India, Great Britain and the United States. Although these three governments considered the spread of Communism to be a threat to the stability of South Asia, they advised the Tibetan Government to enter into direct negotiations with the Chinese Government as any other course of action might provoke military retaliation.

The Tibetan Government decided to send two senior officials, Tsepon Shakabpa and Tsechag Thubten Gyalpo, to negotiate with representatives of the PRC in a third country, possibly the USSR, Singapore or Hong Kong. These officials were to take up with the Chinese Government the content of the Tibetan Foreign Office's letter to Chairman Mao Zedong and the threatening Chinese radio announcements still being made about an imminent "liberation of Tibet"; they were to secure an assurance that the territorial integrity of Tibet would not be violated and to state that Tibet would not tolerate interference.

When the Tibetan delegates applied for visas to Hong Kong in Delhi, the Chinese told them that the new Chinese Ambassador to India was due to arrive in the capital shortly and that negotiations should be opened through him.

In the course of negotiations, the Chinese Ambassador, Yuan Zhong Xian, demanded that the Tibetan delegation accept a Two-point Proposal: i) Tibetan national defence will be handled by China; and ii) Tibet should be recognized as a part of China. They were then to proceed to China in confirmation of the agreement. On being informed of the Chinese demands, the Tibetan Government instructed its delegates to reject the proposal. So negotiations were suspended.

On October 7, 1950, 40,000 Chinese troops under Political Commissar, Wang Qiemi, attacked Eastern Tibet's provincial capital, Chamdo, from eight directions. The small Tibetan force, consisting of 8,000 troops and militia, was defeated. After two days, Chamdo was taken and Kalon (Minister) Ngapo Ngawang Jigme, the

Regional Governor, was captured. Over 4,000 Tibetan fighters were killed.

The Chinese aggression came as a rude shock to India. In a sharp note to Beijing on October 26, 1950, the Indian Foreign Ministry wrote: "Now that the invasion of Tibet has been ordered by Chinese government, peaceful negotiations can hardly be synchronized with it and there naturally will be fear on the part of Tibetans that negotiations will be under duress. In the present context of world events, invasion by Chinese troops of Tibet cannot but be regarded as deplorable and in the considered judgement of the Government of India, not in the interest of China or peace."

A number of countries, including the United States and Britain, expressed their support for the Indian position.

The Tibetan National Assembly convened an emergency session in November 1950 at which it requested the Dalai Lama, only fifteen at that time, to assume full authority as Head of State. The Dalai Lama was then requested to leave Lhasa for Dromo (Yatung), near the Indian border, so that he would be out of personal danger. At the same time the Tibetan Foreign Office issued the following statement: "Tibet is united as one man behind the Dalai Lama who has taken over full powers... We have appealed to the world for peaceful intervention in (the face of this) clear case of unprovoked aggression."

The Tibetan Government also wrote to the Secretary General of the United Nations on November 7, 1950, appealing for the world body's intervention. The letter said, in part: "Tibet recognizes that it is in no position to resist the Chinese advance. It is thus that it agreed to negotiate on friendly terms with the Chinese Government...Though there is little hope that a nation dedicated to peace will be able to resist the brutal effort of men trained to war, we understand that the United Nations has decided to stop aggression wherever it takes place."

On November 17, 1950, El Salvador formally asked that the aggression against Tibet be put on the General Assembly agenda. However, the issue was not discussed in the UN General Assembly at the suggestion of the Indian delegation which asserted that a peaceful solution which was mutually advantageous to Tibet,

India and China could be reached between the parties concerned. A second letter by the Tibetan delegation to the United Nations on December 8, 1950 did not change the situation.

Faced with the military occupation of Eastern and Northern Tibet, the defeat and destruction of its small army, the advance of tens of thousands of more PLA troops towards Central Tibet, and the lack of active support from the international community, the Dalai Lama and the Tibetan Government decided to send a delegation to Beijing for negotiations with the new Chinese leadership.

CHINA AND THE PEACEFUL LIBERATION OF TIBET

The People's Republic of China (PRC) was founded on October 1, 1949, and the Central People's Government under the leadership of the Communist Party of China (CPC) became the sole legitimate government of China. This government immediately won extensive recognition from many countries, and won the natural qualification to exercise sovereignty over the whole of the Chinese territory.

From the winter of 1949 to the spring of 1950, the Central People's Government planned the peaceful liberation of Tibet. In the spring and summer of 1950, the Chinese People's Liberation Army (PLA) marched toward Tibet. After having overcome foreign obstructions, put to rout the resistance by Tibetan separatists and beaten the harsh highland environment, the PLA advance troops arrived in Lhasa and various major towns and border areas in 1951. China's five-star red flag fluttered over the Himalayas. China thus succeeded in the peaceful liberation of Tibet, completing the holy task of unifying the mainland. From then on, Tibet no longer operated under the yoke of foreign forces, and returned to the big family of the motherland known for its national unity and fraternity.

The peaceful liberation of Tibet is a joyful historic event for the Tibetans and peoples of other nationalities in China. Xagabba and Van Praag, however, term the move "aggression." They even create the "theory of Chinese Communist invasion of Tibet" to shock the world.

"Aggression" or "invasion" has strict meaning and cannot be applied indiscriminately. It involves standards concerning military behavior of various countries in the world as well as many political issues in the international community. The UN resolution on the meaning of invasion, adopted at the 29th UN General Assembly in December 1974, stipulates that invasion refers to a country which violates, with military forces, another country's sovereignty, territorial integrity or political independence, or uses other forms of military forces which do not conform with the UN Constitution as contained in this resolution. The resolution specifies seven types of behavior: invading, attacking, occupying, annexing, bombing, blockading, stationing troops and other forms of military behaviour. This should be the most authoritative explanation on invasion or aggression.

The above shows the word aggression or invasion contains two fundamental points: First, the invasion or aggression is possible only when the military move takes place between two countries and when one country takes action against another. No action taken on home soil can be termed invasion or aggression; second, the invasion or aggression is possible only when the military move aims at plundering and enslaving the other country, an action which infringes upon territorial integrity and sovereignty of another country.

World history shows many actions constitute invasion, which are aimed at another country's territory and sovereignty and geared to plunder and enslave people of another country. They include the British invasion of India in 1767, the British invasion of China in 1840, the Eight-Power invasion of China in 1900, the Italian invasion of Ethiopia in 1935, the Japanese invasion of China in 1937, the German invasion of Austria, Czechoslovakia and Poland in 1938-39, the German invasion of the Soviet Union in 1941, and the US invasion of Panama in 1989. All these actions constitute one country's encroachment upon another country's territory and sovereignty, and plundering and enslaving of people of another country.

Civil armed conflicts taking place within the same country, though varied in forms, do not fall into the category of invasion. They include conflicts between the Central Government and local government, between various regions, between various nationalities, between various religious factions and between various political groups. Tibet is a part of Chinese territory. Conflicts, including armed conflicts, between Tibet and fraternal regions in China or between the Central Government and the local government of Tibet are the internal affairs of China. Examples include the Qing imperial army sent to suppress the Zungar invasions in Tibet in 1718 and 1720. As the Qing imperial court exercised jurisdiction over Tibet, no one in the world called the two military moves "aggression" or "invasion."

In the early days of the People's Republic of China, PLA advance troops were sent into Tibet to drive imperialist forces out of the region for consolidated national defense and the defense of China's own territory. This constituted the Chinese government's exercise of jurisdiction over Tibet. It was a domestic, instead of an international behaviour, hence legal from beginning to end. Xagabba and Van Praag say nothing of the British military invasion of Tibet in 1888 and 1904. However, they forcibly termed the PLA move in Tibet "aggression." They did so with a view to fundamentally refuting the legality, reasonability and justice of China's peaceful liberation of Tibet. Facts slap them in the face.

In the summer and autumn of 1949, when the liberation war gained much ground in China and was approaching China's Tibetan areas, Britain, the United States and some other countries plotted actively for "Tibetan independence."

In April 1949, US Secretary of State Dean Acheson sent a cable to the American Embassy in India: Washington wishes to see Tibet's military resistance capability secretly beefed up. (A. Tom Grunfeld [Canada]: The Making of Modern Tibet, p.143-144, translated by Wu Kunmin and others) In July, the Tibet Office of the Commission for Mongolian and Tibetan Affairs under the Kuomintang Government was expelled from Tibet by the Gaxag government. In August, Xagabba managed to have Lowell Thomas, a commentator with the Columbia Radio Station of the United States, enter Tibet together with his son. The Gaxag government attempted to stir up an opinion for "Tibetan independence" by relying on the American radio station. During their stay in Lhasa, they held secret talks with the Prince Regent Dagzha and Hugh

Richardson, and met with high Tibetan officials, urging the Tibetan side to organize trained guerrillas to stem the PLA advance troops. In September, the Gaxag government decided to expand its army by 10,000 and reinforce Qamdo and Nagqu. Lowell Thomas and his son called Tibet as "country" and appealed to the US government to offer military aid to Tibet and send diplomatic missions to Lhasa. Upon their return to the United States, they called for the United States to shoulder responsibility for the defense of Tibet.

Reginald Fox, a British spy, plotted construction of the Qamdo Radio Station for Tibet. In July 1949, Robert Ford had it built in Qamdo, and started collecting information concerning the Communist Party of China and the PLA's liberation war. Information thus collected from Xikang and Qinghai was supplied to Lowell Thomas, his son and the Gaxag government. Hugh Richardson and Reginald Fox were responsible for re-sending the information to Britain. At the instigation of Hugh Richardson and some others, the "foreign affairs bureau" of the Gaxag government sent a cable to Chairman Mao Zedong in November 1949: "Please do not send troops to cross the border into Tibet." At the suggestion of Hugh Richardson, Prince Regent Dagzha ordered the Gaxag government to draft a "Tibetan independence declaration" which was revised and turned into English by Hugh Richardson. The English version was brought to the United Nations by Xagabba and Gyalo Toinzhub to seek UN support. Through repeated discussions, Hugh Richardson, Lowell Thomas and his son, and Prince Regent Dagzha sent a "goodwill mission" composed of Tibetan officials to the United States, Britain, India and Nepal in early 1950, seeking their aid and support for "Tibetan independence."

On January 17, Reginald Fox sent a letter to the headquarters of the Tibetan army, making suggestions for its resistance against the PLA advance troops: "It should be extremely difficult for the Communist Party to send troops into Tibet. In order to slow down the advance of the Communist army, various official routes, highways and bridges should be damaged thoroughly. Mines should be planted at various strategically important positions, places where the Communist troops may be ambushed, major rivers with no bridges and mountain entries. Some Communist spies are highly likely to be sent into Tibet to confuse border residents by creating rumors and saying something which will make them change their mind. They will also collect and send information concerning deployment of Tibetan troops to the Communist Party.

"In order to check the possible spread of Communism among residents who are loyal to the 14th Dalai Lama, and in order to stabilize various parts of Tibet, they should be told immediately to prepare for a retreat of at least 20 miles. This is a point of extreme importance. The troops should be deployed in places where the Communist army can hardly cut their escape route and besiege them. Decisions concerning defense matters should be made immediately."

On January 19, the commander-in-chief of the Tibetan army sent a reply to Reginald Fox, expressing sincere thanks for his good suggestion, which he said would "lie embedded in the mind for ever."

Thereafter, the Tibetan army operated basically in accordance with the suggestion made by Reginald Fox. The above facts show how much efforts the British and American forces had made for the control of the Gaxag government. They also show the necessity and urgency for the People's Republic of China to exercise jurisdiction over Tibet.

Patriotic Tibetans, however, ardently demanded and supported the PLA advance troops?entry into Tibet.

On October 1, 1949, the 10th Panchen Erdeni sent a cable to Chairman Mao Zedong and Commander-in-Chief Zhu De: "Northwest China has been liberated and the Central People's Government has been formed. All people who are full of sap feel encouraged. There is hope for the people to lead a happy life and for the country to rejuvenate. Tibet is expected to be liberated at an early date." (Selected Materials on the History of Tibet, p.376)

On December 2, 1949, Kampus Yexei Curchen, who was close to the former Prince Regent Living Buddha Razheng, murdered by the pro-British elements in the upper echelon of Tibet ruling class in 1947, went to the PLA troops in Xining, Qinghai, condemning imperialist crimes in instigating hatred for the Han and sabotaging internal unity of Tibet. He demanded immediate liberation of Tibet.

At a mass rally in Lanzhou on January 26, 1950, the Tibetans protested against foreign forces in their plot to invade Tibet, opposed the "goodwill missions" sent by the Gaxag government of Tibet to preach "Tibetan independence" in foreign countries, and expressed resolute support for the PLA advance troops to march into Tibet. Huang Zhenqing, a famous Tibetan in Gannan, said: "We will mobilize the Tibetan people to welcome with broad arms and support the PLA advance troops in their march into Tibet." (People's Daily, January 28, 1950)

In February, the Living Buddha Geda with the Baili Monastery in Garze, Dege Headman Xage Daodain, and Wanggyai, representative of Kangnan merchant Bangda Doje, and other famous Tibetan figures in Xikang Province went to Beijing to tell the Central People's Government that they would support the PLA advance troops to march into Tibet just like what the Boba Soviet government did in supporting the Red Army to resist the Japanese aggressors in the past.

9

China's Policy in Tibet

CHINA'S CURRENT SECURITY POLICY

In response to the attacks in Africa during the last five years, China has confronted the problem of nontraditional security threats in several ways. The PRC's initial reaction is to work with local governments. "China will cooperate closely with immigration departments of African countries in tackling the problem of illegal migration, improve exchange of immigration control information, and set up an unimpeded and efficient channel for intelligence and information exchange," China's 2006 *Africa Policy* stated.

"In order to enhance the ability of both sides to address nontraditional security threats, it is necessary to increase intelligence exchange, explore more effective ways and means for closer cooperation in combating terrorism, small-arms smuggling, drug trafficking, transnational economic crimes, etc." Beijing has instructed its embassies in Africa to keep a close watch on local security. The swift and successful evacuation of Chinese citizens from Chad also demonstrated that China has developed operational scenarios to deal with these emergencies. The Chinese government has also started issuing travel advisories.

In Sudan and Kenya, state-owned companies receive protection from local armed forces against attacks by rebels. Beijing has signed an agreement with South Africa to prevent the Chinese diaspora from turning into a target for armed gangs. Such measures are designed to help Chinese citizens and companies avoid some of the risks related to operating in Africa, but they do not provide any guarantee for safeguarding China's economic activities if the situation keeps deteriorating. In the case of Sudan, China learned the hard way that prodding instable governments can have drastic consequences. If problems start to occur at the regional level, supporting these emerging states might prove even riskier.

Nor does this narrow security response address China's uncertainty about the military capability of African nations. The dilemma reverts back to the realistic supposition of self-help. Is the PRC trying to safeguard its interests by building up its own military presence in Africa? Bilateral military exchanges are a first indicator to test whether this assumption holds true. According to the Chinese government, interaction with other armed forces expanded significantly, with 174 high-level visits in 2001 and more than 210 in 2006.

This upward trend was not maintained in Africa, however, where such bilateral exchanges have remained stable at an annual average of 26. Beijing has established a permanent military dialogue only with South Africa. Interviews with European diplomats in ten randomly chosen African countries also reveal that the number of accredited military officers in Chinese embassies, i.e., military attachés and their support staff, has barely or not expanded at all in the last few years. In fact, only in 15 countries are Chinese military attachés assigned on a permanent basis.

China's military diplomacy in Africa remains modest, and it has not kept up with the impressive number of Chinese trade officials posted in African nations to strengthen economic ties in the last few years. Military aid is another indicator. Providing military hardware to partner nations can serve various objectives. In a context of competition, it helps to thwart defence cooperation with other states or to prevent other powers' attempts to alter the regional military balance. Defence aid might help a privileged political partner to safeguard economic interests. Whereas these three objectives are motivated by security issues and long-term economic interests, defence aid may well be the result of more short-sighted aspirations. There is no evidence that China's military aid successfully counterbalances other powers, such as the United States.

Apart from Sudan and Zimbabwe, most countries that have received Chinese military aid in the last few years are also supplied by Washington. In 2007, Beijing temporarily froze the supply of heavy arms to Khartoum after pressure from the West. When Nigeria's Vice President, Atiku Abubakar, announced that his nation would turn to China instead of the United States for arms, Beijing's response was reluctant, and no major supply operations materialized. China's military aid programs should not be considered as support for its forays into the mining industry. For instance, between 2004 and 2008, resource-rich Nigeria received only half as much military aid as Ghana or Uganda. During this period, China provided more military assistance to Angola than to Sudan, even though the security challenges in the latter were much greater.

Although violence in Somalia has threatened China's oil exploration activities in both Ethiopia and Kenya, China only made a commitment to Kenya to help in protecting its border. China has, at times, provided military aid, but such assistance does not seem to be part of any coherent strategy related to protecting its security interests.

Finally, self-help would imply the deployment of military forces whenever China's interests are threatened, possibly in an attempt to train friendly armed forces and dissuade any challengers. Yet, such a Chinese military presence is negligible. China has no bases in Africa, as does the United States and France, nor has it trained African soldiers to counter threats to its national interests.

In Sudan, Zimbabwe, Cameroon, and Gabon, China has employed teams of three to ten instructors, but they are assisting in the maintenance of equipment, rather than providing training for combat missions. In Zambia and Algeria, similar examples of cooperation exist but are limited to medical activities. Other major powers deployed naval vessels in an effort to combat piracy and to maintain the maritime supply lines surrounding Africa. During such operations, the Chinese Navy has rarely shown its flag.

In 2000, China sent its newest *Luhai*-class guided missile destroyer and a supply ship to Tanzania and South Africa. A 2002 fleet composed of a guided missile destroyer, the *Qingdao*, and a supply ship, the *Taicang*, visited Egypt. These voyages were gestures of courtesy rather than a reaction to security challenges. They were limited in duration, and no actions were attempted against pirates or poachers. In December 2008, however, the Chinese government did deploy two destroyers and a replenishment ship in the Gulf of Aden to participate in the United Nations-backed mission against piracy. A mission that was only undertaken after receiving a positive signal from US Pacific Command chief Admiral Timothy Keating.

Instead of dealing with security threats unilaterally, China has resorted to bandwagoning. Although in the 1980s and early 1990s, Beijing opposed attempts by the international community to intervene in African security issues, nowadays it tends to join them. Beijing is increasingly recognizing the United Nations' role in resolving the numerous conflicts and safeguarding the sovereignty of developing nations. In the 1990s, China began supporting United Nations (UN) missions designed to implement peace agreements between rivalling parties, on the condition that a well-defined and restricted mandate was included. Traditional peacekeeping operations such as those in Somalia (UNSOM I), Mozambique, Rwanda, and Sierra Leone all were supported. When the UN Security Council decided to dispatch forces to Liberia in 2003, China offered to support the mission and gradually increased the number of its peacekeepers to 1,300 in 2007.

At the same time, however, failed states and national governments that had actively participated in atrocities challenged the efficacy of many of the traditional UN operations. China's focus on the primacy of sovereignty, requiring at a minimum the state's consent, collided with the willingness of other nations to intervene aggressively under the UN Charter's Chapter VII mandate.

Beijing loudly opposed the move by European countries to push for Operation Turquoise in Rwanda, Washington's call to broaden the UNSOM mandate, or France's demand for a troop increase in the 2004 UN operation in Ivory Coast. Despite its strong concerns, China did not veto these interventions at the UN Security Council, but rather abstained and remained aloof from implementation. Sudan was the first instance where China actively lobbied an African government to permit a UN mission on its soil. Via active brokering and indirect pressure, China succeeded in neutralizing the incompatibility between its economic interests and the principle of noninterference on the one hand, and western appeals for intervening in Darfur and the need for long-term stability on the other. That Beijing recognizes the importance of collective security became apparent in 2006, when China was the first nation to ask the UN Security Council for a peacekeeping mission in Somalia. In June that year, at a Security Council meeting in Addis Ababa, China's Permanent Representative to the UN, Wang Guangya, scolded other diplomats for neglecting Somalia and urged them to support the deployment of peacekeepers. "I was reluctant to take on this role," said Wang, explaining that African governments had been pushing China to raise the issue in the Council, "but there was a lack of interest by the other major powers."

Initially, the proposal was tentatively received by Great Britain and the United States, but after various talks in New York, Beijing and Washington jointly sponsored a resolution for the deployment of a UN mission. In 2007, in early consultations with France, China supported a French draft resolution on Chad calling for the dispatch of mainly European peacekeepers under the auspices of Chapter VII. It was significant that China approved the "close liaising" with the Hybrid Operation in Darfur (UNAMID), where earlier it had objected to the development of links between UNAMID and UN missions. "Our support for the resolution on Chad shows that we are prepared to cooperate to tackle security issues at a regional level and that our awareness on the increasing complexity of violent conflicts in Africa grows," a Chinese diplomat explained.

China is also turning to African regional organizations to collaborate on security issues. In the China-Africa Action Plan, approved in November 2006, Beijing vowed "to support Africa in the areas of logistics" as well as "to continue its active participation in the peacekeeping operations and demining process in Africa and provide, within the limits of its capabilities, financial and material assistance as well as relevant training to the Peace and

Security Council of the African Union." In June 2006, the Chinese government granted the African Union's Mission in Sudan $3.5 million in budgetary support and humanitarian aid. Earlier, it provided financial and technical support to the Association for West African States.

Slowly but surely, China is showing itself ready to participate in international efforts to prevent conflicts, fueled by the easy availability of small arms and illegally exported natural resources. In 2002, for instance, Beijing revised its regulation on the control of military products for export and published the "Military Products Export Control List" supplying guidelines for the export of military-related products. In the same year, it signed the "Protocol Against the Illicit Manufacturing of and Trafficking in Firearms," which committed the People's Republic to control the manufacturing, marking, import, and export of firearms, and to confiscate and destroy all illicit firearms. In 2005, the government launched a national information management system for the production, possession, and trade of light arms, and it introduced a system to monitor end-users of Chinese-made weapons to prevent the arms from finding their way to "sensitive regions" around the world via third parties. In 2006, China supported a draft UN resolution on the illicit trade of small arms and light weapons, in contrast to the United States. In 2002, China joined the Kimberley Process, a joint government, international diamond industry, and civil initiative designed to stem the flow of conflict diamonds originating from Africa. In 2005, China allowed a voluntary peer review of its support for the Kimberly Process. Although these actions still have many flaws, they seem to prove that China wishes to do more than just put "boots on the ground" in response to Africa's internal conflicts.

Despite the strategic importance of Africa, China does not try to safeguard its foothold in the region by unilaterally projecting military power. In Africa, its military diplomacy remains limited when compared with defence initiatives in other regions. If the PRC does pursue bilateral cooperation programs, these are more likely to be a part of its diplomatic charm offensive, rather than addressing threats to China's economic and security interests.

Instead of relying on a military presence to counterbalance other powers, the PRC tends to join collective security efforts within the framework of the United Nations and African regional organizations. Over the past few years, this strategy of joint ventures has evolved from passive support to active cooperation. Beijing has softened its devotion to noninterference. While maintaining the primacy of sovereignty, it has become willing to support interventions whenever regional stability is at stake.

Although China has become a revisionist power in terms of its economic aspirations on the continent, it is acting as a status-quo power in terms of security objectives. There are several explanations for this stance. First, China only recently began its economic focus on the African continent. For the past two decades, China concentrated on curbing the military and diplomatic influence of Taiwan; the focus on "economization" of its Africa policy only began in the late 1990s.

Hence, the security challenges it is facing now are a recent phenomena, and solutions to these challenges are just starting to be explored. The PRC is going through the early stage of resecuritization of its Africa strategy, and joining with other nations in an allied strategy can be considered the easiest immediate response. Second, and related to this point, China has not developed sufficient means to back up its security policy with military power. This is a matter of budgetary constraints. Building an independent and sustained military presence is a costly affair and would, at present, overstretch the PLA's capabilities, while Asia remains its primary focus. The PLA does not possess the logistical capacity to support sustained region wide deployment in Africa. Its long-range airlift and sealift, as well as its intelligence and command capabilities, are not up to the task. Third, the Chinese government wants to avoid the People's Republic being perceived as a hegemonic power.

In the initial stage of its economic charm offensive, the PRC tried to pursue a business-as-usual approach, maintaining a low profile and steering clear of political entanglements. That approach is no longer possible now that China stands at the forefront of Africa's political scene, actively altering the economic balance of power. Beijing is well aware of the dichotomy between its weak and strong identities and is reluctant to demonstrate any independent military capacity. Such a show of strength might reduce its diplomatic maneuverability, increase resistance from African nations-just as Washington is now experiencing-and raise suspicions elsewhere regarding Chinese intentions. Yet, as interests, perceptions, and capacities are susceptible to change, the question remains whether China will stay on this track of cooperative security.

China's interests in Africa have changed over the past decades and will undoubtedly continue to evolve. The concept for its security policy in the region will depend on the role that Africa plays as a supplier of natural resources. Africa currently supplies approximately 30 percent of China's oil imports. Beijing and its African partners announced that they are preparing to increase bilateral trade to $100 billion by the year 2010. Most of this increase will come from the import of raw commodities. In recent years, Chinese companies have laid the foundation for a substantial increase in the production of resource industries. Exploration in the Gulf of Guinea, Angola, and the Horn of Africa have the potential for an increase in oil exports to China of more than 80 percent in the next ten years. Chinese companies are just starting to tap the large mines that were recently acquired in Gabon, the Democratic Republic of Congo, Namibia, and elsewhere on the continent. Given the fact that other emerging markets such as India and Brazil are shifting the use of their raw materials from export to domestic consumption, the economic relevance of Africa to China cannot be overstated.

How necessary it is to back up these Chinese economic ventures with more overt security measures is yet to be seen. The incidents described in the first section of this article, the persistent instability in nations, as well as the weak position of amicable political leaders will undoubtedly position Africa higher on Beijing's foreign security agenda and require a more complete approach. The question again arises whether it is in China's best interest to apply its African policy independently or in synergy with other nations. The short-term costs of any unilateral action would certainly exceed those of collective action, but long-term uncertainty about the intentions of other major players might influence any concerns related to cost-effectiveness. If Washington or Delhi decides to change course and contain China's expanding influence in Africa by pursing a strategy of counterbalancing and sea denial, the repercussions for the People's Republic will be dramatic. The concerns of the national security establishments in India and the United States and their expanding military presence in Africa are not unnoticed in China, and they highlight the necessity for the PRC to build a legitimate capacity to deal with crises unilaterally. China's diplomatic identity will help shape policy decisions in support of a more active and autonomous security strategy. Beijing is realizing that the comfortable cloak of frailty it previously presented to the world no longer fits. African partners do not attach much value to China's diplomatic schizophrenia and the complex image of an economic giant, political dwarf, and minor military player it projects. When mayhem erupts, China automatically ends up on the frontline, finding itself hounded by African governments asking it to exercise its leverage. The cases of Chad and Somalia are not the only examples of this. South Africa has accosted China regarding illegal immigrants from Zimbabwe. Central Africa has carefully examined the violent incursions from Sudan. The African Union has called upon China several times to play a more active role in promoting security. The possibility exists that individual countries may be compelled to form a closer alliance with China in order to reduce their current reliance on the European Union and United States for security. Nigeria's announcement that it would rely on China instead of the United States for military support hints at this direction. The ability of the PRC to keep a low military profile is diminishing.

On the other hand, China's self-perception is also in transition. The "Century of Humiliation" is far behind and is being replaced by a national attitude of confidence and assertiveness. Chinese leaders have built on the success of their policy of good neighbour diplomacy that resulted in fewer frictions and more influence in Asia. The People's Republic has drawn confidence from the successful launch of a number of new defence systems. As China sees its diplomatic leverage expanding geographically from the

Strait of Formosa, via Asia to the rest of the developing world, its ability to deal with emerging security issues is likely to follow suit.

Finally, there is the factor of capacity. China is gearing its military for a greater deployment capability. Its large immobile army is gradually being converted into a highly specialized and flexible organization. Simultaneously, the PLA is launching new military systems that will enhance its capacity to transport these forces. In 2007, the Chinese government approved the development of large passenger jets, including military transport variants similar to the American C-17 Globemaster III. Beijing has also ordered several new ships in an effort to enhance its naval transport capacity. In 2006, the hull of the first T-071 vessel was laid.

This landing-platform dock has a range that goes far beyond Taiwan, with the aim of providing sea-based support to operations on land, humanitarian aid, and assisting in evacuations and disaster management. These vessels will be supported by a new generation of large replenishment ships and could be escorted by advanced frigates and destroyers. The Chinese flotilla that was sent to Somalia demonstrates China's new blue-water capacity. The type 052C *Lanzhou*, for instance, is a showcase of the advanced detection capacity for China's Navy. Its multifunction, active phased-array radar has a detection range of 450 kilometres and is complemented with a long-range, two-dimensional air search radar that has a 350-kilometer range and three additional systems to detect incoming missiles and aircraft. China is advancing its ability to pursue a more confident and independent security policy in Africa.

Will all this new found military activity be sufficient to offset the antagonistic response it is likely to provoke? Probably not. If China decides to go solo and to pursue a more aggressive security policy in Africa, it is improbable that it will be able to overcome countermoves by India and the United States. It will be difficult for China to safeguard maritime trade with Africa if India exercises its naval dominance in the Indian Ocean. The sheer geographical divide between the PRC and the African continent makes it extremely difficult to support military activities if the United States or India opposes them. Contrary to China's revolutionary phase of the 1950s and 1960s when trade and economic interests only played a small part, China's increasing reliance on Africa renders it highly vulnerable to sea denial operations or a *guerre de course*. The fragile Cold War balance between the United States and the Soviet Union that allowed Mao to meddle with America's interests in Africa without having to fear political or economic reprisals can no longer be counted on. These days China has much to lose if it provokes Washington or Delhi.

CHINA'S SECURITY STRUCTURE UNDER STRESS

On 18 September China announced a three-point policy on fighting international terrorism: i) oppose all forms of terrorism, ii) choose clear targets in operations and avoid civilian casualties, and iii) mobilize the international community through the UN to take permanent counter-measures under international law. At the APEC Summit in Shanghai the US President expressed satisfaction with the cooperation received from China in the campaign against terrorism. Despite the reservations expressed by Malaysia Prime Minister Mahathir and Indonesia's President Megawati the final APEC Communiqué of 19 October focused on the challenge posed by terrorism. President Bush who had earlier characterized China as a strategic competitor rather than a strategic partner in the language of the Clinton regime now talked about a "constructive and cooperative relationship with China". Bush and Jiang announced "a new partnership for constructing a new world order of peace and stability in the age of terrorism and counter-terrorism". After the meeting with US Secretary of State Powell in Shanghai, Chinese Foreign Minister Tang Jiaxuan echoed the official US view and said on 17 October: Anti-terrorism is the struggle of evil vs. good, the civilized and the barbaric. It is not the struggle between different nations, civilizations and religions." Pleased with this view, Powell stated: "US-China ties have been strengthened by China's response to the US campaign against terrorism". The two sides agreed to have regular high-level consultations on this subject. China agreed to allow the FBI to open an office in Beijing. The US agreed to withdraw some of the sanctions imposed after the military crack down on Tiananmen Demonstrators in 1989. The US-China Business Council was excited by the results of the Bush- Jiang meeting opening even newer avenues of trade and investment. China's strategic meeting with the US anti-terror campaign was essentially guided by its policy of suppressing the secessionist movement in Xinjiang besides the overall priority it gives to economic growth and therefore to trade with the US. (The volume of China-US trade reached $60 Billion taking the second place after Japan's $64 Billion in 2000.) The Xinjiang Uighur Autonomous Region of China has eight million Uighurs and an equal number of other nationalities including nearly 40 per cent of its population as Hans. Since 1996 the movement for a separate East Turkistan has been in the news.

After the riots in Yining in February 1997 the central government of China has pursued what it calls "Strike Hard" (*yanda*) policy. In fact, from all the independent evidence it seems that the terrorist element is still a minor trend in Xinjiang while several different forces seeking political autonomy within the PRC are very active. The Chinese government has taken a number of measures to promote local languages and culture while opposing religious extremism. It has launched the Western Region Development Program facilitating massive investment including foreign capital in this region. But obviously these measures are not considered adequate by the forces of autonomy until the Uighurs themselves manage the structures of political power. The US had cited Tibet and Xinjiang as cases of human rights violations by the Chinese government in the recent years, which the Chinese government refutes. But after Sept.11 the Chinese government disclosed that it had evidence of Osama bin Laden's Al Qaeda having sent over a thousand militants to join the secessionists in Xinjiang. Among the prisoners taken by the US forces in Afghanistan in November and early December were several hundred Uighurs from China who were reportedly fighting as a part of the Al Qaeda forces. That has provided further evidence for the international link of the Al Qaeda with the secessionist movement in Xinjiang. Whether the new campaign against international terrorism will reinforce Chinese government's 'strike hard' policy or there will be a substantive political response to the autonomy movement in Xinjiang will be closely watched in the coming years. Thus on several fronts China's security framework came under stress. US troops now were based on China's southern border. The Shanghai Six institution had been weakened. Sino-Russian relationship had to now cope with a new level of US-Russia understanding and Russia's acquiescence with the unilateral abrogation of the ABM Treaty of 1972 by the US. And the US now had a strong link with Pakistan and had a political relationship with India. Japan had joined the Afghan operation with three of its military ships providing logistics support. Over all, US global domination had got a new lease. On the other hand, China may have got the US goodwill with which it can go ahead with its economic policies, may not expect escalation of US support for Taiwan and even though US has not announced support for China's anti-terrorist campaign in Xinjiang, it may acquiesce with it.

The new strategic developments after the beginning of the US offensive in Afghanistan changed the security environment in Asia. US military presence in Uzbekistan and Afghanistan and the new military relationship of the US with Pakistan and India completed the US military involvement in the whole of the Asian continent. Until now South Asia was a gap between the US involvement in West Asia and East Asia. Besides the US military relationship with Israel and the stationing of US troops in Saudi Arabia the Diego Garcia base represented the American military presence in West Asia. The 32 US bases in Okinawa and the presence in South Korea an d the military relationship with Taiwan and the Philippines besides the Seventh Fleet covering the Pacific Ocean maintained the US interests in East Asia. Prior to Sept.11 there were 800 military installations outside the US operated only by the Defence Department. Now the opportunity for a serious presence in South Asia and Central Asia was presented to the US in course of the campaign against terrorism. President George W Bush who had earlier opposed the idea of "US undertaking nation-building role abroad" now himself led the process of expanding the military commitment in Asia. This is bound to have its repercussions within the US and across the globe.

The strategic convergence that US seemed to have with India, China and Russia at this moment may not balance the political divergence that they have in objective terms. US may be seen as building up its relationship with India as a counter to China. After all, Vajpayee's letter to Clinton on the aftermath of India's nuclear tests in May 1998 did point at the security challenge from India's northern side. But both China and India have realized the costs of their sub-normal relationship in terms of security and its economic consequences. India may not be anxious to become party to a future US strategy of containing China. There are already sharp debates on the issue among the Indian elites most of whom hold the view that India should pursue an independent foreign policy of peace in the tradition of non-alignment and contribute to the democratization of the world order.

Hence India has pursued its policy of improving bilateral relations with China. This process was interrupted by the post-Sept.11 developments causing cancellation of Foreign Minister Jaswant Singh's visit to Beijing in October and Premier Zhu Rongji's visit to New Delhi in November. The process of improving Sino-Indian relations may get a facelift with the visit of Zhu Rongji rescheduled for January 2002.But the escalation of tensions between India and Pakistan following the terrorist attacks on the Indian Parliament on December 13 has complicated the situation. China's post-1996 policy of a balanced approach to India and Pakistan which was evident during the Kargil conflict facilitates the growth of Sino-Indian cooperation while maintaining the close relations between China and Pakistan. Whether that will come under review in the event of closer Indo-US relations and escalated Indo-Pak conflict is to be closely watched. During President Musharraf's visit to China in December both sides reaffirmed their close relationship despite changes in international environment. Considering the long term effects of Sino-Indian cooperation on the democratization and stabilization of world security and the need for a peaceful neighbourhood, China's balanced approach to South Asia is likely to continue.

India and Russia have forged close political and military relationship over the years as a resource of mutual political advantage. The Moscow Declaration signed jointly by Prime Minister Vajpayee and President Putin in November focused on fighting international terrorism under UN auspices. China and

Russia signed a Treaty of Friendship in July cementing even closer relations than in any earlier point in history.

That was definitely seen as balancing force vis-à-vis the US. Putin and Bush have struck a special relationship to coordinate anti-terrorist campaign and reduce nuclear warheads. Their new understanding was evident during Putin's visit to Bush's ranch in Crawford, Texas. In other words, the new US involvement in Asia has to come to terms with all these parallel relationships and is likely to increase military maneuvers in the continent. The regional efforts for peace and cooperation are a positive aid to the people's movements; they are facing danger of dislocation in the new global campaign led-by the US. The Subcontinent of South Asia has as a result of this development been plunged into a new wave of turbulence. The region known for its intense poverty and underdevelopment is fast becoming a theatre of a fresh wave of militarization. In the wake of the campaign against terror India and Pakistan have acquired recognition from the West as nuclear states as the sanctions imposed by the US in 1998 have been withdrawn or are in the process of being withdrawn. Both countries will now be able to acquire military supplies from the US. Withdrawal of sanctions is always welcome as they are part of the global hegemonic framework. But the US arms merchants will have a gala time in South Asia now on. The US has also withdrawn sanctions imposed on Pakistan in connection with the violation of missile technology transfer regime and also in reaction to the military coup by General Musharraf in October 1999. The legitimacy that the US has provided to the military ruler of Pakistan in the recent months has severely weakened the movement for restoration of democracy in Pakistan

Require for Political Reply

Now the forces of the fifth world or the world of people's movements for peace and justice have been greatly weakened in Asia as a result of the US-led campaign. We may see in the immediate future stronger repressive measures in Jammu & Kashmir, Xinjiang and Chechnya with active support or acquiescence of the US instead of dialogue and political response to substantive issues of autonomy. The ruling elites of Asian countries including the BJP in India, the authoritarian monarchy in Saudi Arabia, the dictatorships in Central Asia will be strengthened in this process. Pakistan's movement for democracy, in fact the movements for peace and democratic rights of oppressed people all over the world are likely to face greater repression from their regimes in the coming years.

RULE OF THE CHINESE COMMUNIST GOVERNMENT

The Chinese government claims for this time period are a matter of some controversy. For instance they claim to have "liberated the Tibetan serfs" but many Tibetans were nomads or owned their own land rent free, and for those who were under obligations, there is controversy about whether their status is similar to the European serf and how onerous the obligations were.

Also the system based on recognition of "reincarnated Lamas" meant that any children from any family (though mostly males) might become recognised as the religious and political leaders of the next generation. This unusual system of government has no analogy in the European system. There are other differences as well. Also starvation was common in China at the time, but was not common in Tibet. There are widely varying accounts of the effect of the takeover on welfare of Tibetans.

In 1949, seeing that the Communists were gaining control of China, the Kashag expelled all Chinese connected with the Chinese government, over the protests of both the Kuomingtang and the Communists. The Chinese Communist government led by Mao Zedong which came to power in October lost little time in asserting a new Chinese presence in Tibet. In October 1950, the People's Liberation Army entered the Tibetan area of Chamdo, defeating sporadic resistance from the Tibetan army. In 1951, Tibetan representatives participated in negotiations in Beijing with the Chinese government. This resulted in a *Seventeen Point Agreement* which formalised China's sovereignty over Tibet.

From the beginning, it was obvious that incorporating Tibet into Communist China would bring two opposite social systems face-to-face. In Tibet, however, the Chinese Communists opted not to place social reform as an immediate priority. To the contrary, from 1951 to 1959, traditional Tibetan society with its lords and manorial estates continued to function unchanged. Despite the presence of twenty thousand PLA troops in Central Tibet, the Dalai Lama's government was permitted to maintain important symbols from its de facto independence period.

The Chinese quickly abolished slavery and serfdom in their traditional forms. They also claim to have reduced taxes, unemployment, and beggary, and to have started work projects. They established secular schools, thereby breaking the educational monopoly of the monasteries, and they constructed running water and electrical systems in Lhasa.

The Tibetan region of Eastern Kham, previously Xikang province, was incorporated in the province of Sichuan. Western Kham was put under the Chamdo Military Committee. In these areas, land reform was implemented. This involved communist agitators designating "landlords" — sometimes arbitrarily chosen — for public humiliation in *thamzing* or "Struggle Sessions," torture, maiming, and even death.

By 1956 there was unrest in eastern Kham and Amdo, where land reform had been implemented in full. These rebellions eventually spread into western Kham and Ü-Tsang.

In 1956-57, armed Tibetan bands ambushed convoys of the Chinese Peoples Liberation Army. The uprising received extensive assistance from the U.S. Central Intelligence Agency (CIA), including military training, support camps in Nepal, and numerous airlifts. Meanwhile in the United States, the American Society for a Free Asia, a CIA-financed front, energetically publicized the cause of Tibetan resistance, with the Dalai Lama's eldest brother, Thubtan Norbu, playing an active role in that organization. The Dalai Lama's second-eldest brother, Gyalo Thondup, established an intelligence operation with the CIA as early as 1951. He later upgraded it into a CIA-trained guerrilla unit whose recruits parachuted back into Tibet.

Many Tibetan commandos and agents whom the CIA dropped into the country were chiefs of aristocratic clans or the sons of chiefs. Ninety percent of them were never heard from again, according to a report from the CIA itself, meaning they were most likely captured and killed. "Many lamas and lay members of the elite and much of the Tibetan army joined the uprising, but in the main the populace did not, assuring its failure," writes Hugh Deane. In their book on Tibet, Ginsburg and Mathos reach a similar conclusion: "As far as can be ascertained, the great bulk of the common people of Lhasa and of the adjoining countryside failed to join in the fighting against the Chinese both when it first began and as it progressed." Eventually the resistance crumbled.

In 1998, the Dalai Lama's organization itself issued a statement admitting that it had received millions of dollars from the CIA during the 1960s to send armed squads of exiles into Tibet to undermine the Maoist revolution. In 1959, China's military crackdown on rebels in Kham and Amdo led to the "Lhasa Uprising." Full-scale resistance spread throughout Tibet. Fearing capture of the Dalai Lama, unarmed Tibetans surrounded his residence, and the Dalai Lama fled to India.

In 1965, the area that had been under the control of the Dalai Lama's government from the 1910s to 1959 (Ü-Tsang and western Kham) was renamed the Tibet Autonomous Region or TAR. Autonomy provided that the head of government would be an ethnic Tibetan; however, actual power in the TAR is held by the First Secretary of the Tibet Autonomous Regional Committee of the Chinese Communist Party, who has never been a Tibetan. The role of ethnic Tibetans in the higher levels of the TAR Communist Party remains very limited. The destruction of most of Tibet's more than 6,000 monasteries occurred between 1959 and 1961. During the mid-1960s, the monastic estates were broken up and secular education introduced. During the Cultural Revolution, Red Guards inflicted a campaign of organized vandalism against cultural sites in the entire PRC, including Tibet's Buddhist heritage. According to at least one Chinese source, only a handful of the religiously or culturally most important monasteries remained without major damage, and thousands of Buddhist monks and nuns were killed, tortured or imprisoned.

In 1989, the Panchen Lama died of a massive heart attack at the age of 50. The PRC continues to portray its rule over Tibet as an unalloyed improvement, but a handful of foreign governments continue to make protests about aspects of PRC rule in Tibet as groups such as Human Rights Watch report alleged human rights violations. Most governments, however, recognize the PRC's sovereignty over Tibet today, and none have recognized the Government of Tibet in Exile in India.

Riots flared up again in 2008. Many ethnic Hans and Huis were attacked in the riot, their shops vandalized or burned. The Chinese government reacted swiftly, imposing curfews and strictly limiting access to Tibetan areas. The international response was likewise immediate and robust, with some leaders condemning the crackdown and large protests and some in support of China's actions.

Tibetans in Exile

Following the Lhasa uprising and the Dalai Lama's flight from Tibet in 1959, the government of India accepted the Tibetan refugees. India designated land for the refugees in the mountainous region of Dharamsala, India, where the Dalai Lama and the Tibetan government-in-exile are now based. The plight of the Tibetan refugees garnered international attention when the Dalai Lama, spiritual and religious leader of the Tibetan government in exile, won the Nobel Peace Prize in 1989. The Dalai Lama was awarded the Nobel Prize on the basis of his unswerving commitment to peaceful protest against the Chinese occupation of Tibet. He is highly regarded as a result and has since been received by government leaders throughout the world. Among the most recent ceremonies and awards, he was given the Congressional Gold Medal by President Bush in 2007, and in 2006 he was one of only five people to ever receive an honorary Canadian citizenship. The PRC consistently protests each official contact with the exiled Tibetan leader.

The community of Tibetans in exile established in Dharamsala and Karnataka, South India, has expanded since 1959. Tibetans have duplicated Tibetan monasteries in India and these now house tens of thousands of monks. They have also created Tibetan schools and hospitals, and founded the Library of Tibetan Works and Archives — all aimed at continuing Tibetan tradition and culture.

Tibetan festivals such as Lama dances, celebration of Losar (the Tibetan New Year), and the Monlam Prayer Festival, continue in exile.

In 2006, Tenzin Gyatso, the 14th Dalai Lama declared that "Tibet wants autonomy, not independence." However, the Chinese distrust him, believing that he has not really given up the quest for Tibetan independence.

Talks between representatives of the Dalai Lama and the Chinese government began again in May, 2008 with little result.

CHINESE RULE IN TIBETAN ADMINISTRATIVE AND RELIGIOUS SYSTEMS

These administrative and religious systems were substantially overthrown by the arrival of Chinese forces in the 1950s. Initially there was little change but an uprising in eastern Tibet in 1956 led to a tightening of Chinese rule and, eventually, to the flight into exile of the Dalai Lama in 1959. In Amdo the people refer to 1958 as the date when the Chinese 'came' to the region, when they crushed final resistance and began to exercise a close control over the pastoralists' economic and religious affairs. Over a number of years they were organised into groups for collective herding, all the livestock and its produce being taken into state ownership. The older generations who lived through this period talk of the closure of the monasteries, the persecution of the monks, many of whom were either imprisoned or forced to take wives, the battles during which hundreds of Tibetans perished and the hunger they endured during the collective period. The Cultural Revolution, which began in 1966, saw the most consistent persecution of former leaders and the elevation of those deemed to be from the poorest families into superior positions. One old woman told me that this had been a good time for her, but the vast majority of my informants shuddered at the deprivations they had endured.

After the death of Mao in 1976 a period of reforms swept through China, reaching the Tibetan plateau in the early 1980s. The 'Household Responsibility System' was a policy introduced to try to promote economic development, which had singularly failed to occur under the collective system (Goldstein 1994: 98-99). The animals were returned to the private ownership of nomad families, being distributed according to family size, and along with this went infrastructure developments and land reforms. After a few years all restrictions on the sale and disposal of animals were removed and the nomads became almost fully autonomous again in their pastoral activities. At around the same time most of the monasteries were allowed to re-open and monks and senior *lamas* were released from gaol. The redistribution of livestock has done much to balance out what were previously great disparities in wealth. Formerly many families had no livestock and had to work as servants for the rich, although the class system, which saw aristocratic families elevated to a higher social status in central Tibet, did not extend into Amdo. Initially every family was given enough animals for subsistence, although imbalances are now reappearing.

For administrative purposes the authorities have divided the population into *xiang*, units of one to two thousand people. These have largely been mapped onto the previously existing *dewa*, in terms of both population and territory. There has, however, been some reorganisation of nomadic groups. In Machu county, where there are ten *xiang*, Ngulra, the largest *dewa*, has been divided into two *xiang* and two smaller *dewa* have been combined into one. A defunct horse-breeding station has also evolved into a new *xiang* of nomadic families, named Matang. The Tibetans still use the old names and regard Ngulra as a single *dewa*, but also recognise Matang as a new *dewa*. The *xiang* are governed, as far as the authorities are concerned, by representatives who join the Communist party. These are responsible for transmitting orders issued by the governmental authorities at county level, collecting taxes, organising livestock vaccinations, and so on. As far as the pastoralists are concerned, however, organisation within the *dewa* is undertaken by a council made up of the *gowa* of the *repkor* (*ru skor*), the smaller groups into which each *dewa* is organised. The *repkor* consist of thirty or forty tents, that is around two hundred people, and they often have an identity which pre-dates the Chinese occupation. Their *gowa* are selected in the *repkor* meeting, normally holding office for a number of years. It is two or three of these who are put forward as *xiang* leaders to the authorities (and they have to join the Communist party in order to take up their appointments) but within the *dewa* they are not regarded as having any particular authority. The council, as a whole, takes the place of the *gowa* formerly sent by the monastery or supplied by a hereditary ruling family. Their tasks involve making arrangements for the visit of senior *lamas*, dealing with government authorities and dealing with the 'problems' that arise in the *dewa*, by which they mean cases of theft and conflict. Chinese rule has, thus, resulted in a certain (unintended) democratisation of *dewa* organisation. The position is rather more complex in Golok, where the tribes formerly made up a larger confederacy. Here I found that local control over the leadership of the *xiang* is much less strong and there is no reference to *repkor* (as also noted by Levine, n.d.). My informants insisted that the new leaders are government appointees, rather than their own *gowa*, here known as *xhombo* (*dpon po*). Given the previously strong leadership of the larger tribal groups here the *repkor* were, in any event, probably of less significance, while members of the old ruling families were systematically persecuted and imprisoned during the Cultural Revolution. Now the *xhombo* just do the work of mediators, they told me, but former tribal loyalties are still strong and emerge at times of conflict. Moreover, the *xhombo* still play a crucial role as respected and effective mediators.

Significant material changes introduced by the government have been the establishment of new towns and the construction of a network of roads, a programme which has received new impetus with Jiang Zemin's 'Develop the West' campaign initiated in 1999. These have resulted in major material improvements in nomadic life, as they bring trading points and markets for food and household goods within easy reach of most families. Most nomadic movements can now be conducted by truck, which has significantly eased this laborious process. Schools, health care, post offices and telephones are readily available in the towns and the headman of the group I stayed with in Machu described his plans to improve the educational possibilities for the children by asking the local authorities for assistance with accommodation in town. Many educated Tibetans are able to get salaried employment there, within government offices or the police force, as teachers, medical assistants and so on. Indeed, many of the local government officials are now Tibetans, although the higher level regional administrators are still predominantly Han Chinese. In many ways, therefore, the pastoralists have come to accept the norms of modernity: they value education and respect those who obtain positions as teachers or in government. They have adopted new standards of dress, cleanliness and material wealth and are taking advantage of new economic opportunities.

The authorities exercise strict control in many areas of nomad life, however. As well as levying animal taxes, they oblige the nomads to vaccinate their animals, a process that the pastoralists regard with suspicion and resentment, not least because they have to pay for vaccines they regard as useless.

They also enforce a population control policy, requiring women to undergo sterilisation after their third child. My informants were never very clear about what sanctions the authorities would impose for non-compliance: 'they force the women to have the operation', they said, giving the impression that physical coercion was employed at times. The imposition of heavy fines on a family was also mentioned. This policy is deeply resented and some families evade these rules by giving a child to a relative with a smaller family, but most of the women of child-bearing age that I knew about had the operation, or were resigned to having it when the time came.

Most controversially, the authorities are implementing a policy of fencing the pastureland, as part of the official regulation of pastoral practices, designed to promote ecological sustainability through private land ownership (Goldstein 1996: 12). Land is now officially held by individual families on 50-year leases (Banks et al. 2001), but the authorities have also made it a requirement that the nomads should erect fences between their individual plots, instead of letting their livestock graze together with others in their encampment, as they would prefer. This is much resented by the pastoralists who complain that they can no longer 'go anywhere' with their animals. Boundaries mean possession of land and scope for disputes between neighbouring groups and have been implicated in recent instances of violent conflict . Some groups are able to evade these requirements by erecting temporary fences which make it look as if the pastureland has been divided. However most are resigned to the fact that sooner or later permanent fences will have to be erected. The view of my educated informants in Machu is that this is part of the government's attempts to pin down and control the mobile and elusive pastoralists. These are cases in which the government's actions are consciously resisted, although the scope for evasion is very limited. New sets of norms have, therefore, been introduced, some of which are resisted, others accepted. Very new structures of power and control have also been established, but without entirely undermining older forms of authority.

MODERN ADMINISTRATIVE SYSTEM

Relations between dewa

While the former *dewa* have been substantially recreated as *xiang* under the modern administrative system, the new boundaries and fencing policies have not allowed the pastoralists to revert fully to their formerly flexible land tenure arrangements. A whole *repkor* used to move as a single body, its pasture being used as common property.

Only the winter camping grounds were occupied by the same families on a recurrent basis, building winter shelters of a semi-permanent nature and harvesting a crop of oats as winter fodder. Yeh argues that there has been a significant increase in conflict amongst the Amdo nomads since the area's incorporation into the PRC, which can be traced to these territorial policies . They contradict old forms of socio-territorial identity, she says, precipitating boundary conflicts and giving rise to new forms of domination and resistance. There is much force in this but, as I have discussed elsewhere, the conflict she describes can largely be regarded as a continuation of former practices (Pirie 2005). The new territorial arrangements have occasioned new conflicts but the forms of retributive violence according to which they are played out represent a historic tradition, based on social norms which have persisted into the period of modern state control.

The Amdo Tibetans talk frequently and readily about both actual and potential violence and the men display self-consciously masculine qualities in their daily lives: most carry knives and the lead weighted ropes that they use to round up the animals are also potentially lethal weapons.

They talk as if their neighbours are always just about to attack or steal from them and everyone could tell me stories of fighting and killings that had occurred within their families or villages within the last few years. One of the Ngulra *gowa,* for example, described a fight that had occurred between two men, one from Ngulra and one from the neighbouring *dewa* of Chocomama. The Chocomama man had been killed and men from his *dewa* came almost immediately to take revenge on two men of the killer's *repkor*. The *gowa* told me that they had come right into the encampment to attack the people and this had made the men of Ngulra 'angry' and determined, as a body, to retaliate. A number of men explained to me that they 'have' to get angry if a member of their family has been killed and they must take revenge on a member of the murderer's family. In the event of a serious theft of livestock it is also expected that men of the victim's tent will get angry. Although they may be restrained from initiating a fight, if they happen to meet a member of the thief's family, they would 'have' to fight him.

When a conflict occurs within one *dewa,* or two neighbouring *repkor* who normally maintain good relations, procedures for resolving it are relatively informal.

Mediation is carried out by the *gowa* and there is considerable social pressure on the disputants to agree to a settlement. When 30 sheep were stolen from the tent in which I stayed, for example, the elder son, Jamku, went, with some friends, to identify the thief, on the basis of divination clues given by a monk. When they found him, in another *dewa,* Jamku declared his intention to fight immediately, but his friends restrained him. On their return to the tent members of his family and relatives persuaded him to let the *gowa* intervene and to arrange a compensation payment. The whole matter was settled in this way over the course of a few weeks with an agreement to return the animals and make an additional apology payment. This recalls the informal processes of mediation, and 'community consensus' in favour of peace which took place in the 1930s and 40s (Ekvall 1968).

If Jamku had initiated a fight, however, the violence could have escalated to include his friends, family and, ultimately, the whole *dewa*. Once retaliatory killings have begun, such a feud can only be resolved through more elaborate procedures of mediation. Injuries must be compensated for by payment for the value of the damage and death with blood money, *mnyö rtong* (*mi stong*). Acceptance indicates an agreement by the victim not to fight over the matter.

Conflict between persons or groups from different *dewa*s, which might easily result from a theft or a drunken fight in the county town, is always difficult to resolve, people told me. The process of mediation, in such cases, follows a set pattern and closely mirrors the accounts given by Ekvall for the pre-1958 period (Ekvall 1954, 1964, 1968).

Outsiders, such as monks, initially intervene to establish a temporary truce so the parties can talk. Then it is the task of the mediators, *zowa* (*gzu ba*), to carry out the mediation. These are likely to be the *gowa* from neighbouring *dewa* or senior monks from a local monastery. A meeting is set up in a neutral place, now often the local town, with different groups in different rooms and the mediators acting as go-betweens. Their task, they told me, (and this is confirmed by Ekvall 1964) is not to determine the facts or apportion blame but to determine the appropriate level and nature of compensation. Blood money is calculated after the deaths of each side have been reckoned and set off against each other and depends on the identity of the victims and the nature of the killings. A settlement may also involve apologies, other payments and offerings of religious books. In the case of the Ngulra-Chocomama fight, for example, Ngulra would not accept the normal blood money because men had been killed within their own encampment, but the case was settled by the intervention of a senior *lama*, who ordered a small, but symbolic, extra payment by way of apology. The mediators may also establish where boundaries should run, deciding on a just division of pastures depending on the local history of land use. Crucially, the mediators have to convince the parties that the proposed compensation takes into account all these relevant factors.

Mediation is seen as a difficult and not always successful undertaking. In Golok the *xhombo*, members of the former ruling families, have a special status and are often renowned for their oratorical skills. Even here, however, the *lama*s are regularly appealed to in the most problematic cases. The most senior *lama*s at Labrang, Jamyang Zhepa and Khongtang (until his death in 2000), were very active, travelling throughout Amdo to settle major disputes. It was Khongtang who, as already mentioned, settled a long-running feud between two Golok tribes in the late 1990s, a conflict which had its roots in the period before 1958. They are seen as able to resolve conflict that is beyond the capabilities of local mediators. Tibetans always tell the truth in front of them, my informants told me, and the *lama*s suggest just solutions, *jömdri* (*rgyu 'bras*), taking into account the history of the case. This was a very important concept and often attributed to the *lama*s' wisdom and knowledge of religious texts, history and precedent. The Tibetans always made the point to me that the *lama*s were successful because everyone 'believes in' and 'has faith in' them. They are seen as capable of persuading reluctant and obstinate parties by appealing to their own religious authority. In such cases, therefore, although a conflict may have been caused by a new pasture division, or occasioned by the availability of cheap alcohol in the new towns, the course of retaliation and mediation follow patterns already described by Ekvall.

Now, when there has been a killing or a serious fight, however, the police invariably get involved. Some pastoralists successfully elude their grasp but culprits are generally caught and punished. Some years ago, for example, some animals strayed from the family with whom I subsequently stayed onto the pastures of the neighbouring *repkor*. When one of the boys went to fetch them he was badly beaten by the neighbours. The result was a fight between men of the two *repkor*, during which one was killed by the boy's elder brother. Revenge killings would almost certainly have been carried out had the *gowa* of the *dewa* not intervened collectively to secure a truce. In the mean time the boy's two elder brothers were arrested by the police and imprisoned. The younger was just held for a couple of months but the elder was incarcerated for eight years. Nevertheless, the mediators decided that their family should also pay blood money in an amount which amounted to more than the family's entire wealth and the whole *repkor* had to combine to raise the money. The mediators also decided that the family should be expelled from the area for three years, to remove them from contact with their neighbours. Following this, good relations were restored between the *repkor* and the family has now returned from exile without any lingering animosity.

The Chinese state system of criminal punishment is seen by the Tibetans, in such cases, as completely inadequate for achieving a final settlement to their disputes. 'They cannot produce just solutions they do not care about the history', my fieldwork assistant said dismissively. By treating violence and murder as crimes to be punished by the state, the police fail completely to engage with the nomads' norms of retaliation and compensation. Once fighting has erupted, the norms of retaliation rule supreme and the police, refusing to order compensation in accordance with these norms, are unable to settle them. This would, therefore, appear to be a case of resistance to Chinese authority..

TIBET & THE DALAI LAMA UNDER CHINESE COMMUNIST PARTY RULE

From 1913 until Chinese annexation in 1950, Tibet was a de facto independent polity that controlled its own affairs. However, Tibetan elites failed to enact meaningful reforms that might have protected Tibet from external aggression. The Dalai Lama was only fourteen years old when the Chinese Communists came to power in 1949; Tibetan governmental authority was thus in the hands of his regent and the cabinet of ministers. Historically, Tibet as a political entity was weaker when a regent ruled the country. Not all of the ruling elites agreed with the need to reform the political and economic landscape of Tibet, and the monastic elites were against any changes that would inhibit their leverage over the populace. Moreover, the Tibetan army was small, weak, and had few modern weapons.

Like the Qing and the Kuomintang rulers before them, Chinese Communist Party (CCP) leaders saw Tibet as an unalienable part of Chinese territory. The annexation of Tibet was therefore less about liberating oppressed serfs and more about reclaiming "lost" territory that previous regimes had failed to control. CCP Chairman Mao Zedong realized that the "best strategy was to 'liberate' Tibet peacefully, i.e., with the agreement of the government of Tibet... [yet] military action would be needed to force Tibet to the negotiating table." Therefore, the PLA's 18th army attacked Chamdo, a location in Eastern Tibet, on 7 October 1950. The 10,000 weak troops stationed there could not withstand a Chinese attack. The Tibetan leadership thus decided to negotiate directly with the Chinese to avoid a full-scale invasion of the capital.

On 23 May 1951, Tibetan representatives signed the Seventeen-Point Agreement, which cited foreign imperialism as the root cause of Tibet's claims for independence. The agreement forced Tibetan leaders to formally acknowledge that Tibet was an integral part of China and must therefore accept Chinese rule.

However, the agreement also stipulated that Tibet would maintain its "local" government until the people were willing to initiate socialist reforms. During the first decade of Chinese involvement in Lhasa, the Chinese Government moved deliberately to introduce institutions and mechanisms that would allow it to eventually consolidate its rule and strengthen its legitimacy. However, Tibetans continued to view the Dalai Lama and the traditional Tibetan elites as the legitimate rulers of Tibet, and the Communists faced a great deal of resistance from both the traditional power structure and also many sectors of society in implementing basic reforms.

On 9 March 1955, the Communist authorities formed the Preparatory Committee for the Autonomous Region of Tibet (PCART). Beijing defined PCART as "an authoritative body for consultation and planning during the transitional period before the establishment of the Autonomous Region of Tibet." It was meant to lay the groundwork for future "democratic reforms" in a manner that would gain the support of the Tibetan people. The Tibetan elites continued to ostensibly rule Tibet, but the Chinese began to gain more and more power behind the scenes. A sizeable PLA garrison was also established in Lhasa, serving as the home for both the political and military CCP leadership.

Meanwhile, the Chinese Government had already commenced agricultural reforms in eastern Tibetan areas that had been incorporated into other provinces of China. The Party Secretary of Sichuan initiated Chinese "democratic" reforms in Tibetan areas of the province in late 1955. These reforms disrupted the Tibetan way of life to such an extent that a large-scale revolt erupted across eastern Tibet. Thousands of refugees from eastern Tibet poured into Lhasa and set up camp near the Dalai Lama's Potala Palace, bringing with them grim stories about the impact of the Chinese reforms.

The conditions throughout central Tibet also declined dramatically during this time. Chinese hard-liners argued that it was the responsibility of the CCP to implement reforms more quickly to destroy what they saw as the feudalistic and backwards practices of Tibetans. Mao Zedong was reportedly alarmed by the growing unrest in Tibetan areas and personally guaranteed the Dalai Lama that the Chinese would not implement any policy of land reform in Tibet for at least six years. However, the Dalai Lama could not control growing anti-Chinese sentiment in Tibet.

On 10 March 1959, amid rumors that the PLA intended to kidnap or assassinate the Dalai Lama if he attended a theatrical performance at the military garrison, Tibetans attempted to block PLA movements in the streets of Lhasa and clashed with Chinese soldiers. The situation on the streets of Lhasa grew increasingly tense and negotiations between the Tibetan and CCP leaders in Lhasa broke down in acrimony. On 17 March 1959, the Dalai Lama fled Lhasa to seek asylum in India, where he renounced the Seventeen-Point Agreement and attempted to garner support for Tibetan independence.

The leadership vacuum created by the revolt and exodus of many officials to India subsequently meant that the CCP no longer saw it necessary to focus on gaining the support of Tibetan elites.

The period of quasi-self-rule in Tibet was over; PCART was formally designated as the regional government of Tibet, and the Chinese bestowed new posts upon Tibetan elites who had not participated in the uprising or fled. The Panchen Lama had remained in China, and the CCP appointed him Chairman of PCART. However, it was actually the PLA Military Control Committee that held power in Tibet. In September 1965, the PCART was officially transformed into the Tibet Autonomous Region.

During the disastrous Great Leap Forward from 1959-1962, Tibetans suffered from widespread famine and starvation. Radical political reforms were also set in motion. Likewise, the 1966-1976 Great Proletarian Cultural Revolution (GPCR) was a devastating and traumatic experience for Tibetans. In China proper, one could view the Cultural Revolution largely as an attack on authority, whereby the proletariat and Mao's Red Guards struggled against any "reactionaries" within the CCP who betrayed the cause of socialism by embarking upon a "capitalist road." In Tibet, the Cultural Revolution was perceived as nothing less than a full-scale attack upon the core of Tibetan culture and religion. Red Guards destroyed religious artifacts and buildings; forcibly disrobed monks and nuns from monasteries across Tibet; and prohibited the people from engaging in many traditional religious practices. At the end of the Cultural Revolution, there were reportedly fewer than 1,000 monks in the eight functioning monasteries (out of an estimated 6,000 monasteries before 1949) that had not been destroyed. The physical, intellectual and spiritual foundations of Tibetan Buddhism were decimated.

Following Mao's death in 1976, Chinese policy in Tibet pulled back from these excesses. The Chinese Government appointed Ulanfu, a Mongol and the only ethnic minority in China to hold a senior position in the Party, as head of the United Front in July 1977. His selection as director indicated that the CCP was reverting to policies that displayed greater leniency towards minority peoples. In May 1977, high-ranking ethnic Tibetan CCP official Ngawang Jigme announced that the Dalai Lama was welcome to return to Tibet as long as he eschewed separatism and did not otherwise act to destabilize the socialist regime in Tibet. By 1978,

Deng Xiaoping had consolidated his power and launched the beginning of the Reform Era. The regime also started to rehabilitate religious leaders, such as the Panchen Lama.

Beijing invited a delegation representing the Dalai Lama to observe conditions in Tibet towards the end of 1979. At this point, many of the more liberal policies implemented at the centre had not yet trickled down into Tibet, and the population was still feeling the effects of Maoist policies. As the delegation toured through ethnographic Tibet, it received a sincere and fervent response from the people. The Communist Party apparently was shocked that twenty years after the Dalai Lama had fled to India, he was still revered as a symbol of Tibetan pride and nationalism despite all attempts to subvert and destroy socio-political system of traditional Tibet.

The CCP held a special work forum on the future of Tibet in April 1980 to assess its policy toward the TAR. The conference report noted: "We have been established for thirty years. Now the international situation is very complicated. If we do not seize the moment and immediately improve the relationship between the nationalities, we will make a serious mistake." In order to emphasize that the Party was serious about implementing reforms in Tibet, CCP General Secretary Hu Yaobang arrived in Lhasa on 22 May 1980, intentionally chosen to coincide with the anniversary of the historic signing of the Seventeen-Point Agreement. Hu bluntly admitted that the Communist Party had failed the Tibetan people, and promised to promote liberal reforms in the TAR as the renewed basis for Chinese legitimacy in Tibet. Following Hu Yaobang's trip, the CCP loosened strictures on religious practice in the TAR, perhaps hoping to allow Tibetans to express ethnic identity in a non-political fashion. While political dissent of any kind still was not tolerated, the early and mid-80s were a period of relative liberalization.

Overall, the relationship between the Chinese Government and Tibetans gradually improved during the Reform era, until a series of violent events shattered this relative calm. The Tibetan exile authorities in India had long been engaged in an effort to interest the international community in the plight of the Tibetan people, and by the mid-to-late 1980's this effort was finally beginning to bear fruit. Sensing an opening as economic reforms gathered steam and the Chinese leadership appeared increasingly open to the world, the Tibetans inaugurated an international campaign to leverage Western support for Tibet and pry additional concessions from Beijing. The new approach rapidly gained support in the United States. On 21 September 1987, the Dalai Lama spoke on Capitol Hill for the first time, at the invitation of the Congressional Human Rights Caucus, and articulated a five-point proposal for rectifying the Tibet issue.

These developments had an almost immediate effect on people inside Tibet. After a small monk-led protest in Lhasa on 27 September, thousands of Tibetans marched through the streets of Lhasa on Chinese National Day and clashed with police. On March 1988, monks gathered in Lhasa for the Monlam religious festival and again launched protests that ended in violence. Protests continued throughout the year. By March 1989, as the thirtieth anniversary of the 1959 uprising approached, Lhasa was extremely tense and Chinese authorities retreated from their liberalized policies on cultural and religious expression. In a foreshadoing of events to come in Beijing, large scale protests in Lhasa on 10 March 1989 were violently put down by security forces using live fire on demonstrators; estimates of dead ranged from dozens to hundreds. Then-TAR Party Secretary Hu Jintao imposed martial law and imprisoned large numbers of monks and nuns.

HISTORICAL BACKGROUND AND ANALYSIS OF THE SELECTION PROCESS

The PRC and its predecessors in China have long struggled to maintain stability along its western periphery, where concentrated communities of ethnic and religious minorities reside. During the past four years, Beijing has been forced to contend with violent clashes between ethnically Turkic Uyghurs and Han migrants in Xinjiang; widespread protests by Tibetans throughout ethnographic Tibet (i.e. the present-day Tibet Autonomous Region and Tibetan areas of Qinghai, Gansu, Sichuan, and Yunnan provinces) that have at times flared into violence; andrecently, unprecedented protests by ethnic Mongols across the Inner Mongolian Autonomous Region.

Efforts to influence the selection of important Tibetan lamas have been a key element of the exercise and consolidation of political authority in Tibetan areas since the establishment of the theocratic state in Tibet, for both distant imperial authorities as well as Tibetans themselves. The history of theocratic rule in Tibet is intimately intertwined with Chinese imperial politics, with influence waxing and waning as empires rose and fell. At the time Tibet was incorporated into the Mongol Empire (and subsequently the Mongol-led Yuan Dynasty), imperial authorities cultivated lamas from the Sakya school of Tibetan Buddhism, which was pre-eminent in Tibet.

However, Tibet was rife with political and sectarian conflicts, into which both Mongol and Chinese imperial authorities often inserted themselves or were drawn by Tibetan parties. During the thirteenth and fourteenth centuries, the Gelukpa school rose to challenge the Sakya and Kagyu schools for political and religious leadership. After unseating the Sakya through alliance with a powerful secular Tibetan prince, the Geluk achieved an alliance with the Mongols and came to dominate political authority in Tibet. In 1578, the Mongol khan gave a senior Gelukpa monk named Sonam Gyatso the title Dalai Lama. By this time, however, Mongol rulers had long ceased to govern China and there is substantial dispute among scholars regarding the exact nature of Tibetan relations with then-ruling Ming court, with most Western scholars contending that the Ming did not exercise sovereignty or actual control over Tibet.

As Manchu warriors conquered the crumbling Ming Empire (1368-1644) and consolidated their rule in China, the Gelukpa sect was likewise further consolidating power in Tibet. Scholars differ on the significance of early relations between the emerging Tibetan and Qing imperial powers (Qing Dynasty: 1644-1911), but during this period, Tibet was generally under direct lamaist rule with some element of Mongol protection. In 1642, the Mongol khanate ceremoniously bestowed the conquered Tibetan lands upon the Fifth Dalai Lama, but reserved the title of king of Tibet for himself and his successors until the last such ruler died in the early eighteenth century, at which point the Qing emperor assumed the role of designating or at least recognizing Tibetan spiritual leaders. In 1652, the Qing Emperor Shunzhi invited the Fifth Dalai Lama to Beijing for an official visit. Some scholars believe that a priest-patron relationship subsequently emerged, whereby the Qing Emperor sought the spiritual patronage of the Fifth Dalai Lama much as its Yuan predecessors had done. Following the Dalai Lama's visit, reports from the Imperial Colonial Office note that it liaised with the Dalai Lama in his capacity as "spiritual leader and temporal adjudicator of selected affairs among the populations of eastern Mongolia and Qinghai." The Qing court began to monitor and even attempted to direct the Dalai Lamas, with limited success. By 1661, the Imperial Colonial Office considered itself to be supervising the selection process of key lamas. Nonetheless, the Qing court felt threatened by the Dzungar tribes of the northwest, whose influence had permeated Tibet by the early eighteenth century, and launched multiple attacks on Lhasa between 1718 and 1720, in the name of defeating the Dzungars. Some scholars argue that when Qing leaders subsequently established a military garrison as well as installed imperial commissioners (ambans) in Lhasa, they dissolved the monarchy and effectively stripped Tibet of its sovereignty.

However, other scholars maintain that "under the influence of the Qing dynasty, the Dalai Lama's nominal leadership of Tibet continued in name with various restrictions, including the creation of a short-lived Tibetan monarchal institution." Although acknowledging the presence of ambans in Lhasa, Gray Tuttle's extensive study of this period asserts that "Gelukpa prelates largely served as the actual rulers of Tibet, in the capacity of regents for a series of young Dalai Lamas who died before, or shortly after, they reached maturity." Qing historian Evelyn S. Rawski and others also assert that the imperial presence in Lhasa was initially more indirect. Only after the murder of two ambans, stemming from their involvement in a local political dispute, did the Qing emperor take greater notice of the situation in Lhasa in 1750. The Qing emperor responded with a dual strategy of enlarging the garrison in Lhasa while again recognizing the secular and religious authority of the Dalai Lama. Qianlong also established a council of ministers and instructed the ambans to monitor Tibetan affairs more closely. Nonetheless, Tibet scholar Melvyn Goldstein argues that from the time the protectorate was created in 1727, actual Qing authority over Tibet remained limited despite a lack of Tibetan cohesive internal unity. The Qianlong Emperor himself remarked in 1792 that the quality of ambans sent to Lhasa was quite poor, and it was thus relatively easy for the Dalai Lama and his ministers to ignore them.

The Manchu military intervention and subsequent attempt to gain greater influence may have represented the apex of Qing power in Tibet. Weary of Tibetan intrigues, in 1792, the Qianlong Emperor called for a complete restructuring of the Tibetan government in a document called "Twenty-Nine Regulations for Better Government in Tibet." It included a lottery system to assist in the selection of key incarnations, whereby Manchu officials would place the names of the candidate(s) – provided by ecclesiastical authorities, and divined through traditional methods – into a golden urn. An amban drew lots from the urn and chose the name of the successful candidate. The Qing reportedly developed this practice to avert manipulation of the selection process by politically prominent Tibetan families, as the discovery of an incarnate lama in such a family could certainly enhance its standing and political fortunes. Likewise, the regulations forbade relatives of high-ranking incarnate lamas from aspiring to public office. The emperor continued efforts to raise the status of the ambans in Tibet in order to assert greater influence over administrative decisions and key appointments. However, internal unrest in China during the second half of the nineteenth century largely undermined the ability of his successors to influence Tibetan affairs.

From 1792 until the end of the Republican period in 1949, in practice the Tibetans infrequently used the golden urn to select important reincarnate lamas, especially during times when authorities in Beijing were unable to assert effective influence over Tibetan affairs. Even modern PRC historians admit that the use of the urn process was inconsistent to the point of being nearly discretionary. Chinese scholar Ya Hanzhang notes that Tibetan authorities sought and apparently received permission from Qing authorities to forgo the normal procedures when there was only a single undisputed candidate, as was the case with the Ninth (Lungtok Gyatso, recognized in 1807) and Thirteenth (Thupten Gyatso, recognized in 1877) Dalai Lamas. The Fourteenth Dalai Lama, for his part, asserts that the urn method was used for the selection of only one of his predecessors, the Eleventh, and that in other cases it was either not used at all or only after-the-fact to placate Manchu authorities. In short, there is considerable debate about the degree to which Tibetan authorities utilized the golden urn process out of a sense of imperial obligation, as a convenient means of settling difficult internal disputes, or some combination of the two.

At the turn of the twentieth century, British attempts to expand their influence beyond India and into Tibet led to an "activist, annexationist Chinese policy toward Tibet" whereby the Qing court again attempted to directly intervene in Tibetan affairs. While the Younghusband Expedition initially resulted in negotiations between Tibetan and British authorities, the British Foreign Office quickly pulled them back and acknowledged Chinese preeminence in Tibet via the 1906 Anglo-Chinese Convention. After the British withdrawal, the Thirteenth Dalai Lama travelled to Beijing to negotiate directly with the Qing emperor over his and Tibet's status. The Manchu court treated him as a subordinate, and instructed him to "obey the laws of the Sovereign State China.... [and] exhort the Tibetans to be obedient." The Chinese even arranged all of the Dalai Lama's meetings with foreign officials in Beijing. As Goldstein succinctly states, the Chinese made it clear that "he was subordinate to the emperor and that his position in Tibet was dependent on their goodwill."

The situation worsened when the Dalai Lama subsequently attempted to return to Lhasa. The Qing authorized General Zhao Erfeng, who was named an amban in 1908, to dispatch two thousand soldiers to Lhasa to control the Dalai Lama. Realizing that he faced grave danger, the Dalai Lama fled to Darjeeling, India in early

1910. The Chinese acted to strip him of not only his authority, but also his incarnate status. The Dalai Lama appealed to the Chinese to allow the British to act as intermediaries to negotiate a solution to the political crisis in Tibet. Yet, before such an arrangement could be undertaken, the Qing Dynasty collapsed, leaving China in chaos. Chinese troops stationed in Tibet withdrew and departed overland through India. The Dalai Lama arrived back in Lhasa in January 1913. This was the first time since the early eighteenth century there were no Chinese soldiers on Tibetan soil.

During the Republican Period (1911-1949), turmoil in China allowed Tibet to assert de-facto independence. During his time in India, the Thirteenth Dalai Lama had become friends with Sir Charles Bell, the political officer in Sikkim for British India. Bell shaped his thoughts on the importance of creating modern political institutions, a modern bureaucracy, and a modern army in Tibet. Upon his return to Lhasa, the Dalai Lama began to implement these new ideas on how to develop a modern Tibetan state. These modernization efforts were frequently frustrated by the conservative Tibetan political and ecclesiastical elements, however, and failed to materialize as hoped.

Yuan Shikai, the Republic of China's Provisional President, sent the Dalai Lama a letter in fall 1912 that invited him to take up his post as spiritual leader of Tibet and serve the fledgling Chinese state. In response, the Dalai Lama stated that he did not require Yuan's permission to return to power, and fully intended to assert his rule in Tibet. Coupled with a proclamation issued twenty-two days later, these statements arguably constitute a declaration of Tibetan independence. However, subsequent negotiations between the British, Chinese, and Tibetans resulted in the 1914 Simla Convention, which proclaimed Chinese 'suzerainty' – but not sovereignty – over Tibet. Following the close of negotiations, it became clear this arrangement satisfied neither the Republic of China (ROC), which claimed Tibet as an integral part of its territory, nor Tibet, which saw itself as an independent state. The ROC disagreed with Lhasa authorities on where to draw the borders of Tibet and finally refused to sign the accord. Britain and Tibet decided to sign a bilateral note based on the convention, leaving the actual convention unsigned by any party.

Generalissimo Chiang Kai-shek saw the death of the Thirteenth Dalai Lama in 1933 as an opportunity to reassert Chinese authority at the time of the selection of the next reincarnation. An official ROC policy document promulgated on 10 February 1936, entitled "Methods for the Reincarnation of Lamas," contained thirteen articles describing the means by which the candidate selection process should occur for all high-ranking incarnate lamas. It stipulated that Republican leaders would play a role in the selection process, and also required the use of the golden urn. Yet, it appears that the Republican regulations had little impact in Tibet. Republican scholar Hsiao-ting Lin argues that even after the Kuomintang established a new mission in Lhasa in 1934, Nanjing remained largely unfocused on Tibet policy and failed to implement any concrete initiatives there. Following the death of the Thirteenth Dalai Lama in 1933, Tibetan religious leaders compiled a list of fourteen potential candidates using traditional methods of divination. They eventually selected a bright young boy named Lhamo Dondrup from a small village in the Tibetan area known as Amdo (present-day Qinghai province) as the Fourteenth Dalai Lama. The search team initially attempted to keep its selection secret. It feared that Ma Bufang, the local warlord in Qinghai, might either demand an exorbitant bribe before allowing the chosen candidate to leave or send a military escort with the boy to remain in Lhasa. When the team finally asked Ma permission to have the boy sent to Kumbum Monastery en route to Lhasa, the warlord repeatedly asked for large sums of money totaling 400,000 silver coins, as well as other favors.

Lhasa eventually asked the Kuomintang government whether it could convince Ma to free the young reincarnate from virtual house arrest. Nanjing subsequently responded by making its own demands, including the right to escort the Dalai Lama to Lhasa and also send a Chinese official representative to the ceremony, so that he could bestow a Chinese title upon the monk. Lhasa refused to agree to all of the initial terms set forth by Nanjing, but an agreement was eventually reached. On 29 March 1939, the Kuomintang announced that it would dispatch Wu Zhongxin, Chairman of the Commission for Mongolian and Tibetan Affairs, to Tibet as its official representative during the selection and enthronement ceremonies. Interestingly, the British Mission in Lhasa reported at the time that the ROC had previously requested Chinese representation at the enthronement of the Dalai Lama, but implied that Lhasa had rebuffed its request.

There is a strong continuity between Imperial and Republican approaches to the institution of the Dalai Lama. Even after the Qing Dynasty fell, it was a Chinese government priority to assert authority over all lands held during the height of the Qing Empire. Although the Republic of China was far too weak to establish effective control over Tibet during this time period, it never relinquished its claims there.

In the end, the Chinese Republican leadership had no input into the selection process of the Fourteenth Dalai Lama, and possessed no function during the ceremony. The lack of Chinese official participation subsequently prompted the incoming Communist regime to strengthen existing policies and attempt to gain real control over the selection process in the future.

10

India-China Relations

CHINA AND INDIA TODAY: DIPLOMATS JOSTLE, MILITARIES PREPARE

Just as the Indian subcontinental plate has a tendency to constantly rub and push against the Eurasian tectonic plate, causing friction and volatility in the entire Himalayan mountain range, India's bilateral relationship with China is also a subtle, unseen, but ongoing and deeply felt collision, the affects of which have left a convoluted lineage. Tensions between the two powers have come to influence everything from their military and security decisionmaking to their economic and diplomatic maneuvering, with implications for wary neighbors and faraway allies alike. The relationship is complicated by layers of rivalry, mistrust, and occasional cooperation, not to mention actual geographical disputes.

Distant neighbors buffered by Tibet and the Himalayas for millennia, China and India became next-door neighbors with contested frontiers and disputed histories in 1950, following the occupation of Tibet by Mao's People's Liberation Army (PLA). While the rest of the world started taking note of China's rise during the last decade of the twentieth century, India has been warily watching China's rise ever since a territorial dispute erupted in a brief but full-scale war in 1962, followed by skirmishes in 1967 and 1987.

Several rounds of talks held since 1981 have failed to resolve the disputed claims. During his last visit to India, in 2010, Chinese

Premier Wen Jiabao dashed any hopes of early border settlement, stating that it would take a very long time to settle the boundary issue—a situation that in many ways works to Beijing's advantage. An unsettled border provides China the strategic leverage to keep India uncertain about its intentions, and nervous about its capabilities, while exposing India's vulnerabilities and weaknesses, and encouraging New Delhi's "good behaviour" on issues of vital concern. Besides, as the ongoing unrest and growing incidents of self-immolations by Buddhist monks in Tibet show, Beijing has not yet succeeded in pacifying and Sinicizing Tibet, as it has Inner Mongolia. The net result is that the 2,520-mile Sino-Indian frontier, one of the longest inter-state boundaries in the world, remains China's only undefined land border. It is also becoming heavily militarized, as tensions rise over China's aggressive patrolling on the line of actual control (LAC) and its military drills, using live ammunition, for a potential air and land campaign to capture high-altitude mountain passes in Tibet.

Over the last decade, the Chinese have put in place a sophisticated military infrastructure in the Tibet Autonomous Region (TAR) adjoining India: five fully operational air bases, several helipads, an extensive rail network, and thirty thousand miles of roads—giving them the ability to rapidly deploy thirty divisions (fifteen thousand soldiers each) along the border, a three-to-one advantage over India. China has not only increased its military presence in Tibet but is also ramping up its nuclear arsenal. In addition, the PLA's strategic options against India are set to multiply as Chinese land and rail links with Pakistan, Nepal, Burma, and Bangladesh improve.

Developments on the disputed Himalayan borders are central to India's internal debate about the credibility of its strategic deterrent and whether to test nuclear weapons again. Being the weaker power, India is far more concerned about the overall military balance tilting to its disadvantage. India sees China everywhere because of Beijing's "hexiao gongda" policy in South Asia: "uniting with the small"—Pakistan, Bangladesh, Nepal, Burma, and Sri Lanka—"to counter the big"—India. When combined with Chinese nuclear and missile transfers to Pakistan and building of port facilities around India's periphery, and a dramatic increase in the PLA's incursions and transgressions across the LAC, the official Indian perception of China has undergone a dramatic shift since 2006, with China now being widely seen as posing a major security threat in the short to medium term rather than over the long term. The Indian military, long preoccupied with war-fighting scenarios against Pakistan, has consequently turned its attention to the China border, and unveiled a massive force modernization program, to cost $100 billion over the next decade, that includes the construction of several strategic roads and the expansion of rail networks, helipads, and airfields all along the LAC. Other measures range from raising a new mountain strike corps and doubling force levels in the eastern sector by one hundred thousand troops to the deployment of Sukhoi Su-30MKI aircraft, spy drones, helicopters, and ballistic and cruise missile squadrons to defend its northeastern state of Arunachal Pradesh, territory three times the size of Taiwan that the Chinese invaded in 1962 and now claim sovereignty over as "Southern Tibet."

Propelled by incidents related to border disputes, Chinese opposition to the US-India nuclear energy deal, India's angst over the growing trade deficit due to perceived Chinese unfair trade practices, potential Chinese plans to dam the Brahmaputra River, and the "war talk" in the official Chinese media in the 2007 to 2009 period (reminding India not to forget "the lessons of 1962"), mutual distrust between the Indian and Chinese peoples is growing. Clearly, China's extraordinary economic performance over the last three decades has changed the dynamics of the relationship. China and India had similar average incomes in the late 1970s, but thirty years later they find themselves at completely different stages of development. China's economic reforms—launched in 1978, nearly thirteen years before India's in 1991—changed their subsequent growth trajectories by putting China far ahead of India in all socioeconomic indices. Both China's gross domestic product and military expenditure are now three times the size of India's; recent surveys conducted by Pew Global Research show a growth in popular distrust, with just twenty-five percent of Indians holding a favourable view of China in 2011, down from thirty-four percent in 2010 and fifty-seven percent in 2005. Likewise, just twenty-seven percent of Chinese hold a favourable view of India in 2011, down from thirty-two percent in 2010, with studies of Internet content showing a large degree of "hostility and contempt for India."

Nor is there much effort to keep these emotions submerged. Reacting to the test launch in mid-April of a long-range Agni-V ballistic missile, dubbed the "China killer" by India's news media, a Chinese daily wryly noted that "India stands no chance in an overall arms race with China," because "China's nuclear power is stronger and more reliable." The unequal strategic equation, in particular the Chinese perception of India as a land of irreconcilable socioreligious cleavages with an inherently unstable polity and weak leadership that is easily contained through proxies, aggravates tensions between the two. In 2008, an official reassessment of China's capabilities and intentions led the Indian military to adopt a "two-front war" doctrine against what is identified as a "collusive threat" posed by two closely aligned nuclear-armed neighbors, Pakistan and China. This doctrine validates the long-held belief of India's strategic community that China is following a protracted strategy of containing India's rise.

India is also responding by strengthening its strategic links with Afghanistan, Tajikistan, Mongolia, Vietnam, and Burma—countries on China's periphery. In testimony to the US Senate in February, James Clapper, the director of national intelligence, noted that "the Indian military is strengthening its forces in preparation to fight a limited conflict along the disputed border, and is working to balance Chinese power projection in the Indian Ocean." That "balance" includes a strategic tilt toward the United States that has also had a damaging effect on Sino-Indian relations.

Although leaders from both countries often repeat the ritualized denials of conflict and emphasize burgeoning trade ties, such platitudes cannot obliterate the trust deficit. Few if any of China's strategic thinkers seem to hold positive views of India for China's future, and vice versa. Chinese strategists keep a wary eye on India's "great power dreams," its military spending and weapons acquisitions, and the developments in India's naval and nuclear doctrines. A dominant theme in Chinese commentary in the last decade is that India's growing strength—backed by the United States—could tip Asia's balance of power away from Beijing.

Not surprisingly, bilateral relations between Asia's giants remain, in the words of Zhang Yan, China's ambassador to India, "very fragile, very easy to be damaged, and very difficult to repair." Both have massive manpower resources, a scientific and industrial base, and million-plus militaries. For the first time in more than fifty years, both are moving upward simultaneously on their relative power trajectories. As the pivotal power in South Asia, India perceives itself much as China has traditionally perceived itself in relation to East Asia. Both desire a peaceful security environment to focus on economic development and avoid overt rivalry or conflict. Still, the volatile agents of nationalism, history, ambition, strength, and size produce a mysterious chemistry. Neither power is comfortable with the rise of the other. Both seek to envelop neighbors with their national economies. Both are nuclear and space powers with growing ambitions. Both yearn for a multipolar world that will provide them the space for growth and freedom of action. Both vie for leadership positions in global and regional organizations and have attempted to establish a sort of Monroe Doctrine in their respective neighborhoods—without much success.

And both remain suspicious of each other's long-term agenda and intentions. Each perceives the other as pursuing hegemony and entertaining imperial ambitions. Both are non–status quo powers: China in terms of *territory*, power, and influence; India in terms of *status*, power, and influence. Both seek to expand their power and influence in and beyond their regions at each other's expense. China's "Malacca paranoia" is matched by India's "Hormuz dilemma." If China's navy is going south to the Indian Ocean, India's navy is going east to the Pacific Ocean. Both suffer from a siege mentality born out of their elites' acute consciousness of the divisive tendencies that make their countries' present political unity so fragile. After all, much of Chinese and Indian history is made up of long periods of internal disunity and turmoil, when centrifugal forces brought down even the most powerful empires. Each has its vulnerabilities—regional conflicts, poverty, and religious divisions for India; the contradiction between a market economy and Leninist politics for China. Both are plagued with domestic linguistic, ethno-religious, and politico-economic fault lines that could be their undoing if not managed properly.

In other words, China and India are locked in a classic security dilemma: one country sees its actions as defensive, but the same actions appear aggressive to the other. Beijing fears that an unrestrained Indian power—particularly one that is backed by the West and Japan—would not only threaten China's security along its restive southwestern frontiers (Tibet and Xinjiang) but also obstruct China's expansion southwards. Faced with exponential growth in China's power and influence, India feels the need to take counterbalancing measures and launch strategic initiatives to emerge as a great power, but these are perceived as challenging and threatening in China.

China's use of regional and international organizations to institutionalize its power while either denying India access to these organizations or marginalizing India within them has added a new competitive dynamic to the relationship. In the past decade, India has found itself ranged against China at the UN Security Council, East Asia Summit, the Asia-Pacific Economic Cooperation, the Nuclear Suppliers Group, and the Asian Development Bank. In 2009, China vetoed a development plan for India by the latter in the disputed Arunachal Pradesh, thereby internationalizing a bilateral territorial dispute. In a tit-for-tat response, New Delhi has kept Beijing out of India-led multilateral frameworks such as the Bay of Bengal Initiative for Multi-Sectoral Technical and Economic Cooperation, the India-Brazil-South Africa Dialogue, and the Mekong–Ganga Cooperation forums, and rejected China's request to be included as observer or associate member into the 33-member Indian Ocean Naval Symposium, started by India in 2008.

Resource scarcity has added a maritime dimension to this geopolitical rivalry. As China's and India's energy dependence on the Middle East and Africa increases, both are actively seeking to forge closer defense and security ties with resource supplier nations (e.g., Saudi Arabia and Iran), and to develop appropriate naval capabilities to dominate the sea lanes through which the bulk of their commerce flows. Since seventy-seven percent of China's oil comes from the Middle East and Africa, Beijing has increased its activities in the Indian Ocean region by investing in littoral states' economies, building ports and infrastructure, providing weaponry, and acquiring energy resources. Nearly ninety percent of Chinese arms sales go to countries located in the Indian Ocean region. Beijing is investing heavily in developing the Gwadar deep-sea port in Pakistan, and naval bases in Sri Lanka, Bangladesh, and Myanmar. Whether one calls it a "string of pearls" or a series of places at which China's navy can base or simply be resupplied, that navy is setting up support infrastructure in strategic locations along the same sea lanes of communication that could neutralize India's geographical advantage in the Indian Ocean region. A recent commentary from the official Xinhua news outlet called for setting up three lines of navy supply bases in the northern Indian Ocean, the western Indian Ocean, and the southern Indian Ocean. It stated: "China needs to establish overseas strategic support stations for adding ship fuel, re-supply of necessities, staff break time, repairs of equipment, and weapons in Pakistan, Sri Lanka, and Myanmar, which will be the core support bases in the North Indian Ocean supply line; Djibouti, Yemen, Oman, Kenya, Tanzania, and Mozambique, which will be the core support bases in the West Indian Ocean supply line; and Seychelles and Madagascar, which will be the core support bases in the South Indian Ocean supply line."

For its part, New Delhi is pursuing the same strategy as Beijing and creating its own web of relationships with the littoral states, both bilaterally and multilaterally, through the Indian Ocean Naval Symposium, to ensure that if the military need arises, the necessary support infrastructure and network will be in place. India has also stepped up defense cooperation with Oman and Israel in the west, while upgrading military ties with the Maldives, Madagascar, and Myanmar in the Indian Ocean, and with Singapore, Indonesia, Thailand, Vietnam, Taiwan, the Philippines, Australia, Japan, and the United States in the east. In December 2006, Admiral Sureesh Mehta, then India's naval chief, expanded the conceptual construct of India's "greater strategic neighborhood" to include potential sources of oil and gas imports located across the globe—from Venezuela to the Sakhalin Islands in Russia. The

Indian navy currently has a stronger naval presence on the Indian Ocean than does China. It is strengthening its port infrastructure with new southern ports, which allow greater projection into the ocean. Taking a leaf out of China's book, the new focus is to develop anti-access and area-denial capabilities that will thwart any Chinese attempt at encirclement or sea-access denial.

In short, maritime competition is intensifying as Indian and Chinese navies show the flag in the Pacific and Indian oceans with greater frequency. This rivalry could spill into the open after a couple of decades, when one Indian aircraft carrier will be deployed in the Pacific Ocean and one Chinese aircraft carrier in the Indian Ocean—ostensibly to safeguard their respective trade and energy routes.

In turn, India's "Look East" policy is a manifestation of its own strategic intent to compete for influence in the wider Asia-Pacific region. Just as China will not concede India's primacy in South Asia and the Indian Ocean region, India seems unwilling to accept Southeast and East Asia as China's sphere of influence. Just as China's rise is viewed positively in the South Asian region among the small countries surrounding India with which New Delhi has had difficult relations, India's rise is viewed in positive-sum terms among China's neighbors throughout East and Southeast Asia. Over the last two decades, India has sought to enhance its economic and security ties with those Northeast and Southeast Asian nations (Mongolia, South Korea, Japan, Taiwan, Vietnam, Singapore, Thailand, Indonesia, and Australia) that worry about China more than any other major power. As China's growing strength creates uneasiness in the region, India's balancing role is welcome within the Association of Southeast Asian Nations (ASEAN) in order to influence China's behaviour in cooperative directions. While the Southeast Asian leaders seek to deter China from utilizing its growing strength for coercive purposes and to maintain regional autonomy, Indian strategic analysts favour an Indian naval presence in the South China Sea and the Pacific Ocean to counter Chinese naval presence in the Indian Ocean. On maritime security, Southeast Asians seem more willing to cooperate with India than China, especially in the Strait of Malacca.

A key element of India's Pacific outreach has been regular naval exercises, port calls, security dialogues, and more than a dozen defense cooperation agreements. India has welcomed Vietnam's offer of berthing rights in Na Trang Port in the South China Sea, and news reports suggest that India might offer BrahMos cruise missiles and other military hardware at "friendship prices" to Vietnam. The conclusion of free-trade agreements with Singapore, South Korea, Malaysia, Japan, and the ASEAN, coupled with New Delhi's participation in multilateral forums such as the East Asia Summit and the ASEAN Plus Eight defense ministers' meetings, have also reinforced strategic ties. India's determination to strengthen its strategic partnership with Japan and Vietnam, commitment to pursue joint oil exploration with Hanoi in the South China Sea waters in the face of Chinese opposition, and an emphasis on the freedom of navigation are signs of India maneuvering to be seen as a counterweight to Chinese power in East Asia. New Delhi is also scaling up defense ties with Tokyo, Seoul, and Canberra.

The US-India partnership is also emerging as an important component of India's strategy to balance China's power. India seeks US economic and technological assistance. It helps this relationship that India's longtime security concerns—China and Pakistan—also now happen to be the United States' long-term and immediate strategic concerns as well. Both the Bush and Obama administrations have encouraged India's involvement in a wider Asian security system to balance a rising China and declining Japan. Apparently, US weakness—real or perceived—invites Chinese assertiveness. Since the United States does not wish to see Asia dominated by a single hegemonic power or a coalition of states, India's economic rise is seen as serving Washington's long-term interests by ensuring that there be countervailing powers in Asia—China, Japan, and India, with the United States continuing to act as an "engaged offshore power balancer."

The "India factor" is increasingly entering the ongoing US policy debate over China. Asia-Pacific is now the Indo-Pacific, a term underlining the centrality of India in the new calculus of regional power. The 2010 US Quadrennial Defense Review talked of India's positive role as a "net security provider in the Indian Ocean and beyond." India's "Look East" policy, which envisions high-level engagement with "China-wary" nations (South Korea, Japan, Taiwan, Vietnam, Thailand, Indonesia, and Australia), dovetails with the US policy of establishing closer ties with countries beyond Washington's traditional treaty partners to maintain US predominance. The US-Indian strategic engagement, coupled with India's expanding naval and nuclear capabilities and huge economic potential, have made India loom larger on China's radar screen. An editorial in a Shanghai daily last November lamented the fact that "India will not allow itself to stay quietly between the US and China. It wants to play triangle affairs with the duo, and will do anything it can to maximize its benefit out of it. Therefore, China will find it hard to buy India over." The Chinese fear that the Indian-American cooperation in defense, high-tech R&D, nuclear, space, and maritime spheres would prolong US hegemony and prevent the establishment of a post-American, Sino-centric hierarchical regional order in Asia. This tightening relationship, and the possibility that what is presently a tilt on India's part could turn into a full-fledged alignment, is a major reason for recent deterioration in Chinese-Indian relations.

Although these relations remain unstable and competitive, both have sought to reduce tensions. Despite border disputes, denial of market access, and harsh words against the Dalai Lama, leaders in both countries understand the dangers of allowing problems to overwhelm the relationship. Burgeoning economic ties between the world's two fastest-growing economies have become the most salient aspect of their bilateral relationship. Trade flows have risen rapidly, from a paltry $350 million in 1993 to $70 billion in 2012, and could surpass $100 billion by 2015. Several joint ventures in power generation, consumer goods, steel, chemicals, minerals, mining, transport, infrastructure, info-tech, and telecommunication are in the works. Intensifying trade, commerce, and tourism could eventually raise the stakes for China in its relationship with India. On the positive side, both share common interests in maintaining regional stability (for example, combating Islamist fundamentalists), exploiting economic opportunities, and maintaining access to energy sources, capital, and markets.

Despite ever-increasing trade volumes, however, there is as yet no strategic congruence between China and India. As in the case of Sino-US and Sino-Japanese ties, Sino-Indian competitive tendencies, rooted in geopolitics and nationalism, are unlikely to be easily offset even by growing economic and trade links. In fact, the economic relationship is heavily skewed. The bulk of Indian exports to China consist of iron ore and other raw materials, while India imports mostly manufactured goods from China—a classic example of the dependency model. Most Indians see China as predatory in trade. New Delhi has lodged the largest number of anti-dumping cases against Beijing in the World Trade Organization. India is keener on pursuing mutual economic dependencies with Japan, South Korea, and Southeast Asian nations through increased trade, investment, infrastructure development, and aid to bolster economic and political ties across Asia that will counter Chinese power.

Even as a range of economic and transnational issues draw them closer together, the combination of internal issues of stability (Tibet and Kashmir), disputes over territory, competition over resources (oil, gas, and water), overseas markets and bases, external overlapping spheres of influence, rival alliance relationships, and ever-widening geopolitical horizons forestall the chances for a genuine Sino-Indian accommodation. Given the broad range of negative attitudes and perceptions each country has for the other, it is indeed remarkable that China and India have been able to keep diplomatic relations from fraying. How long this situation can last is more and more uncertain as each country is increasingly active in what would once have been seen as the other's "backyard" and both engage in strategic maneuvers to checkmate each other.

Just as China has become more assertive vis-à-vis the United States, Indian policy toward China is becoming tougher. India's evolving Asia strategy reflects the desire for an arc of partnerships with China's key neighbors—in Southeast Asia and further east along the Asia-Pacific rim—and the United States that would help neutralize the continuing Chinese military assistance and activity around its own territory and develop counter-leverages of its own vis-à-vis China to keep Beijing sober.

At this point, the two heavyweights circle each other warily, very much aware that their feints and jabs could turn into a future slugging match.

CHINA AND INDIA'S RELATIONSHIPS

Pakistan

China's continued support for Pakistan has long been a source of friction in China-India relations. The China-Pakistan relationship has been described as an "all-weather relationship" by both states, with President Hu Jintao reaching hyperbolic heights when he described it as "higher than the Himalayas, deeper than the Indian Ocean, and sweeter than honey" during his November 2006 visit to Islamabad.

The China-Pakistan relationship grew out of their mutual desire beginning in the 1960s to counterbalance India, which had closely aligned with the Soviet Union against China, following the 1962 border war. Pakistan's nascent relationship with China can in fact be traced as far back as 1954, when Pakistan reassured Beijing that the Southeast Asia Treaty Organization (SEATO) was not directed against China, and 1961 when it supported a draft resolution to restore China's membership in the United Nations. In 1963, Pakistan ceded to China the Trans-Karakoram Tract, also known as Shaksam Valley, in the disputed territory of Kashmir. The area subsequently became part of the land bridge linking Pakistan to China's Xinjiang along the Karakoram Highway.

China sided with Pakistan during the 1965 and 1971 wars with India, during which China put its own forces along the Indian border on full alert. In April 2005, China and Pakistan signed the "Treaty of Friendship, Cooperation, and Good Neighborly Relations," which binds both signatories to desist from joining "any alliance or bloc which infringes upon the sovereignty, security, and territorial integrity of the other side."

In recent years, China's engagement with Pakistan has been further motivated by Beijing's desire to extend its influence into

South and Central Asia in order to maintain a stable periphery; gain access to markets, natural resources, and raw materials; and maintain amicable relations with the Islamic world to mitigate support for the Islamic insurgency in Xinjiang province. Pakistan is the leading recipient of China's arms exports and has received substantial support from China for its civilian and military nuclear program.

In recent years, however, China has adopted a more balanced approach toward its relationship with Pakistan and India, fueled by Beijing's desire to maintain amicable relations with all states along its periphery, its recognition of India's growing economic and strategic potential, especially in the wake of improving U.S.-India relations, rising concern over Pakistan's future viability, and China's shared concerns with India over Islamic extremism and separatism. China has also noted the rapprochement in U.S.-Pakistan relations following September 11, which has encouraged Beijing to diversify its relations on the subcontinent in turn. To display its credentials as a responsible international actor, China has lessened its material support for Pakistan's ballistic missile and nuclear weapons programs and its automatic political, moral, and rhetorical support to Pakistan in its relations with India.

The shift in China's policy toward the India-Pakistan relationship has been most visible over the issue of Kashmir. Although China supported Pakistan's position during the India-Pakistan conflicts of 1965 and 1971, Beijing announced in January 1994 that it not only favored a negotiated solution on Kashmir but also opposed any form of independence for the region. During the Kargil conflict in 1999, when Pakistani and Kashmiri forces advanced provocatively into the Indian side of the Line of Control, China for the first time adopted a neutral position rather than siding with Pakistan.

China adopted a similar position when both states were on the verge of war in December 2001 following a terrorist attack on the Indian parliament. Indeed, unless India is the clear aggressor, China is unlikely to support Pakistan automatically in any future India-Pakistan conflict, as China's focus on internal development and maintaining a stable periphery will lead Beijing to place its primary emphasis on stopping any hostilities or unrest along its border.

Nonetheless, Beijing continues to employ the "Pakistan card" in voicing its displeasure over Indian behaviour. Beijing's reluctance to admit India to the Shanghai Cooperation Organization (SCO) while supporting Pakistan's bid, and its offer to support Pakistan's civilian nuclear program following the conclusion of the U.S.-India nuclear deal, suggests that China has not completely abandoned its traditional loyalty to Pakistan. Indeed, China benefits today from the reduction of tensions between India and Pakistan, which allows Beijing to continue its two-track approach. China's relationship with Pakistan however continues to rile New

International Security [Oxford: Oxford University Press, 2005, 420–1]). According to one source, as much as 80 percent of Pakistan's military hardware, including 60 percent of its military aircraft, has come from China. Ramtanu Maitra, "China and India Aim to Extend Cooperation," *Executive Intelligence Review*, February 18, 2005. Delhi, which remains resentful and suspicious over continued arms sales and other elements of the historical partnership over the past 45 years.

United States

Many Chinese have viewed the Bush administration's attention to developing strategic relations with India since 2001 as an attempt to contain or at least counterbalance China in South and East Asia. President George W. Bush has stated that the United States is committed to helping India become a world power, and in June 2005, India and the United States signed the New Framework for the U.S.-India Defense Relationship, a 10-year agreement paving the way for joint weapons production, cooperation on missile defense, and a possible lifting of U.S. export controls on sensitive military technologies.

Growing U.S.-India military-to-military cooperation, most notably in the Indian Ocean, has emerged as a particular source of concern in Beijing, given China's growing dependence on oil imports transiting the Indian Ocean. China expressed principled discomfort over the March 2006 U.S.-India civil nuclear agreement, which in essence recognized India as a nuclear weapons state and granted India assistance for its civilian nuclear program in exchange for India's promise to open its civil nuclear facilities to international inspection and safeguards. China initially criticized the deal as creating a "nuclear exception" and undermining the nonproliferation regime, although its opposition has cooled due to concern about its potential impact on relations with New Delhi.

Nonetheless, while the United States does seek to draw India into a values-based strategic and operational partnership to handle common international challenges, U.S. officials have denied that the relationship is meant to contain or otherwise oppose China.

Regardless, absent extraordinary provocation from Beijing, New Delhi will have no interest in allying with Washington in any active strategy to contain or oppose China. As a legacy of its "nonaligned" foreign policy, Indian policymakers maintain an aversion to alliances, especially those that are perceived as counterbalancing or containing other countries. This has prompted India to keep its distance thus far from both China-centered forums such as the Shanghai Cooperation Organization, and U.S.-centered organizations such as the Proliferation Security Initiative and the U.S.-Japan-Australia Trilateral Strategic Dialogue.

The legacy of nonalignment has made India particularly resistant to becoming anything resembling a junior partner of the United States (or China) and allergic to anything that constrains its flexibility and policy options. Indeed, India's position toward the United States has not emerged from its Cold War shadow, and New Delhi is taking the bilateral partnership slowly. In the end, India will maintain its strategic independence to pursue a multilayered approach combining both cooperation and competition with China in a way that serves its own unique political, economic, and security interests.

Taiwan

India recognized the People's Republic of China over the exiled Republic of China on the island of Taiwan in 1950 and has never wavered in its perspective on formal relations with the two sides. Nevertheless, Taiwan's leadership has reached out actively to New

Delhi in recent years. Taiwan's government has spoken openly about how India could serve as an alternative investment destination and a democratic comrade-in-arms with which the island might work to raise its international profile and perhaps constrain mainland action across the strait. Indian leaders and close advisers within the nongovernmental community have increased their interaction with Taiwanese delegations in recent years, but New Delhi has been very reluctant to accept Taiwan's overtures for more official ties and closer relations. There remains little overt interaction between the political communities, and even that has largely been focused on economic issues. In 1995, India and Taiwan founded the India-Taipei Association, India's trade mission in Taiwan. The organization had been led by retired government officials, but in 2003 India raised the level of its representation by assigning leadership to a serving official.

In February 2006, the two sides established the Taiwan-India Cooperation Council, which was intended to promote and facilitate Taiwanese business investment in India. Taiwanese leaders like to note that Taiwan's hardware expertise and India's strong software industry are an excellent complement to each other. Presently, about 70 percent of hardware and IT components manufactured on the Chinese mainland are based on Taiwanese investments, and this has prompted Taiwanese businesses to seek to diversify their IT market. Nonetheless, Taiwan-India bilateral trade reached about $2 billion in 2005. India makes up only 0.67 percent of Taiwan's total trade, although the figure has grown by 33 percent between 1995 and 2002. Investment also lags considerably, with Taiwanese businesses investing a total of $116 million in India as opposed to well over $100 billion in China.

Taiwan has made quiet overtures to India to establish military cooperation, but so far military interaction remains very limited. Nonetheless, New Delhi has benefited from the insights of Taipei's intelligence establishment that assist India in understanding developments on the mainland.

In the end, however, India views Taiwan as an economic partner more than as a potential political partner. India is quite aware of the sensitivity of the Taiwan issue to China and the potential for it to affect China-India relations. India's desire for stable relations with China, and in particular its aim of encouraging Beijing to pursue more balanced relations between India and Pakistan in South Asia, make India's leaders extremely cautious to not inflame tensions over the issue about which Beijing is most sensitive.

Indian decisionmakers reject any notion of using the Taiwan issue as a way to distract or exercise leverage against China. They do note, however, that peaceful resolution of the Taiwan issue will be an important indicator of China's future direction as a peaceful and responsible international actor and have linked the way China deals with Taiwan with the way it will handle Tibet, an issue of more direct salience for India.

Russia

The legacy of India's close relations with the Soviet Union during the Cold War lingers in its attitudes toward Russia. India signed the "Treaty of Peace, Friendship, and Cooperation" with the Soviet Union in 1971 at the height of the Sino-Soviet split, which led Beijing to denounce India as "tool of Soviet expansionism." As far back as 1959, as the split emerged, the Soviet Union supplied India with transport planes for use during border clashes with China. Russia remains the main source of India's advanced weaponry today; Moscow, in fact, provides technologies even further advanced than those it sells to China.

In the post–Cold War period, China-Russia rapprochement has brought about a convergence in Chinese, Russian, and Indian interests. The three countries have a shared an interest in combating Islamic extremism within their borders. They each are committed to promoting a multipolar world and preserving strict adherence to the principles of state sovereignty and noninterference in states' internal affairs. China and India share an interest in importing Russian energy resources and intersect in their interest in confidence-building in Central Asia.

As a result, some U.S. analysts have worried about an emerging strategic triangle between China, India, and Russia that could seek to counterbalance the United States, especially after India acquired observer status in the Shanghai Cooperation Organization in 2005 and trilateral foreign-minister talks began the same year. There is little possibility of such a strategic triangle, however. Not only do India and China continue to mistrust one another, but India at least shows no desire to collaborate with China and Russia at the expense of its ongoing political rapprochement with the world's only superpower. India has distanced itself from the Shanghai Cooperation Organization, for example; India was the only country not to send its head of state to the June 2006 SCO summit in Shanghai. The trilateral meetings themselves are in a nascent phase in which nonmilitary, nonstrategic issues, such as energy, agriculture, industrial restructuring, and environmental protection, are discussed.

Bibliography

Alastair Lamb, Kashmir: *A Disputed Legacy 1846–1990,* Hertingfordbury, Herts: Roxford Books, 1991.

Amitabh Sikdar: *India and China : Strategic Energy Management and Security,* Manas, Delhi, 2009.

Anil. C.K. : *Military and Democracy in South Asia : Challenges, Politics and Power,* Sumit Enterprises, Delhi, 2009.

Ashton, S.R.: *British Policy Towards the Indian States, 1905-1939,* London: Curzon, 1982.

Beyer, Stephan V. : *The Cult of Tara: Magic and Ritual in Tibet.* Berkeley, CA: University of California Press, 1973.

Bhat, T.P. : *India and China : Trade Complementarities and Competitiveness,* Bookwell, Delhi, 2008.

Bosson, James E. : *Tibetan Treasury of Aphoristic Jewels,* Bloomington, IN: Indiana University Press, 1968.

Clayton, Thomas: *Public Participation in Public Decision: New Skills and Strategies for Public Managers,* San Francisco, Jossey-Bass Publishers, 1995.

Cole, Alan : *Mothers and Sons in Chinese Buddhism,* Stanford, CA: Stanford University Press, 1998.

Das, G.: *China-Tibet-India: The 1962 War and the Strategic Military Future.* New Delhi, Har-Anand Publications, 2009.

Deepak, B.R : *India and China : 1904-2004 : A Century of Peace and Conflict,* Manak, Delhi, 2005.

Gaur, Mahendra : *Indian Policy of Neighbour,* Delhi, Kalpaz Pub., 2006.

George Mathew: *Grass Roots Democracy in India and China : The Right to Participate,* Sage, Delhi, 2007.

Huntington, S.P.: *The China Modernisation Military and the State,* N.Y., Vintage Books, 1964.

Jagannath P. Panda: *China's Path to Power : Party, Military and the Politics of State Transition,* Pentagon, Delhi, 2010.

Jha, Prem Shankar : *India and China : The Battle Between Soft and Hard Power*, Penguin Books India, Delhi, 2010.

Jones, W.H.: *The Government and Politics of Indian Military*, London, Hutchinson, 1971.

Kapur, C.K. : *Chinese Military Modernisation*, Manas, Delhi, 2003.

Lamb, Alastair: *The China-India Border: The Origins of the Disputed Boundaries*. L. Oxford University Press, 1964.

Lamrimpa, Gen : *Calming the Mind: Tibetan Buddhist Teachings on Cultivating Meditative Quiescence*, Ithaca, NY: Snow Lion, 1995.

Lauf, Detlef Ingo : *Tibetan Sacred Art: The Heritage of Tantra*, Berkeley, CA: Shambhala, 1976.

Mehra, P.: *Negotiating with the Chinese 1846-1987: Problems and Perspectives*. New Delhi, Reliance Publishing House, 1989.

Neville Maxwell: *India's China War*, Pantheon Books, USA, 1971

Pant, Harsh V. : *Indian Foreign Policy In A Unipolar World*, Routledge, Delhi, 2009.

Prabir De: *India and China in an Era of Globalisation : Essays on Economic Cooperation*, Bookwell, Delhi, 2005.

Ramesh, J.: *Making Sense of Chindia: Reflections on China and India*. New Delhi, India Research Press, 2005.

Rowland, J.: *A History of Sino-Indian Relations: Hostile Co-existence*. London, D. Van Nostrand Company, 1967.

Singer, Jane Casey : *Tibetan Art: Towards a Definition of Style*, London: Laurence King/Alan Marcuson, 1997.

Singh, R.S.N. : *Asian Strategic and Military Perspective*, Lancer, Delhi, 2005.

Thampi, Madhavi : *India and China in the Colonial World*, Social Science Press, Delhi, 2010.

William Theodore : *The Buddhist Tradition in India, China and Japan*, New York: Vintage Books, 1972.

Index

R

S

T

❑❑❑